Global Action Networks

BOCCONI ON MANAGEMENT SERIES

Series Editor: **Robert Grant**, Eni Professor of Strategic Management, Department of Management, Universita Commerciale Luigi Bocconi, Italy.

The *Bocconi on Management* series addresses a broad range of contemporary and cutting-edge issues relating to the management of organizations and the environment in which they operate. Consistent with Bocconi University's ongoing mission to link good science with practical usefulness, the series is characterized by its integration of relevance, accessibility, and rigor. It showcases the work of scholars from all over the world, who have produced contributions to the advancement of knowledge building on theoretical, disciplinary, cultural, or methodological traditions with the potential to improve management practice.

The series is edited by the Center for Research in Organization and Management (CROMA) at Bocconi University, and is published through an agreement between Palgrave Macmillan and Bocconi University Press, an imprint of Egea.

For information about submissions of book proposals or the series in general, please contact Maurizio Zollo at maurizio.zollo@unibocconi.it or Robert Grant at grant@unibocconi.it.

Titles include:

Massimo Amato, Luigi Doria and Luca Fantacci (*editors*)
MONEY AND CALCULATION
Economic and Sociological Perspectives

Vittorio Coda
ENTREPRENEURIAL VALUES AND STRATEGIC MANAGEMENT
Essays in Management Theory

Steve Waddell
GLOBAL ACTION NETWORKS
Creating Our Future Together

Bocconi on Management Series
Series Standing Order ISBN 978–0–230–27766–3

You can receive future titles in this series as they are published by placing a standing order. Please contact your bookseller or, in case of difficulty, write to us at the address below with your name and address, the title of the series and the ISBN quoted above.

Customer Services Department, Macmillan Distribution Ltd, Houndmills, Basingstoke, Hampshire RG21 6XS, England

Global Action Networks

Creating Our Future Together

Steve Waddell
Principal, Networking Action

First published 2011 by
PALGRAVE MACMILLAN

Palgrave Macmillan in the UK is an imprint of Macmillan Publishers Limited, registered in England, company number 785998, of Houndmills, Basingstoke, Hampshire RG21 6XS.

Palgrave Macmillan in the US is a division of St Martin's Press LLC, 175 Fifth Avenue, New York, NY 10010.

Palgrave Macmillan is the global academic imprint of the above companies and has companies and representatives throughout the world.

Palgrave® and Macmillan® are registered trademarks in the United States, the United Kingdom, Europe and other countries.

ISBN 978-0-230-28548-4

This book is printed on paper suitable for recycling and made from fully managed and sustained forest sources. Logging, pulping and manufacturing processes are expected to conform to the environmental regulations of the country of origin.

A catalogue record for this book is available from the British Library.

A catalog record for this book is available from the Library of Congress.

10   9   8   7   6   5   4   3   2   1
20   19   18   17   16   15   14   13   12   11

Printed and bound in Great Britain by
CPI Antony Rowe, Chippenham and Eastbourne

This book is dedicated to Ralph Taylor. Without his support over many years, this book would not have been possible.

And it is further dedicated to those many people who have pioneered the development of Global Action Networks and taken time to share their experiences.

CONTENTS

LIST OF FIGURES AND TABLES

Figures

Tables

Although I hope this book will be of interest to academics and students of global governance, change and networks, the book's primary goal is to provide practical assistance to people working in, and associated with, global, multi-stakeholder, inter-organizational change networks that I call Global Action Networks (GANs). Today these people number in the many millions, when all the participating organizations are taken into account. These include people in government and businesses and NGOs of all sizes. They are pioneers in developing an audacious and complex strategy to address the challenges and opportunities presented by globalization. Their success will be judged by their ability to innovate to realize a globalization that works for all: a future that finds strength in diversity, is environmentally sustainable, assures peace, promotes justice, provides health, and generates wealth. It is a very tall order!

In comparison to the scale of their aspirations, these pioneers are working with very modest financial, knowledge, tool, and skill resources. They are entrepreneurs, piecing these together from various sources. They are figuring out things as they go along, since there are no role models. This means that they are often borrowing approaches and ideas from traditions with strategies and goals quite different from their own. Sometimes these can be adapted to a multi-stakeholder, inter-organizational, change network strategy, but often other traditions are problematic and actually hinder GANs' ability to realize their goals.

Such, for example, is the case of the concept of "Secretariat," borrowed from the intergovernmental world of organizations like the UN and World Bank. As this book explains, that concept can be useful for a certain stage of development, but holding onto it will inhibit development of the networks' potential. Likewise, the advocacy traditions of NGOs that focus on telling others what to do can impede GANs' distinctive capacity to grow experiments that develop the "solutions." And similarly, the concept of "brand" can be borrowed from the business world in a way that overruns the importance of local accountability and innovation in response to diversity. These other traditions are valuable for the organizations that developed them and even have limited use for GANs, but when used as organizing principles they can be highly problematic.

The central question behind this book is "What is needed for these networks to realize their potential?" I bring together my decade of experience addressing this question, building on the work of many others. Most people answer this question from a particular angle, such as a political science perspective focusing on governance, or with questions about network leadership, or theories and strategies around change and conflict, or with concerns about measurement and evaluation. My aspiration is to develop a comprehensive response to this question, and bring together all these different aspects. Each angle on its own is necessary, but insufficient.

My biggest assertion is that GANs represent a critical organizing innovation – that they are as different from business, NGOs, and governments as each of those are from each other. When people from the networks are brought together, they resonate strong with this suggestion and discover that they finally have found their tribe and community.

The book begins by describing that tribe. I present ten examples – in fact, there are only several dozen that possess the seven characteristics that I go on to propose as definitional, so ten is a pretty good sample size. The examples are designed to very briefly present the array of issues that a GAN strategy is addressing, and give a feel for the community as a whole. Given the newness of the strategy and its organizational form, it is not surprising that there is significant variability in terms of each GANs' development of each characteristic.

The second chapter focuses on the questions "What is a network? What can a well-functioning network do?" The word "network" is bandied about a lot these days, and usually when I mention it to a stranger they jump to the idea of a computer or technology network. That's actually a pretty good metaphor, but of course creating an inter-organizational network to realize global change presents very different questions and challenges. The UN is also a network – one of governments. And a business corporation is a network – one that brings together suppliers, manufacturers, service providers, communicators, customers, and others. And an NGO is a network of its members and employees. So what is distinctive about a GAN as a network? This question is, of course, critical to developing GANs successfully: we need to know what we are aiming for, if we are going to get there! In fact, for GANs the "there" is still very much in definition.

In Chapter 3 I lay out the process of developing a GAN to its potential. As I explain, I find the core useful concept is "community" development. I find that commonly people focus on *technical physical science solutions* and organizing *events*. They commonly fail to appreciate the core work of creating *processes* that bring together diverse people to be productive as a network that *spurs development and implementation* of solutions.

The development process is described through four development stages and for each are presented key challenges and ways of addressing them. There is now considerable experience with the first three of the stages described. However, I find most people involved in developing the networks are relatively unaware of the tools and experience of others that can assist them, so I hope this will be helpful.

The fourth stage I first hypothesized in a written format in 2006 following some work with GAN leaders. Today this stage is in rapid development with a few GANs, as they become increasingly decentralized and develop inter-GAN ties. However, this is still very much the leading edge.

Perhaps the most tools-based chapter is Chapter 5, where I present eight approaches to visualizing the system that GANs are working in and on. I am constantly amazed at how little use GANs make of these tools that really help getting hands around the complexity of their fields. These tools greatly facilitate making the field discussable and understandable, and consequently can provide great value in strategy development. The lack of familiarity probably arises from the fact that the tools are almost all relatively new, in development themselves, and their modest technical challenges. With greater application to GANs specific needs, these and similar visualization tools will become even more valuable.

The "change" work of GANs is, in my experience, very under-emphasized. I say that because there is little use of the large systems change knowledge, skills, and technology that have blossomed over the past couple of decades. In Chapter 5 I aim to present some core concepts, language, frameworks, and tools to deepen understanding of this field and how to make use of it. I think that this is perhaps the most challenging of all the competencies for GANs to develop, given the scale and complexity of their change challenges. Although I believe that what I present here is very useful and outlines the leading edge of our knowledge, we need to do much more to develop this knowledge and capacity.

Like a moth drawn to light, I find that when many people think about GANs they think about structure and governance issues. I spend Chapter 6 discussing these, so I agree that they are important. However, successfully addressing these issues should be driven by strategy and build upon experience. I remember one GAN leader who was referring to the need to build a "permanent structure." I cautioned that such an entity is usually a dead one, unresponsive to success and failure, and changes in its own working environment. Nevertheless, integration of review and change cycles to ensure living structure is particularly complex for GANs. It should be well connected to the development stages of Chapter 3.

For me Chapter 7 is the most important of the book. This is where I aim to create a comprehensive development framework in response to the question "What is needed for these networks to realize their potential?" Discussing this question with a couple of colleagues, one referred to the need to develop visionary and spiritual aspects that bring a whole-person and interconnected perspective; another referred to systems thinking and building our capacity to see systemic relationships. These might be seen as vision and mission level analyses respectively. I realized that my focus is more at the tactic level, as I focus upon the competencies that need developing.

By "competency" I mean the skills, attributes, tools, and knowledge that are necessary for the networks' full development. Some prefer the word "capacity." Drawing from many years of discussion with people working in GANs, observing how they develop structurally, and seeing what they are struggling with, I propose eight competencies. In this chapter, I aim to give a framework for thinking about these and suggest a strategy for their development. Although the competencies like "leadership" and "communications" are needed by all organizations, I present the unique qualities of these that GANs are challenged to develop. Hopefully I provide sufficiently concrete illustrations that you will find these meaningful.

Chapter 7 aims to also present a development agenda for GANs and those wanting to support their growth. Much work needs to be done. For example, how *do* we create global learning networks (the learning systems competency) that fully integrate emerging technologies, respond to global diversity, and are useful in the action-oriented atmosphere of GANs? What *are* the financial mechanisms (the resource mobilization competency) that will provide the dependable flow of resources at an appropriate level, and how *do* we develop them?

Despite all these unknowns, much has been learned by the GAN pioneers and we should really avoid repeating mistakes and re-learning. Chapter 8 presents nine lessons, drawn from the voices of leaders of GANs. Of course it is one thing to understand these intellectually, but quite another to integrate them into the daily workings of a GAN. Nevertheless, they present a useful list that you can periodically check against, to see how you are doing.

When I talk about GANs realizing their full potential, what am I really talking about? Chapter 9 begins with a brief description from the future, describing GANs in the year 2022. Not so far off, but far enough to provide some space for imagination. The goal is to spur greater discussion

and clarity both about the potential for GANs and what needs be done to
reach that potential.

I suggest a future where GANs represent *the* critical global decision-
making process and forum. For me, that represents a future beyond the
so-called tipping point on key issues in a positive way. However, I suggest nine very possible reasons that a proximity to this scenario will not
occur. But being the optimist and enthusiast for GANs that I am, I end with
four trends that suggest something like the scenario will occur. My personal belief is that we are in an age where some of the basic assumptions
about the way the world works – and *can* work – are changing. Given the
increasing scale of global pressure around issues of social, environmental, economic, and political sustainability, I find hard to believe that basic
assumptions will *not* change. But of course what they will change to is
much more debatable.

Throughout this book I make heavy use of headlines, diagrams, and
tables. By looking at these alone, I hope that you can get the essence of
what I have to say. I hope that you will find the tables useful as frameworks
for taking action. They are interesting simply as intellectual devices, but
the real goal is for them to be used to guide discussions and decisions.
All the words are designed to help you with your particular interests.
And hopefully I have included enough citations to give you even more
to explore, should you want to.

Of course nothing here should be taken as a simple truth – always
test and challenge what is said, to ensure it is appropriate for you and
to improve on it!

My core interest is how to increase happiness. Large-scale possibilities seem to me to be intimately related to the big waves of change – technological, political, cultural, and social. By learning to skillfully surf these waves of energy, surely we can enhance justice, security, environmental sustainability, and wealth. And with the backdrop of impressive transformations such as the collapse of the Soviet Union and the end of apartheid in South Africa, surely we can do it without the painful bloodshed of past revolutions associated with large system change.

Teaching in a leadership and change executive management program I co-founded at Boston College, I like to express entrepreneurial leadership by closing my eyes, stretching my arms out in front of me, taking steps forward purposefully, and feeling for something solid. That's what the experience was like, looking into the networks in this book for ways to increase global well-being. Searching for, in Gertrude Stein's words, a "there there." And I believe I've found it with those working in just such a manner in Global Action Networks (GAN) that are addressing incredibly important and daunting global challenges and opportunities.

My introduction to the networks came in 1999 with a phone call from Wolfgang Reinicke, then Senior Partner with the World Bank's Corporate Strategy Group. I was asked to make a modest contribution to a report for Kofi Annan that became titled *Critical Choices: The United Nations, networks, and the future of global governance*. That call set in motion my work since then, and has resulted in this book.

I was contacted because of my work on multi-stakeholder collaboration. In the 1990s, the concept of business–government–civil society (non-profit) collaboration in problem-solving was still new. Working at the Institute for Development Research, because of the support of David L. Brown and earlier work I'd done on the topic, I had the great fortune to receive funding from USAID, and the Ford and Rockefeller Foundations. They wanted to know more about the value of integrating collaboration strategies into their own work, and how to do so. That led to several years of global exploration, and eventually produced a book entitled *Societal*

Learning and Change: How Governments, Business and Civil Society are Creating Solutions to Complex Multi-Stakeholder Problems.

Wolfgang was a Brookings fellow and produced important scholarly work. Inspired by his concept of "Global Public Policy Networks" (GPPNs) at the core of the report to Kofi Annan, with the financial support and co-creative vision of Ralph Taylor, and the insights and work of many people including Tariq Banuri, I began to look closer at this network phenomenon. I spent a couple of years simply asking questions of people involved with the networks, to better understand them and their potential. By 2003, I felt that I had learned enough to take the daunting step of actually giving the networks of interest a new label: Global Action Networks, or GANs. And with Ralph, Allen White, who had a leading role in founding the Global Reporting Initiative (GRI), and David Stroh, who is a great systems thinker, we founded Global Action Network Net (GAN-Net) to support GANs' development.

I adopted the GAN label instead of continuing with Wolfgang's GPPN one for three reasons. One was that I concluded that I am focusing upon a somewhat different grouping of networks and characteristics, defined in Chapter 1. Another was that while the political science tradition of Wolfgang provides important insights, drawing from the individual-, organizational-, and societal-development and change traditions provides much more powerful insights to support the networks' development. And finally, the people in the networks do not thinking of "global public policy" as a major focus of their work – it is more a by-product or one of many tools. Rather, they are focused upon developing real, meaningful change that requires a comprehensive range of activities and outputs.

My explorations at the beginning of the millennium included organizations that I decided did not fit the GAN label, although they're doing very valuable work. The Climate Action Network (CAN), for example, plays an important role in combining civil society energy to influence the climate change agenda. That includes notably lobbying the United Nations Framework Convention for Climate Change (UNFCCC) process that is behind the Kyoto Protocol and the 2009 Copenhagen climate summit.

On the other hand, I include The Climate Group within the GAN family. That's because unlike the CAN, a major activity of the Group is bridging traditional boundaries between business, government, and civil society. As well, rather than focus on lobbying, advocacy, or at a policy and theoretical level, the Group is actively undertaking projects to realize change such as experimenting globally with LED street-lighting strategies by bringing together city governments, banks, and NGOs.

Of course networks "more or less" fit the GAN characteristics laid out in Chapter 1 – it is a general model, not a dogmatic theory. However, suggesting these characteristics are particularly important is my way of saying that the networks will find assessing themselves against them will prove useful. I think that the most important intervention on my part is to actually suggest that these networks are a new, distinct, and very important organizational innovation. When I began investigating them, people in the networks thought of themselves as a rather odd type of NGO, a weak IGO (intergovernmental organization like the UN), or an entrepreneurial public good type of business. As a community organizer and sociologist, I believe that one of the most powerful forces for change arises out of changing identity, and clarifying identity is critical for it to develop powerfully.

I experimented in many ways with development of the GAN identity. Individual conversations and workshop discussions with individuals working in GANs often produced a palpable sense of relief with the suggestion that they are a new and distinct type of organization. It validated their innate innovative insights about how they can do their work, rather than be limited to traditional concepts about how they should do it.

The most exciting and empowering discussions came when people from the various GANs were brought together. This occurred in numerous action learning groupings such as with the chief executive officers, with communications directors, with those responsible for impact measurement, and with those working on governance and organizational issues. Meetings began often with a sense of intrigue on the part of the participants, about the suggestion that they were an important new way to address global issues called "GANs." When participants first spoke the word "GAN," they did so usually with a slightly uncomfortable inflection, trying it on for the first time, verbally feeling whether it fit.

I remember this in particular with Peter Eigen, founder of both Transparency International (TI) and the Extractive Industries Transparency Initiative (EITI). He agreed to chair meetings of a GAN-Net Council of GAN leaders and others. He said "I'm not quite sure whether or not I am a 'GAN'." And with the wonderful sort of twinkle that can arise in Peter's eyes, he would then declare that he is a GAN – because Steve told him he was.

Some of Peter's questioning arose from TI's global structure. It comprises representatives of national networks that legally are NGOs, but these NGOs are multi-stakeholder. This is simply an organizing variation of the theme of global multi-stakeholder network, and the NGO legal quality should not obscure the critical multi-stakeholder quality. We get far too caught up in the limiting frameworks of legal structures and give them too much power to influence and limit our identity. The three legal options for organizing – for-profit, NGO, government (and intergovernmental) – are simply today's legal constructs. We really need at least a fourth one to appropriately reflect the global, multi-stakeholder nature of GANs.

In any case, those experimental meetings produced wonderful connections, enthusiasm, and energy from the suggestion that participants are working with GANs. The participants had all been in meetings with other types of organizations before. The idea that they actually are a new type of organization was validated by the shared qualities of the challenges they were facing. How *do* we create global conversations, given the complications of time zones, cultures, languages. How *do* we get business, government, and NGOs to work together. And how can we do it all without the authority of government, the resources of business, or the traditional positional assertions of civil society?

I must say that I personally resonate with this "not fitting" theme of GANs, as I've done this work. I grew up in a small town in central British Columbia, the Pacific province of Canada. I spent several years as a freelance journalist, before spending a decade as a Communications Director for a labor union. Over that same decade I was part of an innovative Board of Directors of the world's largest community-based credit union in Vancouver. These were very powerful and visceral experiences in the power of organizational innovation, cross-sectoral work, and community organizing.

In the late 1980s, business–government–civil society collaboration was still thought of as an odd concept, if thought about at all. However, Sev Bruyn at Boston College led editing of a volume called *Beyond the Market and the State* in 1986 based on a conference he organized on the topic. That attracted my attention and led to me to enroll in a joint sociology-management school program Sev started with Bill Torbert, an innovative graduate school of management dean. I went to Boston in 1991 with the goals of credentialing myself and starting something I thought of as a North American institute in business and society. Five years later I had a doctorate in sociology, an MBA, and had organized a wonderful faculty to develop an executive management program called Leadership for Change.

I quickly realized the limitations of academic world for my own entrepreneurial energy. Consequently, although I remained active teaching in the program, I left my Executive Director position and my subsequent work has been without support of a significant organization. Many people view me as an academic, because I publish in academic journals, use analytical frameworks, and stress the value of disciplined interventions. I fit most comfortably in the "action learning" framework that is neither consulting nor traditional scientific investigation, but combines elements of both. It seems to me that the *way* we work *together* in learning and development is key to building new capacity. Personally I think of myself as a community organizer, but working at the global level. The goals concern transformational change, with incremental improvements flowing from that imperative. Working on this scale and depth involves understanding long-term trends and possibilities. It also requires accessing the latest knowledge, technologies, and methodologies and combining them in new and disciplined ways.

Both the networks and my own work are about *emergence,* as this book explains. That's a stance appropriate when working with complex issues, where you don't actually know your goal, but are simply working with a rather broad vision. We talk about "sustainability," but no one actually knows what a twenty-first century version *really* looks like in terms of behaviors, organizations, and societies. We're still deep in the midst of trying to operationalize it, and that requires comfort working with ambiguity.

Complex issues contrast with simple ones with well-defined and limited numbers of linear variables, such as with simple production lines and input/output models. Complex issues also contrast with complicated ones, where there are many interacting but well-defined – or definable – variables and interactions, such as in global production lines. Simply importing into complex situations strategies and tools appropriate for simple and complicated situations will not address complex issues and opportunities. However, one of the qualities of complexity is that it also encompasses simple and complicated situations – although the reverse is not true.

In all this work with GANs, I did not fully appreciate the wonderful network I was developing of impressive individuals who have influenced me and often worked closely with me. Among the closest are those who have joined me in GAN-Net meetings as co-creators. With the Institute for Strategic Clarity, this has in particular included Jim Ritchie-Dunham who, coming from the decision-making sciences, has shared many of the community and methodological development challenges. As well, Luz Maria Puente has demonstrated wonderful leadership by actively experimenting with some of the strategic clarity methodologies in large system development.

Bill Snyder, a well-known colleague of Etienne Wenger in the development of communities of practice and learning systems strategies, continues as a partner who gives feedback and advice. We had lots of fun learning together about application of the community of practice concept to GANs.

And Bettye Pruitt along with co-author Philip Thomas of a wonderful handbook on change, are also great colleagues in developing the knowledge in this book. Bettye and I had the good fortune of being the beneficiary of funding raised by Adam Kahane, another explorer of large change, to investigate GANs from the perspective of their change capacity.

I also count as colleagues Peter Senge, whose work is enormously helpful and relevant to GANs. The Society for Organizational Learning that he founded led to wonderful connections. One of those, and like Peter with an MIT affiliation, is Otto Scharmer who is advancing understanding of deep change processes through study and practice.

The Boston College faculty have been very stimulating and supportive. In particular, there are Sandra Waddock, who is a leading scholar on business and society, Paul Gray, who is a good sociologist buddy in the societal change field, and Bill Torbert, who has influenced me with his work on action inquiry and stages of personal development. And thanks to Charlie Derber for his challenges.

Many others have participated in projects, meetings, and supporting my thinking, such as Pieter Glasbergen at the University of Utrecht, Simon Zadek with a project on the future of GANs, and the wonderful Verna Allee who is a leading thinker in the network and knowledge world.

Another colleague and academic-activist, Sanjeev Khagram, joined me at GAN-Net to lead it to a new level of development. He decided to take it in a very different direction than the association of GANs that I envisioned, and we separated paths. Perhaps the concept I held was too early, simply unworkable or we just did not have the skills and resources needed to make it work. But I see its essence emerging through an increasingly dense relationship between GANs, such as between the Global Compact, Transparency International (TI), the Global Reporting Initiative (GRI), and the Principles for Responsible Investment (PRI).

But of course the greatest debt of appreciation is to the numerous GAN leaders themselves, who took time out of their busy schedules to experiment with me at meetings and in projects. You will meet some of these in the book, who also took time for interviews and to review quotes. I hope that they will find this book worthy of their admirable work, and that it supports them to continue creating our future together that does indeed produce greater happiness.

LIST OF ABBREVIATIONS

ASI	Accreditation Services International
CCM	Country Coordinating Mechanisms (of the Global Fund to Fight AIDS)
CGIAR	Consultative Group on International Agriculture Research (a GAN)
CPWC	Cooperative Programme on Water and Climate (a GAN)
CSO	Civil Society Organizations (NGOs are a sub-set)
EITI	Extractive Industries Transparency Initiative (a GAN)
FSC	Forest Stewardship Council (a GAN)
GAIN	Global Alliance for Improved Nutrition (a GAN)
GAN	Global Action Network
GAVI	Global Alliances for Vaccines and Immunization (a GAN)
GFI	Global Finance Initiative (a project to develop a GAN)
GKP	Global Knowledge Partnership (a GAN)
GPPAC	Global Partnership for the Prevention of Armed Conflict (a GAN)
GRI	Global Reporting Initiative (a GAN)
GWC	Global Water Challenge (a GAN)
GWP	Global Water Partnership (a GAN)
IBJ	International Bridges to Justice (a GAN)
IGO	Intergovernmental organization (like the UN)
ILO	International Labour Organization (a GAN)
ION	Interorganizational network
IPARLS	Impact planning, assessment reporting and learning systems (a measuring impact methodology)
ISEAL Alliance	International Social and Environmental Accreditation and Labelling Alliance (a network of GANs)

IUCN	International Union for the Conservation of Nature (a GAN)
KP	Kimberley Process (a GAN)
MfC	Managing for Clarity (a mapping methodology)
MSC	Marine Stewardship Council (a GAN)
NGO	Non-governmental organization
OM	Outcome Mapping (a measuring impact methodology)
ONA	Organizational network analysis
PRI	Principles for Responsible Investment (a GAN)
SAI	Social Accountability International (a GAN)
SFI	Sustainable Forestry Initiative (a business network)
SFL	Sustainable Food Lab (a GAN)
SG	Secretary General (of the UN)
SI	Systems Intelligent
SLI	Systemic Leverage Index (a measuring impact methodology)
SNA	Social Network Analysis (a mapping methodology)
TAI	The Access Initiative (a GAN)
TI	Transparency International (a GAN)
UNEP	United Nations Environmental Program
USAID	United States Agency for International Development (a government donor organization)
VNA	Value Network Analysis (a mapping methodology)
WWC	World Water Council (a GAN)
YES	Youth Employment and Sustainability (a GAN)

CHAPTER 1

Organizing for the 21st century

The old ways of doing things are not up to the global challenges that we are facing. The Copenhagen 2009 and the Kyoto climate change process have clearly demonstrated the limitations of national governments in global problem-solving. And another finance crisis is inevitable, given that nothing significant has changed with the way the global finance system is organized. These failures are but two giant votes in favor of a new strategy that is rapidly emerging in response to global challenges like corruption, poverty, water, sustainability of forests and fisheries, health, security, and almost anything on the "global agenda." I call this new strategy Global Action Networks (GANs). This is a book about these networks, particularly for people who are working in them and who are interested in developing them.

Networks are perhaps the oldest and most enduring organizational form. Such networks in the form of family ties still dominate most people's lives. For individuals, organizations, and nations, networks have long been important as alliances, coalitions, collaborations, partnerships, and associations.

However, since the end of the twentieth century, networks are taking on new meaning and importance. Of course there are the networks of terrorists and criminals.[1] However, here we are talking about legitimate networks. In his 2000 seminal book, *The Rise of the Network Society*, Castells looks at the entire society through a network prism.[2] In an equally influential book 4 years later titled *A New World Order*, Anne-Marie Slaughter documents the growing importance of networks of government officials – police investigators, financial regulators, even judges and legislators – to combat global crime and address common problems on a global scale.[3]

Business activity is increasingly analyzed as networks between people.[4] In lock-step with globalization business activity increasingly is no longer characterized as centrally owned production processes, but rather long chains with multiple organizations.[5] And civil society's non-governmental organizations (NGOs) are continually forming and reforming networks, to address shifting goals of scale and complexity.[6,7]

The attraction to networks is tied to their ability to do things that other ways of organizing cannot. GANs are, however, a very particular type of network that gives us unusual capacity to create our global future together. Let's begin by taking a look at some of them.

Examples

Example 1. Changing the logic of finance

The "global finance system" hit the wall in 2008 and neared collapse. Although many are working on parts of the solution from nation-state perspectives, the Principles for Responsible Investment aim for basic change at a global level.

In 2005, a group of the world's largest institutional investors, supported by a 70-person multi-stakeholder group of experts from the investment industry, governmental organizations, civil society, and academia, drafted the Principles for Responsible Investment. Those principles aim to change the logic of global finance, so it integrates social, environmental, and economic concerns.

The PRI was launched in April 2006 to give life and meaning to the principles. Key launch partners were the then UN Secretary-General Kofi Annan, the UN Global Compact, and the UN Environmental Program Finance Initiative.

One revolutionary aspect of the PRI is that asset owners such as pension fund trustees are in the drivers' seat and on the PRI board, rather than fund managers and the investment industry. Another distinguishing quality is that individual parts of an organization – such as social responsibility funds existing within an investment firm – cannot become a signatory. Rather, the whole investment firm must commit to the Principles. By 2010, signatories comprised more than 720 institutions, representing in excess of US$ 20 trillion in assets.

Example 2. Transforming forestry

A group of timber users, traders, and representatives of environmental and human-rights organizations met in California in 1990 to discuss how they could combine their interests in improving forest conservation and reducing deforestation. The core ideas of certifying forests that are sustainably harvested through a multi-stakeholder strategy with business, environmentalists, and social activists became the Forest Stewardship Council (FSC) in 1992.

By 2010 the FSC's achievements include:

- FSC-certified products surpassing 50 percent of all timber and panel products produced in and imported to the UK in 2008.
- 120 million hectares of forests certified around the world, representing an area equal to Germany, France, the UK, and Ireland.
- Organizing approximately 16,000 businesses in the forestry-to-retail forest product production chain in almost 100 countries that have a product, process, or service conforming with FSC standards.

Example 3. Addressing AIDS

By the turn of the millennium, AIDS was truly a worldwide epidemic. Over 20 million deaths were attributed to the virus, and an estimated 36 million more were infected. In 2000, there were 4 million new infections in sub-Saharan Africa alone, with approximately 20 percent of those aged 15–49 in seven countries.

And yet, 90 percent of those infected could not access new, effective treatments. Cost was a huge factor, but also the delivery systems were simply not in place. In June 2001, a Special Session on AIDS of the UN General Assembly called for the creation of a global fund to address the scourge. A month later in Genoa, the G8 countries agreed to create such a fund. In January 2002, a Secretariat for the Global Fund to Fight AIDS, Tuberculosis, and Malaria was established, and 3 months later the first grants were given to 36 countries.

By the end of 2008, $14.8 billion in grants had been dispersed, with $3.1 billion in 2008. A quarter of the recipients were in lower-middle income countries; most of the rest in low-income countries. The Fund claimed 3.5 million people who otherwise would have died of AIDS, TB, or malaria over the past 5 years were alive as a result of the interventions.

Example 4. Giving life to the Rio Declaration

The 1992 Rio Earth Summit seemed a watershed event at the time. It was the largest international meeting ever held on the environment. Over 10,000 NGO representatives joined many heads of state and made their global presence felt more strongly than at any other international meeting. One commitment governments signed was the Rio Declaration on Environment and Development that listed 27 principles.

However, the Declaration produced little change. At the turn of the millennium, Frances Seymour and Elena Petkova at the World Resources Institute (WRI) in Washington, DC, began talking about doing something about it. They circulated a paper about what they might do. "It was also an effort to link research more directly to action," commented Elena, "build a constituency and a user base before the research product was ready and thus get a research product that reflects user demand and needs."

Through discussions, Principle 10 of the Rio Declaration surfaced as particularly important. Principle 10 reads:

> Environmental issues are best handled with participation of all concerned citizens, at the relevant level. At the national level, each individual shall have appropriate access to information concerning the environment that is held by public authorities, including information on hazardous materials and activities in their communities, and the opportunity to participate in decision-making processes. States shall facilitate and encourage public awareness and participation by making information widely available. Effective access to judicial and administrative proceedings, including redress and remedy, shall be provided.

In November 2001, about 50 people from NGOs and international government agencies met to discuss action. Rather than a traditional advocacy route to demand government adherence, a more collaborative approach would be developed to engage governments more as colleagues in developing "assessments" of their progress on implementing Principle 10. Zehra Aydin-Zidos of the United Nation's Commission on Sustainable Development commented: "There is lots of resistance to bringing in other actors because (implementation of the Rio Declaration) is seen as a government domain."

Today, through the Aarhus Convention, European countries are advancing the issue of "access rights" (the right to obtain government information, the right to participate in government decision-making, and the right to seek justice are a bundle of valuable rights). However, many countries do not have such strong government commitments. The Access Initiative (TAI) partners work in 50 countries to advance the fundamentals of Principle 10 by:

• conducting research using evidence-based research assessments to advocate for legal, institutional, and practice reforms;

- raising public awareness; and
- engaging their governments and other democratic institutions in a constructive dialogue to create change within their countries.

Guidelines on Principle 10 were adopted in the February of 2010 at the United Nations Global Ministerial meeting in Bali (Environment Forum). The guidelines set out the minimum legal standards for implementation of Principle 10 and mandated UNEP to assist countries in implementing programs and policies around access to information, public participation, and access to justice.

At the national level, most countries now have put in place the basic elements of a legal framework to support access rights. However, there are still wide gaps between law and practice, promises and implementation that TAI is working to address. Profound transformations are still necessary to achieve implementation of access rights in a framework of transparency where governments and civil society share a commitment to environmental democracy.

Example 5. The changing face of labor

Universities across the US know Russell through its brands of athletic clothing, including Russell Athletic, JERZEES, Spalding, and Bike. For about 10,000 Hondurans the US company is their employer.

In 1999, American universities, NGOs, and companies like Russell supplying the universities joined together to form the Fair Labor Association (FLA). The universities and their students wanted to ensure that the billions of dollars of goods they sell in campus stores and to university teams meet fair labor standards.

So when Russell announced its decision to end a Honduran contract at a unionized workplace, its commitment to freedom of association as part of its FLA membership was brought into question. Russell said its decision was simply based on financials: shutting down that plant would save $2 million more than shutting down any other one.

The FLA launched investigations. Students at the universities organized, and 100 universities ended their Russell contracts. NGOs lobbied at the annual meetings of Fruit of the Loom and Berkshire Hathaway who owned Russell. On June 25, 2009, the FLA board, finding grounds for concern about Russell's respect for freedom of association, announced a 90-day special review. On June 29, 2009, the FLA issued a remediation plan setting out specific steps that Russell would have to take in order to come into compliance with FLA standards.

A 45-day extension was approved for the review and on November 14 an agreement was announced. All of the 2000 workers at the first union-ized plant would be rehired with compensation and "collective pacts," (which were seen as anti-freedom of association) covering 8000 other Honduran workers would be phased out to allow for unionization in all facilities.

"In discussions, our corporate members were harder on Russell that our staff," comments FLA President and CEO Auret van Heerden. "They added to the agreement a stipulation that Russell reach out to engage with its stakeholders. Russell saw the stakeholders as the enemy, and said that constructive conversations wouldn't be possible. The corporate members said 'That's your mistake. There's no other way out of this.' "

Example 6. Taking on corruption

In the spring of 1990, representatives of the World Bank stationed in Africa met in Swaziland to discuss an urgent request articulated by African leaders in their famous Long-Term Perspective Study: "Support better governance." Peter Eigen, the World Bank's Director of the Regional Mis-sion for Eastern Africa, talked about corruption as a powerful enemy of good governance. At that time, it was widely regarded as a "cultural" issue not to be discussed, although it sapped hundreds of millions of development dollars.

Participants responded enthusiastically and decided that the World Bank should develop an anticorruption agenda. But it never happened out of fear that it would take the World Bank into forbidden political territory.

Yet some participants remained determined to take action. Eigen left the Bank, and in 1993 founded Transparency International (TI). Today, rather than talking about corruption as a cultural issue and avoiding its political implications, governments are taking action and corporations are being heavily punished. For example:

- On July 2, 2009, the World Bank announced that Siemens was required to pay $100 million to support the global fight against corruption, as part of its settlement with the World Bank Group following bribery by a Siemens' subsidiary in Russia. On December 12, Siemens agreed to pay record fines of $1.6 billion to settle charges of worldwide bribery.
- Anti-corruption conventions have been adopted by the OECD, the UN, and many international development agencies.

- TI is battling corruption through a network of 102 country chapters.
- TI's Corruption Perception Index is widely regarded as important by almost all governments.

Example 7. Creating sustainable fisheries

"To reverse the fisheries crisis," wrote Mike Sutton, at the founding of the Marine Stewardship Council (MSC) in 1996, "we must develop long-term solutions that are environmentally necessary and then, through economic incentives, make them politically feasible. Fortunately, an approach is available that has succeeded in other areas: working in partnership to design and implement market-driven incentives for sustainable fishing."[8] Sutton's comments accompanied a commitment by WWF and the world's largest seafood processor Unilever to partner to form MSC.

In 2010, the MSC topped in an independent assessment of wild capture seafood certification and eco-label programs. It achieved a score of 95.63 against criteria for credible programs, a score that was 30 points higher than the second-place program. The report concluded that the MSC is the only program to be designated "compliant" with the criteria of the evaluation.

Also by this time major retailers like Walmart, Wholefoods, Marks & Spencers, and Sainsbury's had committed to MSC-labeled products. Seafood in the MSC program:

- Produces annual catches of close to 7 million metric tonnes of seafood. This represents over 12 percent of global capture production for direct human consumption.
- The fisheries already certified catch close to 4 million metric tonnes of seafood. This is over 7 percent of the total global capture production for direct human consumption.
- Worldwide, more than 3,000 seafood products, which can be traced back to the certified sustainable fisheries, bear the blue MSC eco-label.

Example 8. Raising the poorest of the poor

Sam Daley-Harris' degree is in music. But in 1977 his Yoga teacher invited him to a meeting on stopping hunger. "If I thought about it, I would have said 'there are no solutions ... someone would have done something about it if there were,'" says Daley-Harris. But that was his beginning. He stresses that he started like almost everyone else does, by feeling hopeless about ending global poverty.

He began organizing and inspiring people to take action through an NGO called Results. "In 1984 we got a video about Grameen Bank, and by 1986 we had legislation introduced on micro-enterprise and had 100 editorials on the topic. Eunnis (Grameen Bank, Nobel Peace Prize Winner) Mohammend joined our Board in '88."

A Results 1994 conference called for reaching 100 million families with microcredit, with a particular emphasis upon women. The goal was to do this by 2005 and the Microcredit Summit Campaign was launched in 1997 when more than 2900 people from 137 countries gathered in Washington, DC.

After reaching its goal, the Microcredit Summit Campaign is now working to ensure that:

- 175 million of the world's poorest families, especially the women of those families, are receiving credit for self-employment and other financial and business services by the end of 2015.
- 100 million families rise above the US$1 a day threshold by 2015.

Example 9. The funding of war

The 1999 movie *Blood Diamonds* presents the story of a fisherman in the war-torn West African country of Sierra Leone. His dreams about his son becoming a doctor are shattered when rebels invade his village and kidnap him to work in the diamond mines. The ensuing story involves a Zimbabwean mercenary smuggler, mercenary South African forces, and rebels who trade the diamonds directly for arms to continue their war and killing. Although the film includes the inevitable Hollywood touches, it tells the basic story of diamonds funding and prolonging chaos, death, and instability.

This cycle spurred a meeting in Kimberley, South Africa, of diamond-producing states, the diamond industry, and NGOs to discuss how to stop the trade in "conflict diamonds." With the support of the UN, in 2003 the Kimberley Process Certification Scheme (KP) began as a joint government, industry, and civil society initiative to stem the flow of conflict diamonds.

Today the trade in conflict diamonds is essentially stopped by the Kimberley Process without offices or staff. However, its participants include 75 countries, the World Diamond Council representing the international diamond industry, and civil society organizations.

The KP imposes extensive requirements on its participants to certify shipments of rough diamonds as 'conflict-free' and prevent conflict diamonds from entering the legitimate trade. Participating countries must put in place national legislation and institutions; export, import, and internal controls; and also commit to transparency and the exchange of statistical data. Participants can only legally trade with other participants who have also met the requirements of the scheme. International shipments of rough diamonds must be accompanied by a KP certificate guaranteeing that they are conflict-free.

Example 10. Changing the definition of success

In the early 1990s, the concept of "triple bottom line" was developed as a new way of thinking about business success. By the middle of that decade, multi-national companies were being overwhelmed with requests for data about their impact on a wide range of issues. CERES, a coalition of environmental organizations and socially responsible investors, decided to see if something could be done to give greater focus to the dispersed activity. It convened a series of meetings with people involved in the various aspects of the emerging field of triple bottom-line accounting.

Out of these meetings, the Global Reporting Initiative (GRI) arose with the vision *that disclosure on economic, environmental, and social performance become as commonplace and comparable as financial reporting, and as important to organizational success.* It is a network of four defined groups: business, labor, civil society, and "mediating institutions" (accounting, foundations, and consultants).

Today it operates with a global office in the Netherlands and focal points in Australia, China, Brazil, and India. It has developed three generations of an evolving Reporting Framework with Guidelines, with numerous supplements for specific industries and NGOs. GRI has tracked more than 1350 organizations that formally issued a GRI-based sustainability report in 2009 – this is a 25 percent increase on the prior year. Studies suggest there are many more GRI reporters that are not formally documented.

The examples' shared characteristics

These networks are dealing with an incredibly diverse array of issues, and they seem to be achieving important results. What is going on here? How are these types of outcomes being achieved? Are these just isolated examples, or do they represent something new and enduring? Do they represent an approach that can address the big challenges of environmental sustainability, equity, economic well-being, peace, and stability? Sure they might do some good things, but they must have big short-comings too! And can they really last, or are they a short-term phenomenon? These questions are at the heart of this book.

I first became aware of these networks while making a modest contribution to a report to Secretary-General Kofi Annan called *Critical Choices: The United Nations, networks, and the future of global governance.*[9] The lead author, Wolfgang Reinicke, is known for his concept of Global Public Policy Networks (GPPNs). I had been working on issues of multi-stakeholder and in particular cross-sectoral (business, government, civil society as three organizational sectors) collaboration. Wolfgang referred to such collaboration as "horizontal" across society, and local-to-global as "vertical" collaboration.

I was inspired by the potential of these networks, put together some money and people, and continued investigating them. However, I found that the people in the networks did not think of their goal as "public policy," but rather transformational change. Moreover, although Wolfgang's political science perspective was useful, I found the organizational-, network-, and societal-development and change traditions I worked with more helpful to them in their development. Consequently, I coined the term "Global Action Networks," popularized as "GANs."

Other people use different terms for a similar group of organizations. This includes nation-state and multi-actor *regimes*,[10,11] *earth governance*,[12] *issue networks*,[13] *collaborative governance*,[14] and *global governance organizations*.[15]

When I refer to GANs I'm speaking of a very specific type of network that combines to a significant degree seven specific characteristics. There are a few dozen similar examples that share seven particular characteristics of these ones. Many others have three or four of these characteristics, but a very modest number combine all seven. Some possess these characteristics "more or less," but they would resonate with them as aspirational.

Characteristic 1. Global and multi-level

GANs aspire to be global, although many are currently active in fewer than 60 countries. One of the amazing qualities of GANs is how rapidly they become global. Outside of businesses conducted over the Internet, creating a global corporation within a few years would be impossible. GANs have a movement- and viral-development approach.

The GANs presume they will be global, and they think globally. That means that they think of the key challenge they are addressing as requiring a global effort, and that they will have a critical role in developing that effort. This criterion eliminates some initiatives that might fit the other ones, such as is the case with the Global Partnership to Eliminate River Blindness, which is really an African activity.

GANs also aim for a local-to-global presence – the multi-level part – sometimes referred to as "glocal." This emphasizes their interest in "where the rubber hits the road" and on-the-ground action. The FSC is not simply advocating forestry standards, it is actively working to apply and further develop them; the Global Water Partnership is not simply interested in a theoretical construct of "integrated water resource management," but in working with partners around the world to give life to it.

Four factors influence how global and multi-level the GANs are:

1. **The role of wealth.** Several of the networks, such as the Global Fund to Fight AIDS, Tuberculosis, and Malaria (the Global Fund), are products of a donor agency mentality with Northern countries aiming to achieve some desired outcome in Southern (developing) countries. Through their government Ministries and Departments, wealthy countries (and some foundations) put money in a common pot to more effectively coordinate their efforts and build the necessary scale to address a problem in poorer countries. In the case of blood diamonds, (brought to attention by a Hollywood movie by the same name) the distinction is between poorer countries where diamonds are mined, and richer countries where they are purchased.
2. **Their stage of development.** Of course physical presence is related to age – unlike Athena who emerged whole from the head of Zeus, a global network does not suddenly appear. Even when sponsored by an existing global network, substantial effort and time is required to give life to a new initiative that spans the world.
3. **Local conditions.** Some countries and cultures are more open to the strategy of GANs and the particular issue of a GAN than others. The Global Compact, for example, had significant initial difficulty in building a presence in the US because the litigious tradition of the US made companies fear their participation would make them vulnerable to suits. In China and Arab countries, the lack of robust civil society organizations makes the GANs' cross-sector organizing strategy problematic.

    Issues of a GAN may simply not be relevant in some countries. For example, the Mountain Forum has no place in the Netherlands, nor in Bangladesh. And some countries have elected a non-GAN route: for example, TAI has little European presence in its work to ensure participatory practices in environmental decision-making since the Europeans have selected a government-led approach with the Aarhus Protocol. Building Partners for Development in Water and Sanitation is quite specialized and would not be of interest to countries committed only to public sector planning, development, and delivery of water and sanitation services.

4. **The GAN membership strategy.** Some of the networks are closed to new members, or set significant hurdles to membership. For example, although anyone can join the Ethical Trading Initiative (ETI), companies must agree to monitoring and ethical performance standards that many would find overly onerous. Although GANs in general are about creating a "vanguard" of standards, GANs like ETI have decided to set themselves on the "elite vanguard."

Characteristic 2. Diversity embracing boundary spanners

To be effective global networks, embracing diversity is absolutely necessary. They must have global representation in their decision-making, and be flexible enough in strategies to be supportive of distinctive local cultures – not just tolerant of them. One huge challenge is linguistic. No one would claim it is satisfactorily addressed, since English is almost always the language of global meetings with little or no provision for translation. And of course embedded in the English language are particular ways of looking at the world.

GANs are also places where people of very different wealth meet. This includes people from wealthy countries meeting people from poor countries, and within countries people of different wealth meeting. Bridging wealth means GANs also bridge traditional donor/recipient divides. And in many of the GANs wealthy corporations with substantial resources work side by side with NGOs.

Particularly distinctive is that GANs have a multi-stakeholder strategy that takes them across the traditional network boundaries of the three organizational sectors of business, government, and civil society (non-profits). A multi-stakeholder strategy also means bringing together the "whole system" of people influenced by, and who influence, an issue. However, occasionally some stakeholders are intentionally excluded, such as with the exclusion of the tobacco companies from the Tobacco-Free Initiative since their interests were diametrically opposite.

For the Cooperative Programme on Water and Climate key bridging was across divides between policy makers (usually governments and international NGOs), techno-experts (scientists, business people, engineers), funders (foundations and donor agencies), and communities (local activists and community members).

Although GANs often start with an emphasis upon global and national, longer-term success usually hinges upon global–regional–national–local boundary spanning. In many ways GANs are the first truly global assemblies. Unlike some traditional global boundary spanners that depend upon creating strong collective identities – such as religious organizations – at least as important for GANs is the ability to preserve the distinct identities of members. If people coming from diverse perspectives cannot successfully articulate and represent them and mobilize the resources of their stakeholder group, their value to the GAN will be lost.

Characteristic 3. Inter-organizational networks

If you are after global action, individuals as an organizing unit provide weak leverage. Most individuals have less influence and resource access than organizations. Organizing individuals to realize the scale of action the GANs aim for would be an even greater organizing challenge than their chosen strategy to network organizations. Sometimes GANs' participants are even associations of organizations – the GAN then being a network of networks like the World Water Council.

Consequently, at the global level the role of individuals as participants and members in the networks is very marginal as opposed to the role of organizations. Transparency International (TI) began as a network of individual members and individuals still have a modest (and diminishing) role, but TI quickly shifted to a network where a specific organization is usually accredited as a national chapter.

In some cases, the distinction between individuals and organizations is finessed – the GRI, for example, specifies that individuals do not represent an organization's interests because of concern that this will undermine the needs of 'the whole' – but in fact, 'Organizational Stakeholders' are a key membership category.

Networks also are associated with a different power dynamic than traditional hierarchical organizations. They support diversity by facilitating marginalized people to find each other and entrepreneurialism by encouraging decentralized action.

Characteristic 4. Systemic change agents

This is perhaps the most complicated of the attributes and is difficult to explain or to assess. By "a system" I mean a set of independent but inter-related elements comprising a whole with regard to an activity, goal, or function. So think of the "system" at play with the issue of corruption. There are those who pay bribes, those who receive them, the legal appara-tus that makes that possible, and the broader social networks and cultural values that are involved. That system is the focus of TI when it brings together the diverse organizations necessary to address corruption.

GANs' core change strategy is to change what is possible, and this usu-ally means changing the very way people think about an issue – TI's Peter Eigen first had to make corruption a discussable issue. Then GANs build visions of how things can be different and create the necessary capacity to go about making them different. This usually means changing rules, procedures, laws, and values.

With its particular issue system, a GAN aims to reach the "tipping point"[16] where organizations will no longer be considered "legitimate" and will be denied opportunities if they don't follow the new rules and integrate the values. For example, the MSC and FSC aim to make selling products that do not reach their certification standard very difficult and costly – their certifications being seen as so desirable that there will be a modest premium for them and that both retail and wholesale purchasers demand the certifications.

Characteristic 5. Entrepreneurial action learners

The truth is that often GANs do not know exactly how to go about imple-menting their strategies, or how successful they will even be. More often than not, they are trying to do things that no one has ever tried to do before, although with books like this one about their experiences they have increasing guidance. This means that GANs are continually involved with experiments and innovating, and they have to develop good learning systems to efficiently and effectively draw appropriate lessons from them.

GANs' learning challenge is complicated by the diversity they embrace and the complexity of the systems and issues they address. They need to draw upon a wide variety of expertise and integrate it into actions. And the expertise is both about content – AIDS, forests, diamond mar-kets, for example – and about processes and structures – about how work gets done, and how to develop a robust network of unprecedented scale and complexity to do it.

This learning involves application and development of new methodologies, tools, and processes. The Sustainable Food Laboratory draws its name from a new methodology referred to as "The Change Lab." It is not only developing a sustainable food system, but also a new approach to change.

A significant challenge for GANs is to pay attention to developing these approaches and use them. People in the GANs find the "action" part much more compelling, and the "learning" part requires much more discipline. However, it is important to avoid repeating mistakes and building a GAN's effectiveness.

Characteristic 6. Voluntary leaders

Bjorn Roberts, Corporate Partnership Manager for The Climate Group, comments: "We're a coalition of the willing...there is the formal membership structure, but we're also a wider group of leading business and government organizations." The GANs are networks of organizations willing to take leadership to address a specific issue. They do not have power of coercion through jail, taxation, or fines. For this, many criticize them. The Global Compact has been accused of "blue-washing" and misuse of the UN's name as cover for bad business practice. The FSC became entangled in enormous controversy in Indonesia and was accused of mis-use of its logo. It was trying to create a strategy to work with large companies who could not immediately make a commitment to ensure all their products are sustainably harvested.

The GANs must walk a difficult line. They must ensure that they are continually advancing the boundaries of good practice, and yet encourage more organizations to adopt the practice. The accompanying strategy is, of course, to influence government regulators who *do* have the power of coercion, and to do this globally.

Characteristic 7. Global public goods producers

> ...public goods are those that share two qualities – non-excludability and non-rivalry, in economists' jargon. This means, respectively, that when provided to one party, the public good is available to all, and consumption of the public good by one party does not reduce the amount available to the others to consume. Traditional examples of national public goods include traffic control systems and national security – goods that benefit all citizens and national private actors but that none could afford to supply on their own initiative.[17]

GANs' public goods creation role is reflected in their activities that:

1. optimize the positive public impacts of public expenditures such as those associated with the Millennium Development Goals and private investment,
2. address negative externalities of globalization,
3. support more equitable development globally,
4. work for an environmentally sustainable future,
5. develop sustainable wealth generation, and
6. nurture greater social cohesion – developing positive relationships between organizational sectors, across national boundaries, and among diverse cultures.

In keeping with this global public good creation, legally GANs are almost always an NGO, a non-profit organization (or a program of one) or, occasionally, an intergovernmental organization as is the case of the Global Compact. The issues GANs focus on in some ways reflect divisions not uncommon with governments, their agencies, and ministries. However, the issues are often relatively specialized – rather than a Ministry of Health, they are constructed around specific health challenges and diseases; rather than a ministry of public works, the Global Water Partnership and World Water Council have much narrower, distinctive, and complementary roles. On the other hand, some of the GANs focus upon cross-cutting issues that traditional governmental structures have great difficulty addressing – such as the International Centre for Trade and Sustainable Development and the Global Reporting Initiative, which are concerned with triple bottom line (economic, social, and environmental) reporting.

A growing phenomenon

GANs arc a post-Cold War phenomenon, for good reason. However, there are three networks that pre-date that period and have most of the GAN characteristics. One is the International Red Cross Red Crescent Movement, with origins in 1863. The International Committee of the Red Cross, part of the Movement, is distinctive because it is an NGO that is "custodian" of the Geneva Conventions that are the product of governments, and because it has a permanent mandate under international law supporting its activities. Other parts of the Movement have a similarly unusual government and NGO character. For example, the American Red Cross Society is established by its own Charter of the Congress of the US.

The Chairman is appointed by the President of the US, but other Board members are elected by members of the Society.

The Movement is an impressive example of a GAN, comprising almost 97 million volunteers, supporters, and staff in 186 countries. It reaches and supports around 250 million people annually through its programs; the value of the contribution made by youth volunteers in Africa alone is estimated to be worth more than $1.4 billion per year.[18]

The second oldest GAN is the International Labour Organization (ILO). It was founded in 1919 in the wake of World War I, in the belief that lasting peace is dependent upon decent treatment of working people. After the UN was established, the ILO became an agency of it. However, it is unique as the only "tri-partite" UN agency. The ILO Governing Body is composed of 28 government members, 14 employer members, and 14 worker members. Countries of chief industrial importance permanently hold ten of the government seats. Government representatives are elected at a Conference every three years, taking into account geographical distribution. The employers and workers elect their own representatives respectively.

The ILO's tasks are promoting rights at work, encouraging opportunities for decent employment, enhancing social protection, and strengthening dialogue on work-related issues. Over the years and through its close UN affiliation, it has become quite bureaucratic and weak in some GAN characteristics like "entrepreneurial action learner."

The third old GAN was founded in 1948 and is IUCN, the International Union for Conservation of Nature. It describes itself as the world's oldest and largest global environmental network – a democratic membership union with more than 1,000 government and NGO member organizations, and almost 11,000 volunteer scientists in more than 160 countries. Although governments usually refuse to be "members" of NGOs, IUCN's members include over 200 government and over 800 non-government organizations.

IUCN is perhaps best known for production of the "Red Book" which catalogues endangered species. It runs thousands of field projects around the world to better manage natural environments and develop leading conservation science.

During the Cold War when groups of countries were split into ideological camps, creating organizations to take truly grounded global action was highly problematic. Moreover, given the heavy dominance of government in Communist countries and the lack of independent business and civil society organizations, multi-stakeholder initiatives were not possible. The best that could be done was academic exchanges, cultural tours, and sports events that were devoted to demonstrating ideological superiority.

Nevertheless, there were a couple of important GAN initiatives in less ideologically charged and yet critical arenas. One is the Consultative Group on International Agriculture Research (CGIAR). It brings together 15 research institutes, funders, national governments, civil society organizations, and the private sector to move research results from laboratories to farmers' fields. Over 300 farmers organizations are currently engaged in collaborative research programs with CGIAR centers. Today more than half the land growing improved varieties of the world's ten most important food crops is growing varieties with CGIAR ancestry.

Additionally, growing out of a 1985 health conference in Canada came the Healthy Cities (Communities) Movement. Although associated with the World Health Organization (WHO) and originating with health professionals, it developed a much broader concept of health. It envisions that people are healthy when they live in nurturing environments and are involved in the life of their community. The key focus is at the local level, and the vision involves connecting diverse people and organizations in communities. Although the Movement as a network continues to be active in Europe with the support of WHO, its global presence has greatly diminished.

But after the fall of the Berlin Wall, new opportunities arose for networks of diverse participants globally. They were inspired by new thinking about traditional divisions, and the FSC was one of the first to explore how adversaries might actually work together. All of the GANs described as examples at the beginning of this chapter are from this period. The fast pace of development of the 1990s slowed with increasing skepticism about networks and "dialogue" associated with them. Today almost every issue has a GAN, and several issues have more than one. Some GANs have died and some are active at a relatively low level. However, there are several dozen today, and about three or four dozen have a significant presence.

They represent an innovation that is as distinct from business, government, and civil society organizations as those three types of organizations are from each other. "We're not a business, not an NGO," comments Ernst Ligteringen, Chief Executive of the GRI. "From a business perspective, we move slowly. From the NGO side, we're moving at a fairly quick pace. I tell NGOs: 'Yes, we consult, but we're not only about consultation. GRI is also focused on maintaining a momentum in the development of sustainability reporting.' " However, the GANs are at an early stage of development and are still not widely recognized as unique.

Their stage of development is comparable to business corporations during the age of the railroad in the late nineteenth century. Only then did the corporate form really take shape, with the demands for coordination of activities with increasing precision over global distances and time zones. Recognition of the importance of the organizational form was marked with the founding of the first business school in 1908, the Harvard Business School.

Governments as we know them today really only developed with the rise of the welfare and nation-state after World War I. Before that they were comparatively modest in extent of activity, and often associated with individuals, ruling families, or oligarchies rather than citizen accountability. Today we have Schools of Government and of Public Administration to train people for those particular institutions.

And at the beginning of the twentieth century civil society organizations were largely associated with religious and labor organizations. Since the 1960s, there has been tremendous growth in NGOs to span almost every issue from human rights, health, and education to the environment, peace, and development. Parallel with these developments we have the rise of centers of learning and capacity development for civil society.

The founding period of a new organizational type like the GANs is a period of general confusion, experimentation, and intense learning. They operate with a different *logic* and *assumptions* that are discussed more in the final chapter that summarizes the experience of GANs and describes their potential future as critical global governance organizations.

People bring to GANs their experiences from other types of organizations, and naturally enough try to apply those experiences. Pioneers in GANs have looked to inter-governmental organizations like the UN and the WHO as possible role models, and this has led to inappropriate appropriation of concepts like "Secretariat", which can limit GANs' development of their potential. Other pioneers have looked to NGOs like Amnesty International as role models, without accounting for the fundamentally different dynamic that embracing of business, government, and civil society generates. Although business corporations have less often been taken as role models, it is not unusual for a person from business – often on a GAN board – to try to make a GAN "more business-like" in its operations.

To realize their potential GANs must be recognized as a distinct type of organization that requires unique skills, structures, processes, and strategies. Given GANs' early development stage, we still do not know what all of these are, but there is rich learning from GAN pioneers. This book aims to present some of that learning to avoid repetition of mistakes and further develop the knowledge and competencies necessary for this type of network to reach its full potential.

Notes

1. Arquilla, J. and D. Ronfeldt (2001). "Networks and Netwars: The Future of Terror, Crime and Militancy." *Networks and Netwars: The Future of Terror, Crime and Militancy*. J. Arquilla and D. Ronfeldt (eds). Santa Monica, CA, USA, Rand Corporation.
2. Castells, M. (2000). *The Rise of the Network Society*. Malden, MA, USA, Blackwell Publishers.
3. Slaughter, A.-M. (2004). *A New World Order*. Princeton, NJ, USA, Princeton University Press.
4. Cross, R. and A. Parker (2004). *The Hidden Power of Social Networks*. Boston, MA, USA, Harvard Business School.
5. Gulati, R. (2007). *Managing Network Resources: Alliances, Affiliations, and Other Relational Assets*. Oxford, UK, Oxford University Press.
6. Khagram, S., et al., eds (2001). "Social Movements, Protest, and Contention." *Restructuring World Politics: Transnational Social Movements, Networks, and Norms*. Minneapolis, MN, USA, University of Minnesota Press.
7. Batliwala, S. (2002). "Grassroots Movements as Transnational Actors: Implications for Global Civil Society." *Voluntas: International Journal of Voluntary and Nonprofit Organizations* 13(4): 393–409.
8. Sutton, M. (1996). "The Marine Stewardship Council: New Hope for Marine Fisheries." *NAGA, The ICLARM Quarterly* (July): 10–12.
9. Reinicke, W. H. and F. M. Deng (2000). *Critical Choices: The United Nations, Networks, and the Future of Global Governance*. Toronto, Canada, International Development Research Council.
10. Ruggie, J. G. (1982). "International Regimes, Transactions, and Change: Embedded Liberalism in the Postwar Economic Order." *International Organization* 36(2): 379–415.
11. Young, O. R., ed. (1999). *The Effectiveness of International Environmental Regimes*. Cambridge, MA, Massachusetts Institute of Technology Press.
12. Biermann, F. (2007). "Earth System Governance' as a Crosscutting Theme." *Global Environmental Change* 17(3–4): 326–337.
13. Rischard, J.-F. (2001). "High Noon: The Urgent Need for New Approaches to Global Problem-Solving." *Journal of International Economic Law* 4(3): 507–525.
14. Zadek, S. and S. Radovich (2006). *Governing Collaborative Governance: Enhancing Development Outcomes by Improving Partnership Governance and Accountability*. Cambridge, MA, USA, Corporate Social Responsibility Initiative – Harvard University.
15. Koppell, J. G. (2010). *World Rule: The Politics of Global Governance*. Chicago, USA, University of Chicago Press.
16. Gladwell, M. (2002). *The Tipping Point: How Little Things Can Make a Big Difference*. Boston, MA, USA, Little, Brown and Company.
17. International Task Force on Global Public Goods (2006). *Meeting Global Challenges: International Cooperation in the National Interest*. Stockholm, Sweden, International Task Force on Global Public Goods, p. 13.
18. ICRC. (2010). "Who We Are." Retrieved March 5, 2010, from http://www.ifrc.org/who/movement.asp.

CHAPTER 2

Understanding networks

The work of 2009 Nobel Prize winners for economics – Oliver Williamson and Elinor Ostrom – is very relevant to Global Action Networks (GANs). These prize-winners' work helps explain what GANs do, when developing GANs as a strategy makes sense, and assessing whether GANs are meeting their potential.

Williamson won the prize for his work on conflicts of interest and how different governance structures address them, with a particular focus upon "transaction costs" – expenses associated with exchanges of goods and services in economic production. In essence, he explains that the control associated with traditional hierarchical organizations like a business corporation makes the best structure for certain types of exchanges. Those would be exchanges that involve uncertainty about their outcome, that occur frequently, and that require significant investment of money, time, or energy. Marketplace exchanges, on the other hand, are best for impersonal exchanges between businesses and/or individuals when the transactions are straightforward, non-repetitive, and require little investment.[1]

In another seminal 1991 article, Walter Powell looked at a third way of organizing: by network. These he defined as "typified by reciprocal patterns of communication and exchange."[2] He compares markets and networks this way:

> In market transactions the benefits to be exchanged are clearly specified, no trust is required, and agreements are bolstered by the power of legal sanction. Network forms of exchange, however, entail indefinite, sequential transactions within the context of a general pattern of interaction. Sanctions are typically normative (peer pressure) rather than legal. The value of goods to be exchanged in markets is much more important that the relationship itself.... In markets, the standard strategy is to drive the hardest possible bargain in the immediate exchange. In networks, the preferred option is often one of creating indebtedness and reliance over the long haul.

> ... *(the) basic assumption of network relationships is that one party is dependent on resources controlled by another, and that there are gains to be had by the pooling of resources. In essence, the parties to a network agree to forego the right to pursue their own interest at the expense of others.*
>
> (pp. 301–303)

In networks, outcomes are associated with what Powell refers to as "exchanges whose value is not easily determined." Reciprocity is central; participants in a network must be willing to contribute and give, as well as take and receive. Reciprocity requires a long-term perspective. In addition, networks are particularly appropriate choice when participation in decision-making is important.

The intent of the network

As Powell also points out, trust is particularly important in networks since dependence upon formal, legalistic mechanisms inhibits reciprocity and robust exchanges. To develop trust and actually assess it within a network, considering three different types is useful. One type is trust of *intent*: that

Table 2.1   Why organize a network?

Desired Outcome	Rationale
Speeding spread of knowledge	Strengthening ties creates more and better paths for knowledge development and dissemination
Realizing benefits of scale	Strengthening ties supports actions on behalf of "the system" and aggregate efforts
Innovating	Creating networks with diverse voices, perspectives, and resources supports emergence of new ways of thinking about issues and integrating resources
Enhancing coherence	Strengthening ties supports actions on behalf of "the system" and the potential for asserting goals of the broader system
Improving coordination	Creating networks broadens the options for action and enhances the potential for reduced friction in exchanges
Integrating resources, knowledge, skills	Networking of complementary assets, (such as competencies and stakeholder connections) is necessary to do a task/realize a goal

This table can help clarify the rationale driving a particular network. Of course there might be more than one. Which ones are internally seen as critical? How do non-participants perceive it? How well does the network achieve its desired outcome, in comparison to other networks? What might it learn from other networks to enhance its outcome?

you and I share a goal. Then there is trust in *competence:* that you and I are actually capable of doing what we say we will do. And third is trust of *understanding:* that you and I have shared understanding of the words and language and commitments.[3]

When arguing in favor of development of an inter-organizational network, advocates often have difficulty in specifying the outcomes that will be realized in measurable terms. In my work I've found that networks may have up to six rationales for their formation. Table 2.1 defines several generic reasons for choosing to organize as a network rather than a traditional hierarchical organization characterized by top-down relationships, or through a market characterized as impersonal exchanges between people who do not know each other. Rationales are particularly important for assessing the effectiveness and relevance of outcomes.

Network advantages

Network connections provide ready conduits for transmission of information. One great attraction of social media, for example, is that it creates networks between people who want to receive the same message, without having to worry about re-sending to many addresses. This is the "narrowcasting" aspect of networks. It is neither "broadcasting" as traditional (hierarchical) media do, nor is it as personalized as one-on-one communications.

A GAN is organized around specific issues and shares information about how to address that issue and its latest developments. They provide ready communication platforms for sub-groups to organize in ever more specialized geographic and sub-issue networks. The Kimberley (conflict diamonds) Process (KP) facilitates not just discussions among its community as a whole, but among the sub-groups of member countries, NGOs, and business. Each of these groups needs their own distinct communications networks, as well as a network for the whole.

"Viral" organizing is often associated with networks, as a way to describe the speed and ease associated with the spread of viruses with networks' easy connection, exchange, and development of joint action. The network structure also allows for reaching a greater scale with less time than hierarchical organizations where there are a lot of gatekeepers, rules, and processes for "approval." Usually GANs simply require that participants abide by a code of conduct that is summarized within a page, leaving participants free to take significant action within that context with trust developed over time.

Julia Marton-Lefevre, Director-General of the conservationist GAN IUCN comments: "A major reason to join IUCN is to strengthen your voice." The viral network organizing is producing vast scale within short periods of time. Networks truly have global reach within a year or two, rather than the years that traditional organizing requires. The Global Compact, in its first assessment a couple of years after its founding, was surprised to learn the extent of the Global Compact national networks; the Secretariat had not "taken charge" of developing them, but rather the local networks grew from local inspiration. Sometimes this admittedly results in problems, such as for Transparency International (TI) when its Kenya Chapter had to be "decertified" because of actions outside of the agreed standards of conduct.

One of the great attractions to networks for global action is that they can accommodate wide diversity and respond to a very broad range of local conditions. The Microcredit Summit Campaign does not direct how its participants should achieve goals defined in the action plans they develop; rather, it sets a global goal and spurs the network participants to focus upon it by getting them to set and report annual commitments. This structure helps create coherence and alignment globally, while permitting innovation locally.

Within the network structure there are sub-groups that want to work together in a more intense manner, and the network supports formation of partnerships among participants. These can form more easily than without the network, because by participating in the network people develop a similar culture, language, values, and orientation. For example, the Global Reporting Initiative (GRI) pulls together people from around the world and from business, labor, academia, and NGOs to develop supplements to its broad framework for triple bottom-line impact assessment for specific industries.

One of the basic rationales for collaboration is that any one organization does not have the skills, resources, and abilities necessary to address an issue. Business, government, and civil society organizations have different logics that let them do very different things.[4] Collaborations also broaden geographic coverage, and ability to engage distinct cultures and social groups.

Different levels of organizing

However, there are very different types of networks, and one way to distinguish between them is by their "level of organizing" described in ypes by organizing level

	Organization	Inter-organizational partnership	Inter-organizational network	System
Legally Distinct Entities	Many	One	Small to modest	Very large	All stakeholders
Organizing Structure	Informal	Hierarchical	Hub and spoke	Multi-hub	Diffuse
Organizing Logic	Personal	Administering/ managing	Coordination	Coherence	Diverse self-direction
Operating Focus	Relation-ships	Organization	Task	System	Definitional
Participation	Open	Closed	Highly controlled	Loosely controlled	External

This table can help analyze the level of activity of a network. Has it got the balance right? Is it good at managing its organizational level? Are its partnerships robust in coordination? Are network activities increasing in coherence? Is there a good theory of change to impact the system?

Source: Adapted from Waddell, S. and S. Khagram (2007). "Multi-stakeholder global networks: emerging systems for the global common good". *Partnerships, Governance And Sustainable Development: Reflections on Theory and Practice*. P. Glasbergen, F. Biermann and A. P. J. Mol. Cheltenham Glos., UK, Edward Elgar Publishing: 261–287.

Table 2.2. From a sociological perspective, an "organization" is simply a network with a formal legal boundary; here the term is used specifically to refer to the traditional hierarchical forms of business, government, and NGO.

I first created a version of Table 2.2 when participating in a seminar on partnerships sponsored by the Royal Netherlands Academy of Arts and Sciences. People were using the terms "network," "partnership," and "organization" inter-changeably and I thought greater clarity in these terms would be helpful. Table 2.2 describes the way terms are used in this book. Others may use the terms differently, but distinguishing between the terms is very useful.

Some may consider what are here referred to as "partnerships" as what I mean when I write "network." Partnerships are defined as task oriented – they have a relatively limited and well-defined objective such as producing a report or constructing a water system. The main rationale behind them is to coordinate activities, resources, and skills. There are perhaps as many as a couple of dozen participants, a small enough number for people (or organizational representatives) to know each other and coordinate activities. They are organized on a hub and spoke model, with a central coordinating committee or organization of some sort.

In contrast, GANs are inter-organizational networks. They may have thousands of participating organizations and tens of thousands of people from those organizations participating – many more than can possibly know each other. They come together because they are participants in a system that they want to move in a certain direction – they want to create greater "coherence" between their activities and that of others. For example, the Forest Stewardship Council (FSC) wants to move all stakeholders in the "forest and forest-product system" in a direction that supports sustainable forestry practices. This includes forest companies, manufacturers of forest products and retailers of those products, environmentalists, the forest communities, consumers, financiers, and others.

But the FSC's success is not dependent upon its ability to engage every stakeholder organization as a participant. In fact, it can achieve its goal with only a minority of stakeholder organizations participating. Its goal is to influence the whole system by engaging enough stakeholders so that it can change the rules of the system and the way it operates. The "system" is very diffuse, and does not have any particular organizing focus although many organizations would be sub-network nodes, such as commercial timber company associations.

One important complication is that a GAN is here described as an inter-organizational network, but it has many "partnerships" within it working on particular projects. For example, the Global Water Partnership (GWP) has local partnerships working on a particular water basin. But a GAN also has an element of "organization" in the form of what is usually referred to as a Secretariat. This central node has staff and a reporting structure that is no different from other traditional hierarchies.

This usually is confusing for GANs. They must effectively incorporate the elements of networks, partnerships, and organizations. They must understand which is doing what, and why; they must be able to apply the appropriate "organizing logic" in each situation. They must be excellent at managing Secretariat staff, at coordinating partner projects, and creating coherence for the network as a whole.

Who makes the rules?

So this brings us to the work of the other 2009 Nobel Prize winner in economics, Elinor Ostrom. She focuses upon a particular type of network and how they enforce rules: networks organized by stakeholders in a system. Her work is summed up in her best-known book titled *Governing the Commons: The Evolution of Institutions for Collective Action.*[5] The media release announcing that she won the Nobel Prize described it this way:

> *(Ostrom) has challenged the conventional wisdom that common property is poorly managed and should be either regulated by central authorities or privatized .... She observes that resource users frequently develop sophisticated mechanisms for decision-making and rule enforcement to handle conflicts of interest, and she characterizes the rules that promote successful outcomes.*[6]

Ostrom worked with local cases addressing the challenges of what she referred to as "common resource pools" (CRPs). GANs deal with significantly larger scale, but much the same challenge. For example, the fisheries that Ostrom studied in Turkey developed an approach at a local level that is much like the approach the Marine Stewardship Council (MSC) is developing globally.

This perspective relates to GANs' role as producers of global public goods, and how to avoid what biologist Garrett Hardin called "the tragedy of the commons." This describes the situation when many people make use of a common resource, such as fisheries, to the point that they are depleted even when it is clear that it is not in anyone's long-term interest for this to happen.[7] The Principles for Responsible Investment (PRI) are, for example, trying to establish rules that will address problems where investors benefit in the short-term by damaging our long-term sustainability.

Three solutions have been proposed to address the tragedy of the commons problems. One is to privatize the common resource, seen in the proposal to sell rights to pollute. Second is through the government, either with taxation (such as taxing polluters), with government ownership (such as ownership of forests), or with regulation (fines and jail for transgressions).

The third approach is represented by Ostrom's work and GANs: bringing together stakeholders in a resource or issue to establish rules through mutual agreement and collective enforcement. In effect, this is where economics moves into the realm of political science where GANs are seen from a perspective of decision-making, power, and addressing the lack of global government. (This perspective is further explored in the final chapter.)

But how are these rules established and global public goods produced? Table 2.3 summarizes the functions or roles of GANs in this work.

Table 2.3   What GANs do

Function	Goal
Shared visioning	Creating events and interactions that generate shared understanding and vision
System organizing	Bringing together an emerging global system of diverse stakeholders to generate coherence in strategies
Learning, Research, Cap. Dev.	Developing and disseminating new knowledge and tools with research, piloting new approaches, and training
Measuring/certifying	Developing indices, assessments, and/or certification processes
Financing	Combining forces to aggregate their impact and create a more efficient funding vehicle than any one could do on its own
Advocating	Mobilizing voice and increasing pressure upon specific stakeholders who are blocking (actively or inactively) change

This table can be used to assess a network's activities. Is it using all the activities? If not, why not? Does it need to do all of them? Which activities is it particularly good at? Which should it strengthen? How?

Shared visioning

GANs always have an important role in developing a shared vision. This is associated not just with a visionary statement, but also a statement of principles and ways to operationalize that vision. However, this vision is never really "complete." The vision needs continual renewal with new participants as they join. Also, the vision continues to develop as GANs operationalize it and give greater precision and meaning to it.

The visioning is often associated with putting an issue on "the global agenda" – making it something people take up as an issue and challenge. The Global Partnership for the Prevention of Armed Conflict (GPPAC), for example, put "conflict prevention" with NGOs having a key role on the global agenda. Paul Faeth, President of the Global Water Challenge (GWC), comments: "It's surprising that there simply isn't enough awareness about the lack of access . . . so that's goal number one."

The visioning activity also engages people and organizations that are not participants in the GANs, typically through "campaigns." The Climate Group organizes big events with big names at strategic moments. For example, it organized Climate Week in New York four months in advance of the Copenhagen Climate Summit, with the UN, the City, business leaders, the Carbon Disclosure Project, and others. Participants included the Secretary General of the UN and former UK Prime Minister Tony Blair.

For the PRI, this is represented by the six principles themselves. The opening statement of the principles refers to "...act(ing) in the best long-term interests of our beneficiaries" as an overall vision. One of the PRI principles that follows is "We (signatories) will incorporate environmental, social, and corporate governance (ESG) issues into investment analysis and decision-making processes." What that means in actual action is a key part of PRI's work. PRI gives an illustration on its web-site of seven types of action this can involve. The initial vision-setting can take considerable time and effort, as described in the next chapter on development stages.

Developing the vision without good participation of the diverse perspectives within a GANs' issue arena is, however, pointless. Diversity is key to making the vision relevant, comprehensible, and legitimate with the stakeholders who have to realize it. Diversity is also key to generating innovations to overcome problems with other approaches. Realizing this diverse participation is the first step in a GAN's system organizing function. However, those participating should be leaders in addressing the issue.

System organizing

System organizing is a key, ongoing piece of almost all GANs' work. This can vary with the GAN's particular development stage and shifting priorities. For Ecoagriculture Partners, organizing was an initial driver, then people realized that there needed greater clarity about what it wanted participants to actually do. Therefore, increasing numbers of participants were put on the back burner for a while. A GAN might stall in its push for system organizing and essentially become a "club" for a small group of organizations in more of a partnership-like mode.

Ernst Ligteringen, Chief Executive of the GRI, points to the importance of system organizing, saying: "It is really being multi-stakeholder, building bridges, helping different groups to understand each other. There's still a big gulf between civil society and business. In the mainstream the views are still informed by prejudices and vie from one's own constituencies rather than experience working with the other."

System organizing is also associated with questions about governance renewal. As a GAN grows, it must find new ways of engaging increasing numbers of participants in the decision-making processes.

Learning and research

Learning is a core part of most GANs' work as well, since how to realize their goals is not always obvious and participants' capacity to contribute to reaching them must be developed. However, GANs often have a remarkably underdeveloped sense of this work. At a meeting of GAN staff who had roles in developing knowledge and learning, they all said that they had very few resources and learning outcomes and strategies were poorly defined. Nevertheless, GANs put an enormous part of their resources into learning, when all the meetings and time in conversation to develop knowledge and capacity are taken into account.

Learning is a key activity of the Global Compact, as it develops lessons to share amongst companies on how the UN principles it promotes can be implemented. It is also a key activity of the GPPAC, which similarly organizes participants into regional learning groups and shares lessons across them.

For the GANs in health care, research is a particularly important activity. Half of the Stop TB's 10-year work plan is R&D for new vaccines. The GANs support collaborative development of this research, bringing together government, civil society, and commercial organizations with their distinctive expertise and capabilities.

Measuring and certifying

Certification is a popular organizing strategy to realize impact. Production of goods and services is assessed in terms of social, environmental, and economic standards, and the GAN certifies whether those standards have been met. The International Social and Environmental Accreditation and Labelling Alliance (ISEAL) is an association of GANs, including the MSC, Social Accountability International (SAI), and the International Federation of Organic Agriculture Movements (IFOAM) and the fair trade groups represented by the Fair Labelling Organization.

Several GANs make development of impact measurement frameworks and infrastructure a core part of their work. Although the GRI does not actually get involved in measurement or certification, it develops the frameworks for companies to assess their impact in terms of social, economic, and environmental outcomes. And in fact, most ISEAL members do not actually do the certification, although they certify the certifiers. TI also has an important measurement program, with its Corruption Perceptions Index that rates countries. And The Access Initiative's (TAI's) core strategy has to do with the broader measurement concept of "assessing" countries' fulfillment of their commitments in the Rio Declaration to provide access to information, participation, and justice in environmental decision-making.

Finance

The GWP exemplifies a GAN formed by donors who wanted to give scale to their efforts by pooling financial resources. The network has been supported financially by Canada, Denmark, the European Commission, Finland, France, Germany, the Netherlands, Norway, Sweden, Spain, Switzerland, the UK, and the US. For these funders, the GWP is an economical way to achieve the overall goals of promoting social equity, economic efficiency, and environmental sustainability, by improving the way water is managed and developed.

This pooling of financial resources is at the heart of most of the health GANs, like the GAIN, the Stop TB Partnership, and the Global Fund to Fight AIDS, Tuberculosis, and Malaria. The latter is financially by far the largest of any GAN: in the 8 years following its 2002 founding it had approved funding of US$19.3 billion for more than 572 programs in 144 countries.

Advocating

GANs' advocating strategy usually resembles a co-learning approach – one across traditional divides, rather than a traditional lobbying and pressuring strategy. This is demonstrated by TAI. TAI takes a learning approach when conducting "assessments" of governments' performance vis-à-vis their commitments to provide access to information, participation, and justice in environmental decision-making. Although NGOs are in control of TAI, "TAI members recognize that governments are not monolithic; they are filled with allies and opponents," comments Joe Foti, TAI Associate.

This leads to a diversity of TAI advocacy strategies with the goal of governments co-participating in the actual process of making assessments. TAI country coalitions find that it usually helps to conduct the assessments in close relationship with a supportive government agency, such as the national Ministry of Environment that is usually weak on finance, political power, and science. In Thailand the TAI coalition includes an institute sponsored by the King of Thailand, which gives it legitimacy in government eyes. And in Africa, the TAI–Cameroon representative was actually asked to advocate to other governments and speak on his government's behalf at a UNEP Governing Council meeting on access to information, participation, and justice in environmental decision-making.

Of course GANs integrate these strategies. For example, The Climate Group focuses in particular on bringing together local and state/provincial governments and business. One project demonstrates the effectiveness of outdoor LED lighting with city government. This requires bringing together LED experts, financial institutions to finance the city's investments, and local government. Bjorn Roberts, Corporate Partnership Manager for The Climate Group, comments: "We make (climate change) a compelling topic for all, and put it on their agenda. The conversations don't happen unless people are put together." Through The Climate Group, a local city project becomes a global pilot. It combines the strategies of shared visioning of green cities, system organizing by bringing together the diverse partners, learning with the pilot, financing through developing new financial instruments, and advocating with other cities to follow the pilot.

Networks as complex systems

When discussing the barriers to realizing the potential for multi-stakeholder change strategies, Marianne Hughes, Executive Director of the Interaction Institute for Social Change commented:

> A great obstacle is our capacity to see system relationships, capacities to see and move through processes of real innovation with multi-stakeholders coming together, transcending differences.

Jim Woodhill, Director of the Centre for Development Innovation added:

> How to understand systemic interactions . . . having that capacity to see this. And how that connects to a spiritual dimension . . . about people's emotions, cognition, how people see the world, the wider institutional environment . . . science has cut three quarters of that out of picture in the way it tries to tackle problems.

Networks are more productively approached as living systems, rather than as engineered and built structures. But what does this really mean, and what are the implications? Some of this is described in a wonderful report *Capacity, Change and Performance.*[8] The report nicely summarizes four key points about a complex adaptive system (CAS) perspective. It:

1. Focuses on *processes* more than structures or outcomes as a way of managing;
2. Defines systems on the basis of *interrelationships* between people, groups, structures, and ideas and the behavior, events, and outcomes they produce;
3. Emphasizes *emergence* as the way human systems change on the basis of countless interactions amongst a huge number of elements; and
4. Brings out in-built tendencies toward *self-organization* that drive the emergence of order, direction, and capacity from within the system itself.

The systems aspect of CAS is related to "systems thinking," an approach popularized by Peter Senge with his 1990 classic *The Fifth Discipline,*[9] based on which the System Archetypes of Chapter 4 were generated. Other key concepts are:

- "feedback loops": the processes that an action (input) sets in motion that re-enforce and/or undermine the action; and
- "unintended consequences": a feedback loop to undermine the original intention.

Systems dynamics guru Jay Forrester pointed out in a classic 1971 paper *Counterintuitive Behavior of Social Systems* that "The human mind is not adapted to interpreting how social systems behave. We think simplistically and linearly."[10]

These comments followed analysis of four programs to address inner city problems. "All of these were shown to lie between neutral and highly detrimental regardless of the criteria used for judgment," Forrester found. "The investigation showed how depressed areas in cities arise from excess low-income housing rather than from a commonly presumed housing shortage."[11]

Jay points to "Three counterintuitive behaviors of social systems (that) are especially dangerous":

- Social systems are inherently insensitive to most policy changes that people choose in an effort to alter the behavior of systems. Policy support results from human intuition that develops from exposure to simple systems.

- Social systems seem to have a few sensitive influence points through which behavior can be changed. These high-influence points are not where most people would expect them.
- Social systems exhibit a conflict between short-term and long-term consequences of a policy change. A policy that produces improvement in the short run is usually one that degrades a system in the long run.

Networks, particularly global, multi-stakeholder change ones, are CAS beasts. Their core strategy is one that assumes a CAS approach is required. If they are to integrate this systems thinking wisdom, they must be experts at such things as identifying and working with "high-influence points." These are actions that can be modest in effort but large in impact because of their connection to the feedback loops.

The "complex" part of CAS is now receiving significant attention. Definitions of "complexity" are quite simple. There are three core concepts: a whole, parts of the whole, and *emergence* – the inter-weaving and relationships between the parts with feedback; in addition there is the factor of time, and the question of the environment the whole fits in.

Complexity theory is associated with the notion that "the whole is more than the sum of the parts". "Complex" is typically contrasted to "simple", where relationships are linear and the whole *is* the sum of the parts, or where a part is the focus, without considering its relationship to other parts.[12] Complexity is also compared with "complicated" which describes service networks as opposed to change ones.[13] The focus of *simple* can be defined as a single set of objectives. This compares to a complicated situation that is characterized by a focus on different objectives valued by different stakeholders, multiple competing imperatives, and objectives at multiple levels of a system. Governance in simple situations is typically a single organization, and for complicated situations multiple organizations.[14]

In the systems thinking and complex systems world, the idea of "emergence" is particularly important. The focus of complexity is emergent objectives; the governance in complex situations is associated with emergent organizations. One team described "emergence" this way:

Emergence is a descriptive term that seeks to convey how big systems change and how capacity develops within them. Emergence is an unplanned and uncontrollable process in which properties such as capacity emerge from the complex interactions among all actors in the system and produce characteristics not found in any of the elements of the system. The process is not driven by purposeful intervention and therefore cannot be managed in a conventional sense. Nor can it can be marshaled and adopted as a technique. However, it can be understood and influenced. The power and influence of emergence grows as complexity and uncertainty increase.[15]

Another important concept is "chaos," which simply refers to the lack of apparent order and difficulty of predicting the impact of an action. But again, this does not mean that taking action is pointless. It means that nothing is guaranteed, and that in fact a small action can have a big impact because of the feedback loops... popularly referred to as the "butterfly effect." The image of when a butterfly flaps its wings has an impact far away is used as a metaphor to describe how very small changes can have very big effects, particularly over time. So in fact this is a rationale for the GANs themselves, as well as a caution against hubris and over-confidence.

GANs aim to guide the emergence and direction of systems. As explained earlier, they are not "the system," but rather an active player in it, pushing for particular values and priorities. One way to think of development of a GAN is to think of it as a steward for the emergence of system change.

All this has an impact upon the type of strategy GANs should develop. Complex systems require strategies that are based on being: (1) robust rather than focused; (2) a continuous adaptor rather than commanding a onetime competitive advantage; (3) a radical innovator rather than conservative operator; (4) diverse rather than routinized; and (5) flexible rather than monolithic.[16]

The *Capacity, Change and Performance* report summarizes some of the CAS implications in a marvelous table shown here as Table 2.4. The shifts in the table describe differences between competencies that may have the same name in a traditional organization, and those for GANs.

Table 2.4 Traditional versus complex adaptive systems approaches

Aspect	Traditional planning approaches	Complex adaptive systems
Source of direction	Often top-down with inputs from partners	Depends on connecting between the system agents
Role of variables	Few variables determine the outcome	Innumerable variables determine outcomes
Focus of attention	The whole is equal to the sum of the parts	The whole is different than the sum of the parts
Sense of the structure	Hierarchical	Interconnected web
Shadow system	Try to ignore or weaken	Accept that most mental models, legitimacy, and motivation for action is coming out of this source

Table 2.4   (Continued)

Aspect	Traditional planning approaches	Complex adaptive systems
Measures of success	Efficiency and reliability are measures of value	Responsiveness to the environment is the measure of value
Paradox	Ignore or choose	Accept and work with paradox, counter-forces, and tension
View on planning	Individual or system behavior is knowable, predictable, and controllable	Individual and system behavior is unknowable, unpredictable, and uncontrollable
Attitude to diversity and conflict	Drive for shared understanding and consensus	Diverse knowledge and particular viewpoints
Leadership	Strategy formulation and heroic leader	Facilitative and catalytic
Nature of direction	Control and direction from the top	Self-organization emerging from the bottom
Control	Designed up front and then imposed from the center	Gained through adaptation and self-organization
History	Can be engineered in the present	Path dependent
External interventions	Direct	Indirect and helps create the conditions for emergence
Vision and planning	Detailed design and prediction Need to be explicit, clear, and measurable	A few simple explicit rules and some minimum specifications. But leading to a strategy that is complex but implicit
Point of intervention	Design for large, integrated interventions	Where opportunities for change present themselves
Reaction to uncertainty	Try to control	Work with chaos
Effectiveness	Defines success as closing the gap with a preferred future	Defines success as fit with the environment

Source: Baser, H. and P. Morgan (2008). "Capacity, Change and Performance." *Discussion Paper No 59B*. Brussels, Belgium, European Centre for Development Policy Management.

Complexity, however, comes in many forms. For GANs, perhaps the most important forms of complexity are:

1. *Spatial*: The GANs must be able to work at the local–national–regional–global levels.
2. *Knowledge centered*: GANs must be able to turn data into universal understanding or union, to take from the knowledge hierarchy as described by Verna Allee summarizing the work of others:

a. *Data*: raw data without significance on their own
b. *Information*: data that are organized and linked
c. *Knowledge*: information that is analyzed, linked to other information, and compared to what is known already
d. *Meaning*: knowledge in the larger social context, which encompasses social and cultural biases and interpretations
e. *Philosophy*: meaning placed in the larger abstract realm of assumptions, beliefs, and theories about the way things work
f. *Wisdom*: evaluated understanding that encompasses the totality of our worldview
g. *Union*: an open, all-inclusive, expansive feeling state of oneness.[17]

3. *Cultural*: Cultural issues include ethic and linguistic, belief systems, and the differences between business, government, and civil society.
4. *Change oriented*: Chapter 5 describes three different types of change that require different amounts of effort and time:

a. *Scaling up*: doing more of the same
b. *Reform*: changing rules and policies, within current power structures to provide for the ability to develop new solutions
c. *Transformation*: fundamental realignments of power and relationships to realize previously unfathomed possibilities

5. *Dynamic*: There are many actions being taken concurrently that influence the developments in the issue arenas.

This gives rise to a comprehensive typology of networks summarized in Figure 2.1, with the explanation that since only three dimensions can be graphically presented, the spatial dimension means that there could be a figure like this for each of the local–national–regional–global levels. Knowledge management and value network expert Verna Allee and I developed this figure out of our work together. This diagram should not be taken literally, but used as an illustrative tool to better understand GANs and support their development – what academics call a "heuristic device."

This typology suggests that GANs actually comprise several different types of networks, and that they are the type of network that is dealing with the highest possible levels of complexity in the four dimensions mentioned.

In the diagram GANs are at the highest level of complexity, up in the top right-hand corner. This is where the "ideal" GAN would be. It is the aspiration place for them and the one that represents their highest stage of development. This illustrates the scale of challenge GANs are taking on.

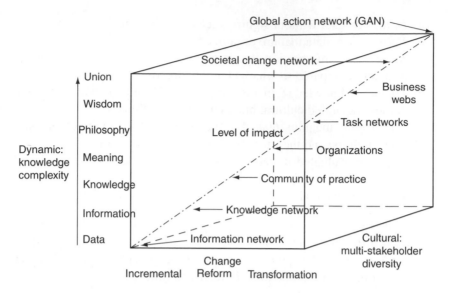

Figure 2.1   Network typology by complexity dimensions

These types of complexity combine in various ways, represented by the diagonal line. This is another device to suggest that there are numerous combinations of these types and levels of complexity that can produce various types of networks that are low or high in particular aspects of complexity. The diagonal further suggests that a GAN actually comprises several different types of networks, and to reach its highest aspirations it must be good at supporting all these network types.

For example, a GAN has information networks where participants share databases. They contain knowledge networks where they are developing and sharing learning, perhaps within a particular sector and geographic region. "Organization" in Figure 2.1 is similar to the concept presented earlier, with management around activity that requires frequent exchanges, significant investment, and uncertainty. Task networks are the partnerships described earlier. Business webs are unisectoral networks; social change ones are like GANs, but more modest in terms of such things as geography and diversity.

The point of all this is not to suggest an overwhelmingly complex management agenda to develop all these network types. The concepts of "emergence" and "self-organizing" are important for their development. Rather, the point is to understand what you are seeing when you are seeing sub-GAN action, and to understand the type of support and interventions that might be critical at certain moments to help a sub-network's evolution.

Communities of practice

All of this is further explored in Chapter 6. However, because I think that Communities of Practice (CoP) as a network type is particularly important for GANs' development, I want to take a moment to further explore this.

Etienne Wenger has popularized the concept of CoPs.[18] Etienne and I have also both worked with Bill Snyder[19] to further develop the concept. My work with Bill was specifically focused upon GANs.

CoPs are particularly valuable for multi-stakeholder change networks because they present a model of very flexible and low-investment support for the learning and its dissemination that are critical for the networks' success. They require very light infrastructure and enhance inter-personal ties that also are key to success.

Three core concepts are behind CoPs: 1) the community (*who*), 2) the domain (*what* – it might be an issue like "sustainable water use" or a sub-issue such as "communications strategies in water"), and 3) the practice (activities to support development of capacity to address the what). The two infrastructure components needed to develop the CoP are a Sponsorship Team and a Support Group. These concepts collectively build applied learning communities.[20]

In 2003, Bill and I worked with the Cooperative Programme on Water and Climate (CPWC). At that time the network's aim to generate learning across 18 initiatives around the world that were working on implications of climate change related to water. Our overall approach was to think of each initiative as an affiliated CoP and the CPWC as a whole as a CoP, so we wanted to explore the value and implications of thinking of the CPWC as a CoP of CoPs.

We organized a pilot initiative to explore application of the CoP model that included three initiatives: Central America (addressing flood impacts of increasing storms in small valleys), Bangladesh (addressing salination issues with rising sea levels), and West Africa (addressing increasing drought). We aimed to create interactions within and between them that could be a microcosm for CPWC as a whole.

In terms of the model in Figure 2.1, this CoP was focused upon the mid-level of dynamic complexity as it aimed for knowledge development to support improved action; it was at the high end of geographic complexity, being global; it was also at the high end of cultural diversity both due to its ethnic and sectoral diversity, and it was at the low-to-medium end of temporal complexity since it was seen as a relatively short-term project to support incremental improvement.

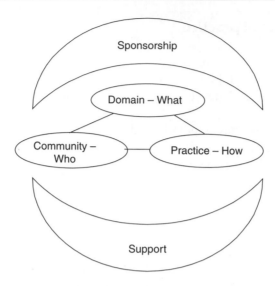

Figure 2.2   CoP learning system

Source: Snyder, W. M. (2005). *Developing Global Action Networks as Communities of Practice: An Initial Investigation with the Cooperative Programme on Water and Climate.* Boston, MA, USA, Global Action Networks Net http://networkingaction.net/5.html.

Figure 2.2 presents the major components in the system we developed.

What: The over-arching questions concerned how climate change can be mitigated.
How: Electronic interactions – telephone, email, and webinar – between (1) each of the three sites and Bill and me, and (2) between all of us and the CPWC Secretariat collectively.
Who: The people involved in the initiatives and the Secretariat.

The CoP infrastructure comprised two key components. One was *sponsors* who included the CPWC secretariat itself and a funder, whose functions included:

- Developing strategic goals for the community;
- Providing funding for the support team and regional coordinators; and
- Participating in ongoing reviews to assess progress and foster development.

The other component was *support* for the daily activities came in the form of Bill and me in terms of CoP development. Our activities included:

- Coaching regional coordinators;
- Guiding case development;
- Coordinating the global community;
- Liaising with sponsors;
- Developing the technology platform – including teleconference events and the web-site (for storing documents, posting messages, member directory, etc.); and
- Documenting the methods, results, lessons learned, and proposals for next steps.

Support locally came in the form of the *local coordinators* – the lead contacts at each of the sites – who led activities at the regional level with the roles of:

- Identifying local players to participate in a regional learning system initiative;
- Developing regional case studies – as a baseline for identifying local improvement opportunities and for sharing insights and innovations across regions;
- Coordinating peer-to-peer and cross-level learning at the regional level; and
- Liaising with local institutions: government agencies, NGO's, funders, and others.

While Bill and I considered the CPWC project a successful learning experience, we did not generate a robust or ongoing CoP infrastructure. There were several reasons for this. At the time (2003), the webinar/teleconference/internet connections we were using were not sufficiently advanced. As well, there was too much divergence in the site issues (the "what") to inspire an ongoing CoP – the local impact of the concept of "water and climate" was too diverse.

Nevertheless, the learning within sites and across them generated deeper understanding by everyone of the system they were trying to organize, and there was value in sharing the lessons about how to connect the parts. There were generic parts identified in the form of four general types of stakeholder communities:

- local communities;
- policy makers;
- socio-techno-science experts; and
- funders.

In a disciplined but light-structure manner, the CoP framing helps address core questions: Who is in the communities? What can they do to address the issue? How can they improve the way they are addressing it?

This approach significantly shifts the focus of many people from engineering-type technical solutions to understand that their work also involves creating new types of social inter-personal ties and a robust learning system.

This case description draws from Synder (2005).[21]

Notes

1. Williamson, O. E. (1975). *Markets and Hierarchies: Analysis and Antitrust Implications.* New York, Free Press; Williamson, O. (1985). *The Economic Institutions of Capitalism.* New York, Free Press.
2. Powell, W. W. (1990). "Neither Market nor Hierarchy: Network Forms of Organization". *Research in Organizational Behavior.* B. Staw and L. L. Cummings (eds). Greenwich, CT, JAI Press 12: 295–336.
3. Luhmann, N. (1979). *Trust and Power.* Chichester, UK, Wiley.
4. Waddell, S. (2002). "Core Competencies: A Key Force in Business-Government-Civil Society Collaborations." *Journal of Corporate Citizenship* (7): 43–56; Waddell, S. (2005). *Societal Learning and Change: How Governments, Business and Civil Society are Creating Solutions to Complex Multi-Stakeholder Problems.* Sheffield, UK, Greenleaf Publishing.
5. Ostrom, E. (1990). Governing the Commons: *The Evolution of Institutions for Collective Action.* Cambridge, UK, Cambridge University Press.
6. Royal Swedish Academy of Sciences (2009). "Economic Governance: The Organization of Cooperation." *The Prize in Economic Sciences 2009 (Press Release).* Stockholm, Sweden, Royal Swedish Academy of Sciences October 12.
7. Hardin, G. (1968). "The Tragedy of the Commons." *Science* 162: 1243–1248.
8. Baser, H. and P. Morgan (2008). "Capacity, Change and Performance." *Discussion Paper No 59B.* Brussels, Belgium, European Centre for Development Policy Management.
9. Senge, P. M. (1990). *The Fifth Discipline: The Art and Practice of the Learning Organization.* New York, Doubleday; Senge, P., et al. (1994). *The Fifth Discipline Fieldbook.* New York, NY, Currency Doubleday.
10. Forrester, J. (1971 (1995 reprint)). "Counterintuitive Behavior of Social Systems." *Theory and Decision* 2(2), p. 1.
11. Ibid., pp. 6–7.
12. Bar-Yam, Y. (2003). *Dynamics of Complex Systems.* Boulder, CO, USA, Westview Pressl; Johnson, N. (2007). *Simply Complexity: A Clear Guide to Complexity Theory.* Oxford, UK, Oneworld Publication.
13. Rogers, P. J. and S. C. Funnell (2011). *Purposeful Program Theory: Effective Use of Theories of Change and Logic Models.* San Francisco, CA, USA, John Wiley/Jossey-Bass.
14. Ibid.

15. Land, T., et al. (2009). "Capacity Development: Between Planned Interventions and Emergent Processes. Implications for Development Cooperation." *Policy Management Brief.* Brussels, Belgium, European Centre for Development Policy Management 22.
16. Johnson, N. (2007). Op.cit.
17. Allee, V. (1997). *The Knowledge Evolution: Expanding Organizational Intelligence.* Boston, MA, USA, Butterworth-Neinemann.
18. Wenger, E. (1998). *Communities of Practice.* New York, NY, Cambridge University Press.
19. Wenger, E. C. and W. M. Snyder (2000). "Communities of Practice: The Organizational Frontier." *Harvard Business Review* (January–February): 139–145; Wenger, E., et al. (2002). *Cultivating Communities of Practice.* Boston, MA, USA, Harvard Business School Press.
20. Allee, V. (2000). "Knowledge Networks and Communities of Practice." *OD Practitioner* 32(4); Wenger, E., et al. (2002); Snyder, W. M. and X. d. S. Briggs (2003). *Communities of Practice: A New Tool for Government Managers.* Arlington, VA, USA, IBM Center for the Business of Government; Sapsed, J. and A. Salter (2007). "Postcards from the Edge: Local Communities, Global Programs and Boundary Objects." *Organization Studies* 25(9): 1515–1534.
21. Snyder, W. M. (2005). *Developing Global Action Networks as Communities of Practice: An Initial Investigation with the Cooperative Programme on Water and Climate.* Boston, MA, USA, Global Action Networks Net http://networkingaction.net/5.html.

CHAPTER 3

GAN development strategies

Perhaps there is nothing more important to guide development of a GAN (Global Action Network) than the famous principle of management guru Alfred Chandler that *structure should follow strategy*. This means *figure out what you want to do, and let that drive the network design.* The principle contrasts with many people's initial focus on formalizing decision-making processes and creating structures that abide by philosophical and theoretical perspectives based in erroneous assumptions, and thereby impede their ability to realize the ends that they aspire for. Over-formalization often indicates lack of trust, and no network is going to be successful without sufficient trust.

Over-formalization can also represent a lack of openness to learning and discomfort with paradox and ambiguity, all of which are part and parcel of GANs. The second, associated principle is *let the network design arise out of your success.* So this means you should have a history before you design and it also implies the need to regularly review your experience to change your design as you grow. These reviews usually are every 3–5 years, and form the basis for moving through "development stages."

Despite this emphasis upon your own networks' experience, there is no need to continually reinvent the wheel. Innumerable times I have met senior people in networks who are excited about "new" discoveries about how to organize and develop a GAN that follows much – often painful and expensive – investment. I am left thinking how much benefit would be gained from receiving advice from other GAN leaders. This led me to form Global Action Network Net (GAN-Net) in 2003 to spur these connections, and its successor organization NetworkingAction.

Very often I find advice coming from the wrong people. There are inevitable attractions to "names" either as famous people or firms, who will bring in frameworks, templates, and experience from non-GANs – businesses, NGOs, government – that can actually hurt a GANs development. A key argument of this book, as presented at the end of Chapter 1 and in later chapters, is to understand that GANs are as distinct from these other organizational types as those types are from each other.

The core development challenge

On the one hand, globalization appears to suppress diversity as languages and cultural traditions disappear. But the reality is much more complex. Today people combine much more diversity than ever before. A black lesbian Buddhist living in New York's Brooklyn borough, but born and raised in French-speaking Senegal, and who is a world music aficionado making her living as a bio-chemist, has a multitude of allegiances, identities, and networks. She represents the paradoxical concurrent trends of globalization and specialization that have their counterparts with organizations. Evolutionary sociology documents these trends as increasing *differentiation* and the need to find new ways of *integration* to transcend the differentiation and address collective challenges and aspirations. GANs present a mechanism for supporting both this differentiation and integration in response to threatening challenges and new opportunities.

Expanding knowledge and increasing ease of interacting globally are driving this integration–differentiation challenge. In the nineteenth century, this was described by Comte as evolutionary theory characterized by movement from simplicity to complexity.[1] Herbert Spencer used a biological metaphor, with new types of social structures being the sociological analogue to plants adapting through mutation to new environmental conditions.[2] The social evolutionary theme was reformulated in a more sophisticated way by Talcott Parsons who distinguished between *segmentation* where similar social structures are replicated in different locations, and *stratification* where units become more specialized and form hierarchies as structures of integration. Although the latter allows for more sophisticated societies, he commented that "... segmentation can occur only if the solidarity of members of society is sufficient to overcome the centrifugal forces of social differentiation."[3]

This differentiation/integration process produces a paradox. Differentiation increases the number and types of NGOs, government agencies, and businesses. However, this results in "underorganization" that becomes increasingly important in terms of inter-organizational linkages like collaborations that can build mutual visions and take collective action.[4]

Adam Kahane has worked with many multi-stakeholder collaborations to solve tough, stuck problems ranging from conflict in Guatemala, to apartheid in South Africa, to child nutrition in India.[5] In a 2010 book he names the same differentiation force *power* as both "power-to" do something in its more creative form, and "power-over" others in its more oppressive form. He names integration *love* by citing Paul Tullich's definition as "the drive towards the unity of the separated."[6] He describes the need for successful multi-stakeholder change initiatives to work with both of these forces. GANs are challenged to create a rhythm in their activities and long-term development processes that categorically honor and work with these two important, complementary forces.

The dynamics of differentiation and power

This is the more difficult dynamic for GANs. They prefer to focus on what joins and brings together, and (like most people) to be conflict adverse and pretend that there is only harmony and agreement. GANs must recognize and make explicit differentiation as well. Suppressing or ignoring difference will not work – it will bubble up as crisis sooner or later. Or, partners will simply drift away because they find the network insufficiently productive and rewarding for them.

One of the most basic of tools to honor differentiation is to identify distinct goals of participants. Often people lose themselves in the comfort of shared goals that are real, but insufficient to hold together collaborations. Participating organizations should be encouraged to clearly articulate their distinct goals in participating, and other partners have to either commit to supporting their achievement or convince the partner that the goal should be changed. This is where the creative juices of collaboration come in, and true innovation arises such as with new multi-stakeholder certification strategies. Participants uncover unrecognized, limiting assumptions that can be invalidated through new information or new relationships.

These distinct goals must be taken seriously. That means not simply identifying them, but actually creating processes and procedures for measuring their attainment as well as attainment of the shared goals. As well, processes for renewing the goals at regular intervals are important.

Three development dynamics

One way to think of GANs' integration strategy is through three themes that continue throughout their development. One of these is community-organizing. Yes, GANs must have technical expertise in the engineering and physical science sense, but they are fundamentally a community-organizing strategy. They are about getting people and organizations together, and developing robust connections for large impact where conflict, confusion, and multi-directionality previously existed.

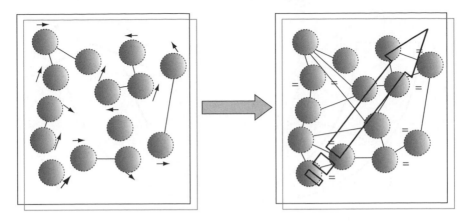

Figure 3.1 The community development dynamic

Figure 3.1 represents the movement that indicates success. You start with poorly connected organizations that, very often, do not even understand that they are working in the same field or that see themselves even as enemies. For example, forest companies and environmentalists were in exhausting pitched battles, and then the Forest Stewardship Council formed. The goal is to develop their connections and create peer, mutual respectful relationships that are grounded in joint activities that generate mutual benefit. This is the picture of alignment around a collective vision and identity.

The second core dynamic is a drive for change of Figure 3.2. Colleague Otto Scharmer of Massachusetts Institute of Technology developed this figure to describe transformational change processes after interviewing over 150 leaders around the world who are associated with being able to realize such change.[7] GANs are about realizing this type of profound change with their diverse participants.

The process is sometimes referred to as the "U" process because of the shape of Figure 3.2 that Otto depicted and was recognized by other change investigators as well. It begins with "co-sensing" to develop a collective understanding of "the current situation" with respect to an issue that appears "stuck," complicated, and of high complexity; Otto often uses a version of scenario development to help people realize particular patterns that can make sense of diverse perspectives. This might take a year or two.

This moves people into a space of co-inspiring, what Otto also refers to as "presencing".[8] This requires a process such as a retreat where people can get in touch with what might be and "what is possible" to "emerge" from "what is." This might take 6 months to a year.

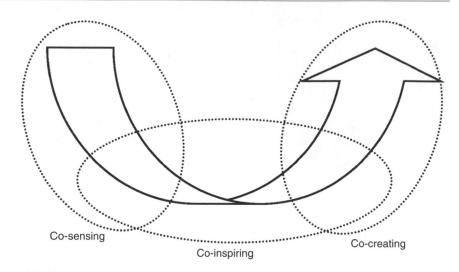

Co-sensing

Co-inspiring

Co-creating

Figure 3.2   The deep change dynamic

Source: Scharmer, C. O. (2007). *Theory U: Leading from the Future as it Emerges.* Boston, MA, USA, Society for Organizational Learning.

The next stage is the "co-creating" which is my particular focus with GANs as vehicles for this: development of the strategies, relationships, resources, skills, structures, processes, and cultures to support the development of responses to the issue. This involves fundamental realignment of power relationships that are deeply challenging to traditional organizations and individuals. For global impact, this takes a couple of decades.

This change process involves significant "shifts" in power and relationships amongst individuals, organizations, and with society as a whole. It is a process that I describe as "societal learning and change."[9]

Learning processes are the third dynamic theme present throughout GANs' development. Sometimes people refer to Otto's dynamic as one of "learning from the future," which means going through a process of deep reflection upon the current state, possibilities to address some issue, and how to realize those possibilities. Traditional learning is about learning from experience and the past. This is often referred to as the Kolb or Experiential Learning Cycle of Figure 3.3.[10]

This is the essence of creating a learning network: creating processes and a culture that encourages reflection upon what has been done, and integration into future actions. This should not be thought of as a great chore or require some huge effort. Rather, it is something that is integrated into the daily, weekly, monthly, and annual rhythms of a GAN. I prefer the term "action learning"[11] to emphasize that there are not huge gaps between

Figure 3.3   Experiential learning cycle

the steps in the cycle, but that they should happen as decisions are being made. On a daily basis, this is quite in-the-moment. Chapter 7 looks at creating this further, by looking at the competencies necessary to develop a learning network.

These three dynamics are ongoing and never really end. They usually begin with a small group of organizations with a global vision that go through the cycles, and the GAN sustains continual expansion of the number of people going through these cycles until the global change is realized. It is not enough for a small group of founders to experience the deep change dynamic – the GAN must support others to go through it, as well. In addition, at a certain stage a GAN may find itself again "stuck" and unproductive, and return to this deep change process.

Development stages

From my work with GANs, I see them moving through four distinct development stages. By a development stage I mean a structure of relationships, decision-making, and power that is stable over a period of time. In these days of network-as-internet, "stage" is often associated with versions of software releases. When working with the Global Knowledge Partnership, we referred to GKP Version3.0 as the stage we are working to emerge or develop.

With each stage come particular questions and challenges, and tools, activities and methodologies to move through them. However, the stages are not distinct and development is messy.

Stage 1: Exploration

Peter Eigen is founder of Transparency International (TI) and the associated GAN called the Extractive Industries Transparency Initiative (EITI).

Table 3.1 Stage 1: Exploration

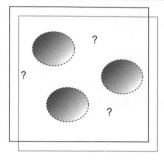

Key questions	• Is the issue ready for multi-stakeholder convening?
	• What is the issue?
	• What is the vision?
	• Who should we convene?
	• How do we convene?
Key challenges	• Identifying stakeholders
	• Convening
	• Visioning
Activities	**Action**
	• Issue analysis
	Infrastructure
	• Action research project
Tools and methods	• Mapping
	• Interviews
	• Infrastructure
Potential impediments	• Too early
	• Too weak of sponsorship

EITI aims to end the insidious secrecy of payments by extractive industry companies to government leaders to receive mineral rights. Peter recalls that in 1999–2000:

> We started out with a campaign, initiated by Global Witness, TI, Oxfam and one or two other British NGOs, to call on companies to publish what they pay. The coalition was very well accepted by NGOs and companies. We found a number of big companies like Shell and BP willing to publish what they pay. But they were told by host countries, like Angola, that they were not allowed to publish what they pay . . . that they had to observe a confidentiality clause in their investment agreement, and that if they violated that they would not get their production rights renewed. The companies said 'We'd love to work with you, but we can't.' So the idea arose that we also had to approach the host countries.

The breakthrough was when President Obasanyo of Nigeria in 2003 addressed a big audience in Berlin to celebrate TI's 10th anniversary. He said "I will not only allow companies operating in Nigeria to publish what they pay; I will make it mandatory for them. And I will publish what I receive."

This type of entrepreneurial persistence is the beginning of many GANs. In this case, Peter knew the field well, he had already founded TI, but he did an enormous amount of investigation to see what would work.

A GAN represents very substantial investment of time and resources. Highly recommended is a significant research effort to see if such a solution is both possible and warranted with respect to a specific issue. Over the past few years, even since the founding of EITI, we have new tools to help the process. Table 3.1 summarizes Exploration Stage learning.

For years I thought that a GAN on global finance was a great idea, but a quick investigation suggested the time was not right. But a quick look in 2007 suggested the time could be right and led to the Global Finance Initiative (GFI) with the goal of developing a strategy to integrate social and environmental concerns into the "logic" (way of working) of global finance. How did I conclude this? I asked three questions:

- Are there relatively well-organized sectoral networks? The presence of global industry associations, inter-government ones such as a dynamic UN committee, and a network of NGOs demonstrates a level organizing that can provide important building blocks. *Finance example:* Industry and government were well-organized decision-makers, but until recently other stakeholders like investors and civil society were not. In 2007, NGOs had become active as a closely connected global community around the UN "financing for development" conferences. Socially responsible investors were forming national groups and connecting cross-border.
- Is there a crisis or a driver for innovation and change? A positive vision can also be a driver. *Finance example:* The Mexican and Asian crises and intensified globalization of finance without any accompanying regulatory structures made another crisis simply a question of time; the rise of social investment movement globally was an example of a positive innovation pushing for change.
- Are there inter-sectoral "spaces" that are active? The presence of business–government–civil society forums/networks/joint events suggests capacity and interest in "transcending" their respective positions.

Finance example: The UN financing for development conferences began in Monterrey in 2002 and brought together the sectors.

The GFI was funded at the end of 2007 and launched in January 2008 just as the global finance crisis was about to hit. An initial exploration question is "What is the issue?" A framing must be defined that can accommodate diverse perspectives and provide an opportunity for transcending them. When GFI began, people would not accept the frame of "global finance," claiming that the risk profiles of banking, equity, and insurance are so different that they cannot be combined like that. However, as the crisis advanced "global finance" became *the* dominant frame.

The other issue framing question relates more to the vision – what is the direction for change? With extensive interviews we looked at several possible frames to accommodate "integration of environmental and social" and discovered (1) that we should include economic (the "real economy" as opposed to the finance industry), and (2) the arising frame is "environmental–social–governance" or ESG.

To understand who to interview and convene, we did extensive mapping (described in Chapter 4 in more detail). This helped us understand the social structure of relationships on an organizational level: who is working in the "issue domain," and who is connected to whom. This led to three important insights: (1) 13 significant global inter-sectoral initiatives in finance had developed over the past 5 years, (2) civil society (NGOs) was focused upon the UN – which has no importance in global finance decision-making – and the World Bank; they ignored the most important global financial institutions: the Bank for International Settlements and the Financial Stability Board, and (3) thinking of the issue domain as containing two stakeholder groups is useful: the insiders comprising traditional decision-makers (commercial finance, regulators, policy makers) and outsiders comprising all the rest who are pushing for significant change.

These mapping insights led to a strategy to focus upon organizing the outsiders. The insiders were already well-organized and bringing together all stakeholders at that time would not be productive – there was also a great deal of imbalance in sophistication, organization, and power. We also concluded that bringing together the intersectoral initiatives could be particularly impactful. Note that we had essentially taken a step back from organizing a true GAN with all the stakeholders.

We did two research convenings of outsider stakeholders and produced a strategy that I still think of as very viable. Essentially the goal was to develop a sufficiently clear and motivating vision through a global process that would also develop the network with the political power to realize movement toward that vision.

However, we could not move to the next development stage for a couple of reasons. The biggest one, ironically, was financial. Although the financial crisis involved evaporation of trillions of dollars, we could not raise additional money. An associated problem was inadequate sponsorship. We tried several strategies to engage networks with good legitimacy in the arena, unsuccessfully. In the end, it may be interpreted as still too early to develop the step we envisioned to develop a GAN.

All of this GFI activity was organized as an *action research* project. This is distinguished as a research approach by participation of stakeholders in the research issue arena, reflexivity (ongoing adjustment in response to what is being learned), an orientation toward taking action, and a goal of realizing impacts through the participation. For the GFI a small group of researchers ensured a disciplined data-gathering and analysis process, but the activities were focused on engaging stakeholders and developing action plans.

Stage 2: Initiation

The convenings for the GFI were really part of the exploration of the potential opportunity. In Stage 2, convenings take place on a larger scale. Two particular traditions are helpful for designing these meetings: scenario development and search conferences.[12]

It is worthwhile to say what these traditions are *not* as well used as they should be, and often big mistakes are made at this stage. Particularly in the inter-governmental and academic world there is a tendency to fall back on events with people making presentations as experts, or engaging in debate or negotiations. These approaches tend to reinforce individual perspectives. In contrast, scenario development and search conferences presume everyone is an expert and the goal is to draw out and integrate their expertise to transcend the individual perspectives. Therefore, there is a lot of small group and collective discussion.

The year or two of Stage 2 is summarized in Table 3.2. It begins with a "widening" period when diverse perspectives and ideas are brought in, followed by a "narrowing period" when people decide what to do. Carson identifies three additional qualities that should be reflected in these processes:

- Forward-looking and promoting futures where all can see benefits for their individual organizations as well as for the whole and the key issue;

- Efficient and seen as good time/resource investment for participants; and
- Fair and seen as embodying integrity.[13]

Although the general principle is that you want to have "the whole system" represented, sometimes this is not the case. For example, the World Health Organization's (WHO's) Tobacco-Free Initiative specifically decided not to engage tobacco companies, since their interests are so diametrically opposed to those of the Initiative.

The Sustainable Food Lab (SFL), aiming to transform the food and agriculture system into a sustainable one, is a good example of a disciplined and thoughtful initiation process. It was designed around a large

Table 3.2   Stage 2: Initiation

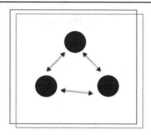

Key questions	• What is holding us back from realizing the vision? • What are possible technical responses? • What are individual stakeholders' roles in developing the responses? • What outcomes would individual stakeholders value?
Key challenges	• Defining the problem • Piloting a core physical technology solution • Building initial centralized network piloting structure
Activities	**Action** • Visioning • Developing a core function/tool • Building core team **Infrastructure** • Communications & learning network
Tools and methods	• Learning journeys • Scenario development • Search conferences • Action learning
Potential Impediments	• Insufficiently tight problem definition • Too loose problem definition • Unclear tool focus – spreading too thin • Crowded issue field • Operational issues

system change process called "The Change Lab" that draws inspiration from the "U-Process" and scenario development. The exploration stage began with social entrepreneurs Peter Senge (*The Fifth Discipline*), Adam Kahane (South African scenario leader, now Reos Partners), and Don Seville and Hal Hamilton (from the Sustainability Institute). They stimulated interest of the Kellogg Foundation and food giant Unilever. "Doing something about sustainable agriculture," commented Unilever's Andre van Heemstra, "will require bringing parties together that normally do not cooperate."

The SFL involved 46 stakeholders with 33 at its first meeting. There were five gatherings over the course of a 2-year project. Participants included leaders from businesses, governments, farm groups, and non-governmental organizations. They worked on the left-hand side of the deep change dynamic – the "U Process" – with the vision of a "sustainable food system" and developed a working understanding of a sustainable food system as one that *produces enough food to feed people affordably, nutritionally, and safely in a way that sustains the economic, environmental, and social systems in which the food system is embedded.*[14]

Developing this shared understanding and identifying the projects were supported by "learning journeys": visits to food-related businesses and farms. The discussions arising from these helped to develop shared understanding and intent that are important ingredients in trust necessary to move ahead.

While exploring the current reality, they identified a number of systemic challenges that the project needs to address, such as the need to increase productivity while stewarding biodiversity and reducing energy use. As the SFL learning history records:

> *The focus on practical initiatives, beginning with new or improved food supply chains, developed as a central focus of the Food Lab from the determination expressed by many Team Members and Executive Champions to make change "on the ground" through practical action, pilot projects and viable full-scale food system interventions.*[15]

These practical initiatives became the focus of the SFL over this initiation period. They undertook several projects that included:

- enhancing consumer understanding of the concept of sustainable fishery management and creating economically viable models of marine resource management;

- developing a benchmarking tool aimed at improving the way agricultural commodities are produced through clearer focus on key, measurable impacts; and
- exploring infrastructure and policy changes that would increase the health, freshness, and local sourcing of food served in institutional and catered settings.[16]

At this stage there are a very modest number of participants, but they are leaders in thinking about the issue. The organizational infrastructure simply needs to support ongoing communication and development of pilots. There are three types of structural arrangements that support the initiatives' development. One is as a project of an organization, which was the case for the SFL that developed as a project of the Sustainability Institute. The Global Reporting Initiative (GRI) similarly began as a project of the Tellus Institute; the Global Partnership for the Prevention of Armed Conflict (GPPAC) began as a project of an European NGO with the same focus. In addition to these NGO initiators, the World Bank and World Economic Forum are incubators for a number of GANs.

A second initiating structure is to immediately start up a new entity that the stakeholders co-own. After 2 years of Stage 1 consultations among sustainable forestry stakeholders, this was the strategy they elected to establish the Forest Stewardship Council (FSC). The Fair Labor Association (FLA) grew out of an initiative of the White House convening of stakeholders. A third strategy is very similar to this, but heavily dominated by a particular social entrepreneur. TI, which is closely associated with Peter Eigen's dynamic energy, is perhaps the best example.

At this stage, particularly important is that a GAN develop a core technology or strategy to tackle its issue that appeals to the diverse stakeholders and moves them to their vision. For the FSC, Marine Stewardship Council (MSC), and a number of other initiatives this core technology is a certification or, in the case of The Access Initiative (TAI), an assessment process. The Global Water Partnership (GWP) developed Integrated Water Resource Management (IWRM). These help quantify the impact of the issue and create shared understanding of the steps necessary to move toward the vision.

The World Commission on Dams (WCD) represents a special case for a GAN at this stage. The WCD was a multi-stakeholder process designed to create comprehensive guidelines for the building of large dams in response to environmental and social disasters associated with large dams funded by the World Bank. It had a very specific 2-year life to achieve this outcome, after which it would be dissolved. From its launch to the final report issued in November 2000, its activities included (1) holding hearings in the affected communities and (2) undertaking conventional research into the issues. Although the diverse Commissioners reached consensus in a final report, the WCD did not translate into agreement among the broader stakeholders' communities, and responsibility for next steps was delegated to the UNEP that proved incapable administratively or authoritatively to effect pursuit of the Commission's work.[17]

Whereas the WCD's development was hobbled by its time-restricted mandate, another challenge that can prevent an initiative from moving to Stage 3 includes the issue field being too crowded. For example, the Global Alliance of Workers and Communities no longer exists at least in part because there are several other GANs working on global labor issues; the Global Water Challenge is operating in a field where several GANs already exist, but is managing this issue by specifically engaging business which is weakly represented in the other water GANs, and geographically having a North American base whereas other GANs are more global but developing country focused.

Sometimes the problem does not have a broad enough definition to be engaging, which is arguably the situation with Building Partnerships in Development for Water and Sanitation and the Cooperative Programme on Water and Climate. Although doing valued work, these have stayed essentially at the partnership level by focusing on the narrower goal of knowledge development. But too broad a definition can also be a problem, since the lack of focus can prevent the needed energy from developing to move the GAN along. In the fair trade arena, both of the too-broad and too-narrow approaches are a challenge: the networks are split around division about whether or not to include large commercial operations, and they are having trouble getting outside of a narrow food and handicrafts niche.

Another challenge can be to spread too thin. Ecoagriculture Partners has had difficulty taking off in part because its core concept of "ecoagriculture" has proven very complex and difficult to operationalize.

And of course there are a number of associated operational issues that can prevent further development. Perhaps the most common is inability to mobilize financial resources to continue development; another is being smothered by a bureaucracy, which is arguably what happened with the WCD when it transferred to the UNEP.

Stage 3: Infrastructure development

The GAN now has legitimacy amongst, and support of, a small but leading multi-stakeholder group, and it has a tool to take it toward its vision. It now needs to engage more people and organizations to reach its vision.

Table 3.3 Stage 3: Infrastructure development early and late

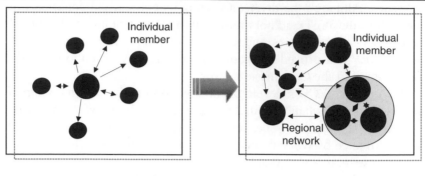

Key questions	• How do we bring in new participants? • How do we manage global diversity? • How do we create robust sub-global structures?
Key challenges	• Broadening application of the physical technology solution • Deepening understanding of the problem and social technology solutions • Increasing network membership and decentralizing structure
Activities	**Action** • Broadening application of core tool • Developing more functions/tools • Making an issue of the issue **Infrastructure** • Secretariat development • Key sub-node development
Tools and methods	• Mapping • Action learning • Planning conferences
Potential impediments	• Leadership holds on • Holding onto core tool as identity • Cannot get economic model • Happy where they are

At Stage 3 there is a significant shift from the physical technologies such as IWRM and certification to social technologies associated more categorically with network development.

One major task is simply to make an issue of the issue the group has been working on. They have developed by this time an "elevator speech" about why it is important and they must be somewhat evangelical about spreading the word. For Transparency, simply making the topic of corruption discussable with aid and donor agencies was a significant achievement. It had to overturn perceptions that corruption was a "cultural" issue and that talking about it was "unwarranted political interference."

Structurally this stage is characterized by the development of a "Secretariat." Personally I dislike this term since it is obviously borrowed from inter-governmental organizations (IGOs) like the UN and World Bank and their agencies. It implies a governmental and bureaucratic logic that can be difficult to escape and continue later development. I encourage that the GAN use a term with "name-Global," such as "FSC-Global." This helps lead the GAN into Stage 4 when the central coordinating functions become much less important, but interaction with global organizations is important.

The role of the Secretariat is usually associated with coordination at early Stage 3, since there are usually still few enough involved to think of the GAN being a larger partnership as described in Chapter 2. By the end of Stage 3, there are well-developed sub-global nodes.

How to organize should grow out of the dynamics and logic of the key issue being addressed. Again taking a lead from IGOs with nations that have geographic boundaries, the natural tendency is to organize around geography. Some, like the GRI, have resisted this in favor of organizing around a core logic associated with their strategy to create reporting frameworks for business. The GRI therefore organized around industries, and a key Stage 3 expansion activity was to take the general Stage 2 triple bottom-line reporting framework and create "sector (industry) supplements." So it created financial, automotive, and food processing sub-groups. Eventually some type of matrix structure usually evolves that includes coordination by geography and sub-issue/activity.

The FSC was also reluctant to organize around geography, although the natural logic is to organize around types of forests or watersheds. In 2009, it finally moved to formally incorporate National Initiatives into its structure.

TI had a very interesting experience and strategy at this stage, which helped it grow quickly. Originally Peter Eigen went about connecting a network of individuals who were committed to fighting corruption. With his long World Bank career, he was well-connected to do this with significant government and business figures. But increasing challenges came from NGOs who had been working on the issue already. Their question was "What is your legitimacy for doing this? Why should we join you? You should join us!"

Transparency's strategy became connecting and strengthening organizations already working in the field of corruption, although to this day it still has a role for individual members. This evolved into development of a system of "national chapters" with multi-stakeholder complexion.

In 2009–10, the Global Alliance for Improved Nutrition (GAIN) was beginning to move into this Stage with greater force. The GAN had spent considerable effort getting the right people to the table, and was particularly successful with governments and business. However, it still lacked local networks that could really do the doing. "After 6 years we must spend more on capacity development," explained former GAIN Partnership Manager Berangere Magarinos. "The partnerships don't just grow naturally."

At Stage 3 the key physical technology tool is being applied more broadly and refined. For FSC this is its process to certify forests as being responsibly managed. However, over this stage other tools are also developed; for FSC this includes development of its brand and ability to derive revenue from it. FSC Executive Director Andre de Freitas points to another challenge they experience with growth. "The issue is more social than environmental when you go to large-scale," he observes. Differences in social impact are much more politically contentious, less resolvable by objective science, and of a much greater variation.

For the GWP the core tool was "integrated water resource management" which is an engineers' tool; application of it demanded building competency in multi-stakeholder development. TI's original tool was "corruption compacts" where organizations involved in a specific contract agreed to abide by a set of rules and standards; at Stage 3 a number of other tools were developed, perhaps most famously its Transparency Perceptions Corruption Index measuring national levels of corruption that is now widely cited.

In all this work, the tools should be understood as vehicles for diverse stakeholders to get together, exchange views, and transcend them to realize the vision. This is the core activity of Fair Labor Association's businesses and NGOs deciding whether fair labor standards are being applied; it is the core activity of deciding how to apply the Principles for Responsible Investment (PRI). Surprisingly, however, the importance of dialogue skill development is severely underrated by GANs. There is a wide range of knowledge and expertise in this arena that they rarely tap as they are still caught in a parochial approach and focused upon the physical technologies.

In this stage mapping again is an important tool to support the network development. Working with GRI as it contemplated developing a South African network, I led a mapping project that defined a methodology for developing sub-networks. This methodology begins by defining the core strategies of the GAN's change theory, and then identifying organizations that have a role in developing those strategies (in the GRI case, in South Africa). For GRI the core strategies of its change process are two: one is to focus upon the triple bottom-line (social, environmental, economic) impact of an organization's activities, and the second is to do this with multi-stakeholder processes.

Once the organizations and their current relationships are identified, then the task is to "weave together" those relationships into a more effective sub-network. This is much better than either coming in and starting something new, and/or GANs beginning with their own partial understanding of who is doing what. If Peter Eigen had first done this with TI, its development would have been significantly accelerated (although in fairness the mapping technologies did not exist when TI was founded in 1993!).

Action learning, described in Chapter 2 and in the Competencies Chapter 7, at this stage should grow into a core dynamic of the entire network.

Another set of methods that GANs make weak use of is the large system planning processes that have been developed over the past few years. These are associated with the large system scenario development and search conference processes of Stage 2. These should replace or at least supplement the cycle of annual to every 4 years (in the case of IUCN) meetings at the regional and global levels. The usual format for these meetings is around two concepts: one is sharing learning in relatively formal and traditional workshop styles of expert-and-receiver of expertise, and the second is around defining the networks' direction with formal motions and debate structures that draw from parliamentary processes, and NGO and business annual meetings.

These two traditions neglect two key distinctive qualities of GANs. As a learning network, the goal is about sharing expertise with the viewpoint that everyone is an expert. And as participant-led collaborations aimed to transcend divides and support transformational change, GANs should develop dialogues rather than debates and negotiations in these meetings.

The meetings should be organized as the product of all the activities that occur between them, so they are not events but part of an ongoing process and rhythm of activity. When people arrive at the meeting they are already informed through a variety of local-to-global forums. When they leave the meeting they know and support the plans that have emerged and they know their roles in realizing the plans and the next steps they are going to take. Moreover, they have had face-to-face connection with people who have similar roles and with whom they will be connected for shared learning as the plans come to life.

Moving into Stage 3 and to the other end of it with well-developed sub-networks may be inhibited by a number of factors. One is that the leadership arising out of Stage 2 may find difficult letting go and encouraging the development of the next generation of leaders. Sometimes this refers to the "executive director" who may have been great at leading the small action research community of Stage 2, but not the hub-and-spoke Secretariat with robust sub-networks structure and dynamic of Stage 3. At least as often the leadership change is required in the Board, to broaden ownership and participation in the network and bring in new ideas.

Another challenge is to broaden the physical technology tools. People in the network may associate their identity so closely with the tool that they have difficulty imagining and developing new ones. This then becomes a network focused upon endless refining of a tool, and the GAN loses its focus upon realizing change. The tool will only be as good as the change it inspires, and it is difficult to conceive of any one tool being powerful enough to realize the scale of change that the GANs envision.

In some ways, TAI has grabbled with these issues. A decade after its founding it still had basically the same "core team" (Board) participants (people *and* organizations) and it was still having difficulty developing tools in addition to its assessment process.

Stage 4: Realizing the potential

By this Stage a GAN has global recognition as a mover and shaker in its issue arena, and it has convinced people of the importance of its issue and the value of its strategy to tackle it. Moreover, there is an extensive and growing group of organizations that consider themselves participants in the network.

However, there is much work still to be done to realize the scale of change that the GAN envisions. "We could have 10 times . . . 100 times the activity on corruption, and we still wouldn't get to where we want to go," commented Cobus de Swardt, Managing Director of Transparency which is among the most advanced of GANs.

In this Stage, the network nodes become well-developed. There is a systematic approach to organizing geographic- and issue-based groups in a type of matrix structure. When a new challenge arises, people from diverse geographies affected by it connect and take action relatively easily.

The Secretariat becomes simply another node in the network rather than a key coordinator between the networks. It is not thought of as "headquarters," nor is it deferred to in decision-making except when an issue concerns global organizations that the Secretariat interacts with. It is its own "region" – global. Just like a South East Asia region working with other agencies operating in its region, the Secretariat focuses on interactions with those in its global regions, such as the UN, World Bank, OECD, and other global organizations. It becomes the "global node."

And just as the South East Asia region will have a key leadership role for communications within it, the Secretariat will have leadership for communications among the nodes globally. However, even this function might be undertaken by another network node. The Mountain Forum, for example, periodically puts out a Request for Proposals to its nodes to contract for the global communications function.

There is deepening of activities, as the networks increasingly work at the sub-national level. In this Stage the Global Compact shifts from global corporations to include small and medium enterprises. Cities and eco-regions become more important organizing units. In Transparency there are now 34 centers in Bangladesh, and Cobus de Swardt, TI Managing Director, comments "We should take our issue into every household." Rather than interacting simply with highly placed persons, the networks become integrated into the fabric of communities.

Another set of growth activities is with traditional scaling up – taking successful pilots from one part of the network and growing them throughout the network.

Stage 4 expansion also generates "spin-offs" which are other networks dealing with the core issue with a particular group of stakeholders or on a sub-topic. For example, TI supported development of the EITI and the Water Integrity Network (WIN). For Peter Eigen, EITI responded to more specialized needs.

> TI wasn't making any progress (with extractive industries). So we wanted an additional approach that would tie in the companies from the beginning. In most countries fighting corruption is mainly the government and civil society. In the big oil producing companies, it's the government, the big oil companies and the people. And the government doesn't dare do anything without asking the companies. You're talking about billions and billions of dollars ... in small countries, the poorest in the world. That's different from TI's work, such as getting a school teacher to give a student a good grade, without a bribe.

Spin-offs do not necessarily come from the efforts of the global node, but can arise spontaneously. The Cities Network of the Global Compact, for example, arose from the efforts of Melbourne out of frustration with the national government's lack of Compact action. This has grown into a global network with little input from the Global Compact New York office.

Table 3.4 Stage 4: Realizing the potential early and late

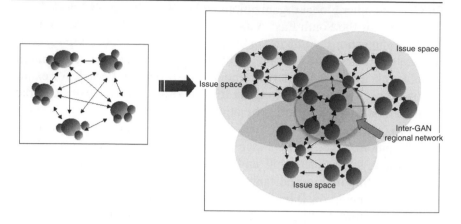

Key questions	• How do we create robust interactions between network nodes? • How do we change the culture globally to support our vision? • How can we organize ourselves to manage legitimacy, accountability, transparency, and value at massive scale? • How do we manage the "tipping point"?
Key challenges	• Re-organizing to address scale • Enhancing legitimacy and value • Creating inter-GAN connections • Creating global action norms • Maintaining the cutting edge
Activities	**Action** • Broadening participation to the grassroots • Spin-offs • Mainstream issue into other organizations • Traditional scaling up **Infrastructure** • From hub and spoke to multi-node • Integrated connections with other issue networks
Tools and methods	• Mapping • Planning conferences • Action learning • Dialogues, search conferences, scenario development
Potential impediments	• Secretariat resistance – fear of letting go – bureaucracy • Nodes resistance – fear of being let go • Inability to transcend issue • Inability to adapt to success and move on

At this stage, GANs must broaden their issue as well. For example, the GWP is becoming increasingly engaged with the climate change issue. "We joined the UN Framework Convention on Climate Change (which leads the Kyoto/Copenhagen process) formally last year so we have observer status," commented GWP Executive Secretary Ania Grobicki in early 2010. "It was a case of coming into the discussions from the cold."

"In the water arena" she continued, "you've got a multiplicity of actors emerging, so we have to find new ways of cooperating and creating coherence. The big shift is to building water security. IWRM (Integrated Water Resource Management – the original core tool of GWP) is a technical concept for water managers, but the broader concept of water security is what enables our partners to work with other sectors. The huge challenges around food security, energy security, each of those has a crucial role for water. It's not helpful when talking with people in other sectors to talk technical jargon. Talking about water security' really helps us to broaden out."

This is a perfect description of how a GAN broadens its activity by not always pushing its own agenda, but understanding the agenda of others and how they might work together productively.

This continued expansion is led entrepreneurially throughout the network. For example, in GWP it is the Regional Water Partnerships and country-level partnerships that are creating dialogues with the disaster relief and climate change communities. At this stage the scenario development and search conferences change processes can take place around sub-issues and in sub-regions.

At Stage 4, the number of organizations integrating the GANs' values and norms increases significantly. For certification GANs, this is done by integrating standards of the certification into their operations; for a forestry company with the FSC, this means making the FSC standards part of their own global operating standards rather than with respect to just a subset of forests. For retailers, it means buying only certified products, as Wal-Mart has committed to do with MSC-certified fish products.

Dissemination occurs most easily through organizations that have a similar organizing logic – in other words, through other GANs that have the same design guidelines and values. The GRI and TI both have their work integrated into that of the Global Compact. The International Union for the Conservation of Nature IUCN has a myriad of GAN relationships, including the GWP, the FSC, and TI.

As attractive and exciting as this Stage can be, there are significant impediments to realizing it. There is a real danger of bureaucratization that drives out the entrepreneurial energy that is critical for GANs. There is ongoing need to balance "administrative/efficiency" concerns with "movement/effectiveness" concerns and the way to do this is not always obvious. Tipping too much in the former direction means a debilitating approval and consensus-building process that is associated with the UN; tipping too much in the latter direction means losing coherence and legitimacy with some key stakeholders.

But the Secretariat and network nodes may well have built a symbiotic relationship in Stage 3 that is hard to break. The nodes may like the way the Secretariat has responsibility for some activities like fundraising and communications, and be loath to take on responsibility themselves.

There is also a danger of being issue myopic – not being able to transcend the focal issue and vision of the GAN, to meaningfully connect with others so the GANs can work together productively.

But perhaps the greatest Stage 4 challenge is to maintain the cutting edge. By this Stage the GAN has become relatively large and successful, and that success can breed complacency. GANs are supposed to be coalitions of those committed to advance an issue, but cutting-edge standards of a few years earlier become dull. A GAN may be seduced by the siren call of size, and equate success with wealth and number of participants, rather than the change it is generating.

Summary

All of this requires that a GAN maintain a forward-tipping inertia. It must always be "moving into the future," broadening the extent of engagement, and deepening understanding of its issue and how to address it. This is not about evangelizing, because no one has "the right answer". Rather, it is about learning and developing answers that work and make sense in particular contexts and situations while keeping in mind the big vision.

These Stages are not, of course, as distinct and clear-cut as they are presented here. A GAN may be at Stage 2, but engage participants in another GAN, for example, which I have described as a Stage 4 activity. The Stages are presented simply as a device to help networks move through them with greater clarity and to identify priorities.

A network does not necessarily *have to* move to another stage of development to be considered valuable. People may be quite happy with the limited but useful activity that they are undertaking. The important point is to be conscious of the choice rather than continually fret about it. However, this probably means modifying the vision and accepting that there are potentially greater outcomes that people have decided not to pursue.

And of course a network may "die" because it cannot address the challenges or because it is successful. An ongoing debate is whether GANs will ever self-dissolve because they reach their goal, or whether they will find renewal through modifying and adjusting their goal. The Microcredit Summit Campaign realized its 10-year goal, but concluded that it still had much to contribute to the poverty-fighting agenda and renewed itself with another goal.

Notes

1. Comte, A. (1855 (1974)). *The Positive Philosophy*. New York, AMS Press, Inc.
2. Spencer, H. (1857/1924). "Progress: Its Law and Cause". *Essays on Education, Etc.* New York, E.P. Dutton & Co.
3. Parsons, T. (1949). "Position and Prospects of Systematic Theory in Sociology". *Talcott Parsons Essays in Sociological Theory*. New York, NY, USA, The Free Press: 212–237.
4. Brown, L. D. (1980). "Planned Change in Underorganized Systems". *Systems Theory for Organization Development*. T. G. Cummings (ed.). Chichester, UK, Wiley: 181–208.
5. Kahane, A. (2004). *Solving Tough Problems: An Open Way of Talking, Listening, and Creating New Realities*. San Francisco, CA, USA, Berrett-Kohler.
6. Kahane, A. (2010). *The Power of Love: A Theory and Practice of Social Change*. San Francisco, CA, USA, Berrett-Koehler.
7. Scharmer, C. O. (2007). *Theory U: Leading from the Future as it Emerges*. Boston, MA, USA, Society for Organizational Learning.
8. Jaworski, J., et al. (2004). *Presence: Human Purpose and the Field of the Future*. Cambridge, MA, USA, Society for Organizational Learning.
9. Waddell, S. (2005). *Societal Learning and Change: How Governments, Business and Civil Society are Creating Solutions to Complex Multi-Stakeholder Problems*. Sheffield, UK, Greenleaf Publishing.
10. Kolb, D. A. (1984). *Organizational Psychology: An Experiential Approach to Organizational Behavior*. Englewood Cliffs, NJ, Prentice-Hall.
11. Revans, R. (1982). *Action Learning*. Charwell-Bratt, Bromley, UK; Morgan, G. and R. Ramirez (1983). "Action Learning: A Holographic Metaphor for Guiding Social Change." *Human Relations* 37(1): 1–28.
12. Weisbord, M. (1992). *Discovering Common Ground*. San Francisco, CA, Berrett-Koehler; Bunker, B. and B. Alban (1997). *Large Group Interventions: Engaging the Whole System for Rapid Change*. San Francisco, CA, USA, Jossey-Bass; Holman, P. and T. Devane (eds) (1999). *The Change Handbook: Group Methods for Shaping the Future*. San Francisco, CA, USA, Berrett-Koehler; Bojer, M. M., et al. (2006). *Mapping Dialogue: A Research Project Profiling Dialogue Tools and Processes for Social Change*. Johannesburg, South Africa, German Technical Co-Operation (GTZ) and Pioneers of Change; Ramirez, R., et al. (2008). *Business Planning in Turbulent Times: New Methods for Applying Scenarios*. London, UK, Earthscan; Wilkinson, A. and E. Eidinow (2008). "Evolving Practices in Environmental Scenarios: A New Scenario Typology." *Environmental Research Letters* 3 (October–December).

13. Carson, A. S. (2002). *Establishing Public-Private Partnerships: Three Tests of a Good Process*. Puerto Vallarta, Mexico, International Applied Business Research Conference.
14. Sweitzer, S. (2004). *Sustainable Food Laboratory Foundation Workshop Learning History Chapter 1*. Hartland, VT, USA, Sustainability Institute.
15. Ibid., p. 5.
16. Sweitzer, S. (2006). *Sustainable Food Laboratory Foundation Workshop Learning History Chapter 4*. Hartland, VT, USA, Sustainability Institute.
17. World Commission on Dams (WCD) (2000). *Dams and Development: A New Framework for Decision-Making*, Earthscan; Dubash, N., et al. (2001). "An Independent Assessment on the World Commission on Dams: Preliminary Report". http://www.wcdassessment.org, World Resources Institute, Washington DC; Lokayan, Delhi; Lawyers Environmental Action Team, Dar es Salaam; Khagram, S. (2004). *Dams and Development: Transnational Struggles for Water and Power*. Cornell, NY, USA, Cornell University Press; Dingwerth, K. (2005). "The Democratic Legitimacy of Public-Private Rule Making: What Can we Learn from the World Commission on Dams?" *Global Governance* 11: 65–83.

CHAPTER 4

Seeing the whole

- When the Global Finance Initiative (GFI) wanted to understand how to define the "global finance system" and identify its stakeholders to develop a strategy to integrate social and environmental concerns into the system, it began with *issue crawls.*
- When the Global Reporting Initiative (GRI) considered its strategy for developing a South African network to advance GRI's triple-bottom-line accountability agenda, *social network analysis (SNA)* was used.
- When the European Commission wanted to understand how to enhance the process of innovation, it used an approach called *value network analysis (VNA).*
- When Youth Enterprise and Sustainability (YES) in Latin America wanted to develop its network strategy it turned to an approach called *managing for Clarity (MfC).*
- When wanting to understand the role of GANs (Global Action Networks) in responding to the Tragedy of the Commons, *systems archetypes* are useful.
- When the Mass Atrocities Project wanted to understand use of specific words, it undertook *web scrapes* to produce *semantic clouds.*
- When the Global Public Policy Research Group wanted to understand the relationships between various organizations in the climate change domain, it developed a *concept map.*

All these organizations turned to tools that can be broadly called *visual diagnostics mapping.* They are tremendously useful when complexity is a big issue, when formal structures are obscuring what is actually happening, and when different ways of thinking about the world are creating conflict.

These visual diagnostics communicate tremendous amounts of information visually, much more easily than volumes of text. They are a product of the vastly enhanced computing power and software developed over the past decade. These tools are an important new resource that has been moving out of academia over the past half dozen years. However, like any innovation at an early stage, they can be very confusing. The language describing them is still evolving, and the limitations and benefits of the various approaches are just becoming clear.

The mapping tools require openness to learning new ways of approaching challenges and looking at opportunities. One necessary shift is to think in terms of "systems," a concept perhaps most powerfully popularized by Peter Senge.[1] Everyone works with "systems" – internal systems relating to how work gets done, issue systems relating to the topic that a GAN is working to address, and mental model systems about how people understand a strategy. Clearly "seeing" those systems is important for success.

Another necessary shift is that participants identify with the issue system. Stakeholders may or may not identify themselves as participants in the system as a GAN frames it. Building this participant identity is critical to creating effective action to realize opportunities, address needs, and respond to challenges. In visual diagnostics mapping, individuals, organizations, or core concepts are depicted as nodes in networks. These diagrams graphically highlight the range of their actions, their ways of thinking *vis-à-vis* the issue, and the natural and man-created environmental factors that influence the issue system.

These maps can include literally hundreds of nodes and arrows, or very few. Experience working with people around the world proves that even relatively complex systems with a couple of hundred nodes can be understood by people with very limited education. Key is a *participatory development process*. I worked with Jim Ritchie-Dunham who developed the MfC mapping approach on a project with CARE in Guatemala to vastly enhance its impact.[2] The final map appears overwhelmingly complicated. However, because of the development process it was well understood by the participants. An evaluation a year later showed that the process was transformational from two perspectives: people had significantly changed their relationships (*who* they were working with) and they had significantly changed *how* they understood their work *vis-à-vis* others.

The visual diagnostic methodologies presented here are not a comprehensive list, but they are ones I'm familiar with and have found useful. They are presented in a very rough order from the most simple to the most complicated. This order also roughly reflects an order of usefulness to describe the various types of complexity presented in Chapter 2 and the degree of complication and effort required to develop the maps. The discussion here is illustrative; whole books are written on the individual methods.

Methodologies

Semantic clouds

Every issue field has many terms and phrases that have close or associated meanings. Using one can open some doors and close others. Who is using which ones? Which ones are emerging as dominant at a particular time? How might usage differ by type of organization or location of organization? One easy way to investigate this is by web scraping: scrapes search the web for usage of a list of terms by a specific list of URLs.

The Mass Atrocities project wanted to understand language in and around the issue arena of mass atrocities – think Darfur and Liberia with systemic rape, civilian murder, human mutilation, and recruitment of child soldiers. A list of terms was compiled as possible ways organizations involved in the arena might describe their work. Using scrapeGoogle, a web scrape then was done for the web-sites of a list of organizations known to be operating in the arena. Such a scrape can specify restrictions such as "by language" and "by country." This produced "semantic clouds" available in several formats:

- All hosts for each issue
- Issue returns per host
- Google count of issue returns per host
- Host recognition per issue
- URL recognition per issue
- Cumulative Google count per issue

Figure 4.1 is the product of the Mass Atrocities scrape for "Host recognition per issue." In this cloud the size of the font is related to the number

Armed Conflict (23) Children in Conflict (10) Civilian Protection (13) Conflict Prevention (21) Conflict Resolution (23) Conflict Transformation (18) Crimes Against Humanity (20) Ethnic Cleansing (18) Genocide (24) Governance (22) Human Security (20) Mass Atrocities (12) Peace building (23) Peacekeeping (23) Reintegration Rehabilitation and Recovery (0) Responsibility to Protect (17) Rule of Law (22) Security Sector Reform (18) War Crimes (20)

Figure 4.1   Semantic cloud for mass atrocities project

of times it appears in comparison to other sites which appear in brackets. In this diagram, there is a clear popularity of terms in the 17–24 range. The preferred term of the investigators, "Mass Atrocity", clearly is at the bottom of usage. This allows for a clear strategic decision, about whether to continue to focus upon this term knowing this, or to change terms.

Issue crawl mapping

One of the easiest form of mapping in terms of effort is issue crawls. The Internet has an increasing role in communications and daily life. People have personal as well as organizational web-sites. Sites bringing people together around shared interests and concerns are numerous. The importance of the Internet in political and other campaigns is unquestioned. Although web presence is not uniform around the world, certainly for global issues and increasingly for local ones the Internet presents an incredible information resource for mapping.

The Internet is structured around sites that have unique URL addresses. And most sites have (hyper) links to other sites that you click on to take you to other sites or pages. These are inserted because they have more detailed information with regard to a topic (including, of course, ads), because the host wants to connect people to allies or colleagues, or because they may be foes on an issue.

These connections between unique URLs provide the basis for mapping relationships by doing an issue crawl. A software program can draw the relationships between organizations' web links, to give a description of the virtual network of the organization.

Figure 4.2 is such a map of an issue system.[1] It shows links between URLs that can collectively be called "the global commercial finance public issue arena." These are the organizations to which global commercial finance institutions link.

The crawl identified 282 URLs; only the top 100 are shown in the map. Key public policy institutions like the World Bank are shown as stars, the UN as a square. Separate data list the number of links to each URL and the direction – whether they go to a URL or come from it – which is important to understand who thinks who is worth attention. Another list summarizes the number of links. In this case URLs with 20+ links are:

---

[1] This was generated using the Issue Crawler (issuecrawler.net) from the Govcom.org Foundation, directed by Prof. Richard Rogers, Chair in New Media & Digital Culture, University of Amsterdam.

1. worldbank.org – 36
2. sec.gov – 26
3. imf.org – 26
4. oecd.org – 22
5. unpri.org – 22
6. whitehouse.gov – 21
7. calpers.ca.gov – 21

Together with this map, the data illustrate the following:

1) There is quite a division in the map with the US Federal Reserve playing a key link between the global and US-based organizations.
2) The World Bank, IMF, Bank for International Settlements, and OECD (the stars) are key global public finance institutions for commercial finance.
3) There also is a group of "shadow" public institutions working in the responsible investment arena in the top-middle-left with the GRI having an important linking role.

Figure 4.2   Issue crawl of global commercial finance public issue Arena

Of course as with any methodology, this presents only a limited picture. However, the crawl suggests that for anyone looking to reform the global finance system, there might be an important role for the responsible investment organizations. The UN Global Compact and GRI should be investigated for potential in playing a role in bridging between non-traditional industry players and others. In this case, one of the most important uses of the data is the other crawls that could be undertaken – depending upon the questions driving the inquiry. The remaining URLs generated give you a large database for further investigation. You can identify the top NGOs and commercial firms in the arena easily, and run different crawls with each of them separately in order to find top organizations in each sector. You can suppress the World Bank (so its site is ignored) or other highly ranked organizations to see if other responsible investment bridges emerge.

Issue crawls are particularly useful when used with other network analysis methodologies, because they help identify organizations in a field to further investigate.

Systems archetypes

In systems thinking there are ten archetypes that can prove very helpful to analyzing complex change challenges. These are causal loop diagrams – ones with arrows indicating whether an action re-enforces or inhibits a particular factor. These have been popularized by Peter Senge[3] and Daniel Kim.[4] They are referred to by titles that describe the fundamental dynamic they analyze.

1. Limits to Growth (aka Limits to Success)
2. Shifting the Burden
3. Eroding Goals
4. Escalation
5. Success to the Successful
6. Tragedy of the Commons
7. Fixes that Fail
8. Growth and Underinvestment
9. Accidental Adversaries
10. Attractiveness Principle

On a global scale, GANs can be seen as responses to the "tragedy of the commons". In the absence of effective global public policy making, the commons, such as the air we breathe and the financial systems we use, become abused. We have been trying to solve these problems through the nation-state, but as Albert Einstein said, "Problems cannot be solved at the same level of awareness that created them." The solution will be found either at a level "below" nation-states, with the elements that make up a nation-state such as people and their organizations, provinces/states – or at a level beyond the nation-states, one that does not operate within the confines of national boundaries.

The Tragedy of the Commons archetype is presented in Figure 4.3 with actors (individuals, organizations, or nations) A and B. Arrows represent direction of a force; (+) indicates an increase, (−) represents a decrease; ‖ across an arrow represents a time delay. Cycles R1 and R2 describe that each person derives benefits from drawing from a limited resource. The critical causal link in 4.3 is the arrow that points to "Gain per Individual Activity"; this Gain will decrease, but with a time delay.

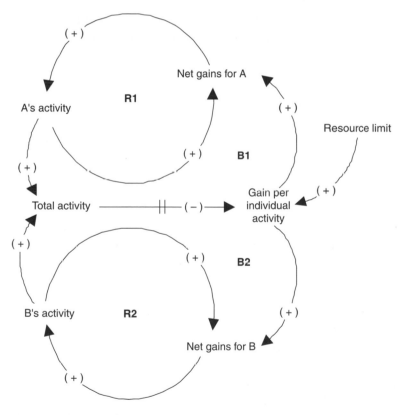

Figure 4.3   Tragedy of the commons

Analyst William Braun explains that "As each person or team increases their demands and expectations of the commons in the name of their own goals, the commons itself finds itself under steadily increasing pressure to perform while simultaneously feeling that its control over its own destiny steadily erodes toward collapse."[5]

To paraphrase Daniel Kim, the tragedy of the global commons requires that:

• Questions be asked such as, "What are the incentives for nations to persist in their actions?" and "Can the long-term collective loss be made more real and immediate to the nations?", and
• Ways be found to reconcile short-term national rewards with long-term cumulative consequences.

This is just a single example of a single archetype. Typically there are two or more archetypes at play with any issue. The diagrams are enormously helpful for people to collectively understand what is happening and define a strategy to change the situation. This approach is particularly valuable, because if used properly, it helps identify unintended consequences of strategies, and to take action to avoid them.

Concept mapping

Sometimes several different aspects are wanted in a particular map – such as geography, players, and roles in a development process. Concept mapping can take any number of perspectives to describe a space in ways that provide strategic insight. This approach is associated with mind-mapping, an approach commonly used in planning meetings.

One example of this is with the climate change arena. This is an extremely complex field, and the multitude of relationships is very difficult to grasp. How can all this be described in a way that is sufficiently comprehensive, relatively easily understood, and summarized on a page?

Several years ago the map below was developed by Tariq Banuri and myself to understand the development of climate policy. It really integrates a type of SNA with networks and their role in three major concept activities of (1) science and policy support, (2) research and advocacy, and (3) climate policy.

Figure 4.4 shows how we mapped this. Policy is the central process, and the United Nations Framework Convention on Climate Change (UNFCCC) and the Kyoto Protocol are central to policy development so we put them at the center. Then we analyzed the major roles of *networks*

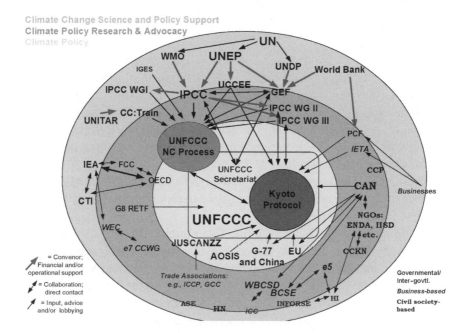

Figure 4.4   Concept map of the climate change system

(rather than organizations, to cut down on the number of actors) – there is a wide range of players who provide support, advocacy, research, lobbying, citizen voices, and information.

The sector (business, government, civil society) was thought important to distinguish since they come with such different concerns – hence, different type faces for the acronyms. There is a slew of alliances between networks that are also important to describe, so connecting lines were introduced. And the players have different roles in the process, so arrows were placed on the lines to distinguish between three particularly important roles. Some actors are more influential than others, so as a very rough estimate of influence some organizations have larger acronyms than others.

The completed diagram describes the dynamics and participants in the arena in a succinct way that facilitates discussion. Are the stakeholders who should be engaged, engaged? Sufficiently engaged? Engaged in the appropriate way? Are there ways relationships should be changed – perhaps made more direct? Should some "new space" be created because some stakeholders need connection in a different way? Maybe the whole arena needs some fundamental rethinking – what could that look like? The diagram facilitates addressing all these questions.

Geo mapping

Geo mapping is a very old concept that is being given brilliant new life with new technologies. Old-timers will remember atlases that showed countries of different size, depending upon a factor like GNP per capita. "Mash-up" technologies on the web combine information from more than one source – combining notably a geographic mapping program, GPS, and cellular phones – to give combining place, time, and some particular information; it can be provided real time.

Disaster relief and human rights networks find this approach very helpful since the average citizen can be engaged to report events via cell phone. Figure 4.5 is an example of this.

Kristin Antin, New Tactics Online Community Builder, explains that "(T)he Kenyan post-election violence map reflects a collection of citizen reports, incidents. These incidents are documented and visualized in a map to see trends and assess risks – and the reports are collected so that journalists can investigate the reports afterwards. In essence – this is a powerful tool for journalists that are working to document and report the violence."

Another mash-up is with databases and Geographic Information System (GIS) technologies. An example is the Millennium Development Goals (MDG) Monitor, a project between the UNDP and the Parsons Institute for Information Mapping. It is a web-based system that enhances and

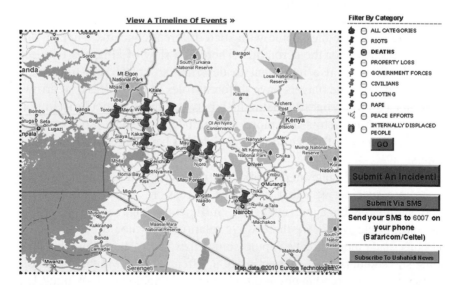

Figure 4.5 Geo mapping post-election violence in Kenya

Source: ushahidi.com/ (2008). "Kenya Post-Election Violence." Retrieved April 8, 2010, from http://legacy.ushahidi.com/.

expands the UNDP's capabilities to assess, evaluate, and enable success of United Nation's partner country goals. The outputs are maps of geographic regions that can be coded in a variety of ways (color, size, pattern, etc.) to easily represent information in visually sophisticated ways that used to take very complex procedures to produce.[6]

Social network mapping

To support GRI development in South Africa, we used perhaps the most common type of visual diagnostic mapping approach: social network analysis (SNA) that describes relationships with a single line or arrow between *nodes,* where nodes are individuals, parts of organizations, or organizations. There are several softwares that can be used for SNA; the best known being Ucinet.

Figure 4.6[II] is a very simple example of an inter-organizational network (ION) that was developed with the GRI when it was thinking about establishing a South African GRI network. Surveys conducted identified organizations and their relationships with two particular characteristics that drew from GRI's core strategy: organizations that were involved with triple-bottom-line analysis and development (social–economic–environmental impact), and organizations that engaged in multi-stakeholder processes. (This type of "boundary setting" is a critical part of mapping.)

This resulting issue system map illustrates the following:

1) There are six different stakeholder groups with these characteristics: labor, business, academic, new South African leaders, associates of an organization for Directors, and environmental organizations.
2) Environmental organizations – the ones in the top center – do not have any powerful linkages to the other organizations.
3) There are some key bridging organizations that connect groups: Business SA, Stellenbosch, Transparency International (TI), and the King Commission.
4) Each stakeholder group except new South African leaders has important hubs: NEDLAC (labor), Business Council Sustainability (business), Ethics South Africa (academics), Institute of Directors (Directors), and IA Impact Assessment (environment).

[II] This was generated using *Visone,* developed under the leadership of Ulrik Brandes (University of Konstanz) and Dorothea Wagner (Karlsruher Institut für Technologie (KIT) in Germany.

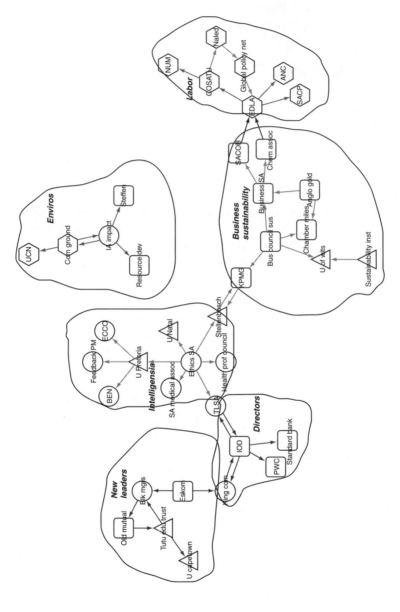

Figure 4.6 Social network of GRI-issue domain networks in South Africa

This descriptive analysis suggests the following strategy:

1) Put the environment on the back burner for the moment, since economic–social issues are more dominant;
2) Consult with the bridging organizations as key informants and perhaps engage them in initial convening to form a GRI South Africa network; and
3) When creating a leadership group or board, make sure you engage the nodes of each group.

The descriptive analysis therefore supports a strategy of firmly building on the current, local orientation, social structure, and capacity to develop a GRI approach. Rather than GRI being a foreign entity coming in through a particular stakeholder group as is often the way an organization enters a new region – raising great suspicions among other groups – GRI can begin with a much more comprehensive strategy that weaves together current social relationships in a new way.

The analysis also supports developing an impact measurement assessment. GRI could imagine what a map of relationships would look like to realize its goals, and repeat the analysis at a later date to see if the relationships have changed.

This is a very simple example of social network mapping. A more comprehensive analysis could describe the types of contacts/relationships (what is being exchanged, how frequently, etc.) and sub-networks in more detail.

Social network mapping can describe inter-personal networks, key thought leaders, and gatekeepers (those who can inhibit or facilitate entry to a network). This type of analysis can help identify and describe political difficulties that an organizing strategy should be aware of.

Organizational analysis could describe the influence of GRI within an organization. For example, a specific person in a company is usually charged with representing a company to GRI. That person and GRI might want to develop a strategy for promoting GRI and building internal corporate capacity to apply the GRI framework, in a large corporation. This can be a huge challenge. Formal reporting structures ignore how most work actually gets done, but internal organizational analysis can help develop a strategy that is built upon the way people actually interact.

Value network analysis

ValueNet Works™ is a mapping methodology developed by Verna Allee.[7] The methodology maps issue systems in terms of *roles* and *exchanges*

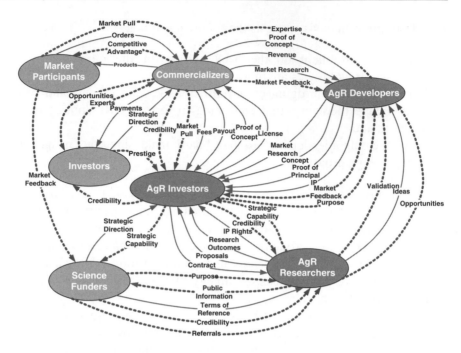

Figure 4.7   Value network of commercializing scientific discoveries

Note: Dotted lines indicate intangible exchanges, solid tangible exchanges

between roles. This is very useful when you want to understand what roles are necessary for a healthy issue system, what roles need more attention, and which might be so well-resourced that competition is creating problems. In Figure 4.7 of the innovation production system, there are seven roles represented by the nodes; the exchanges between them are represented by the arrows where broken lines represent intangible exchanges and solid lines represent tangibles. Most organizations play more than one role – there are actually more than 30 organizations behind the map and many of these would play at least one role and sometimes two or three. This particular map was done with a government agency in New Zealand that commercializes scientific discoveries. In other work with the European Union a similar analysis identified four stages or "phase changes" with different value network models for each. The effort resulted in numerous policy recommendations.

These visual representations are valuable as:

1) Issue framers – Complex issues systems are difficult to put hands around. They seem overwhelming in scale, with a confusing array of ideas about "who is in" and "who is out" of the issue boundaries.

This mapping transforms highly emotional definitions about which organizations should be considered part of an issue system into much less emotional questions about the key roles that are necessary for the issue system to be healthy. In large systems, the number of roles is easier to talk about since they are many fewer than the number of people or organizations.

2) Conversation starters – The VNA methodology should not be treated like a highly accurate one that can measure small transactions in detail, as taking it to that level can be an exhausting exercise. Rather its strength is about overall flows and exchanges. It creates good conversations about what those should be, what roles are well-developed, and which ones need more attention, before getting to the question of who should play which role.

3) Consensus builders – Because the data are a visual representation on one or a few sheets of paper or slides, people much more easily identify and agree upon key points than with long wordy reports. VNA is a method of synthesizing enormous amounts of data that people will otherwise have trouble consuming or agreeing upon. It provides a transparent way for people to negotiate expectations.

4) A strategic development tool – The map provides a means to understand important dynamics of a system and to identify key strategic actions and priorities to shift it.

5) As an impact assessment tool and monitoring – The mapping can be replicated periodically over time, to understand if interventions aimed at addressing specific shortcomings are being addressed.

Managing for clarity mapping

Different people in any GAN issue system (such as water, peacekeeping, global finance, and health care) have different goals, they focus upon different parts of the system and they have different understandings of how "the system" works. Mapping with the strategic clarity methodology developed by Jim Ritichi-Dunham aims to make these differences explicit so that the "whole system" can see itself.[8]

The map includes a description of how the actions and incentives of each stakeholder impact the intended and unintended actions of other stakeholders, and how this set of actions impacts the overall intention of the system. The methodology provides the basis for identifying the highly strategic leverage points that could "shift" the system's behavior in the desired direction.

This methodology for mapping based upon mental models is grounded in systems theory and the decision sciences. The MfC framework provides five principles to describe a complex issue system: **G**oal, **R**esources, **A**ctions, **S**tructure, and **P**eople (GRASP).

- **Goal**: Why does the network exist?
- **Resources**: Which resources drive value for stakeholders and which resources enable work to be done that creates value for the stakeholders?
- **Actions**: Which actions most effectively leverage the enabling resources?
- **Structure**: What are the linkages among the goals, resources, and actions?
- **People**: What do people care about in this system?

These principles are structured in a map in a specific order, as shown in the generic MfC map in Figure 4.8 where actions are at the bottom and goal at the top.

This mapping approach was used by Lu Maria Puente with Youth Employment and Sustainability (YES), a GAN operating in 55 countries. It was applied to YES' Latin America network to investigate its utility as a strategic visualization and planning tool. Maps were created for individual countries and for YES as a whole. Each country map looks different, because each country has a very unique way of doing its work. For example, some countries focus on increasing youth technical and business skills; some focus on developing the internal side with entrepreneurship

Figure 4.8   Generic MfC map

courses; and some focus on strengthening the incubator infrastructure to help youth create new business.

GANs like YES may pay insufficient attention to the needs of different key stakeholders and what they require from the network in order to keep them engaged and participating over time. The MfC framework specifically articulates stakeholders' diverse needs and how they impact the rest of the network. If the network is not satisfying its stakeholders, the stakeholders will leave the network, limiting the network's impact or even putting at risk its survival. Therefore, knowing what they require is critical. Mapping these for YES Latin America as the MfC framework's value-driving resources produced Figure 4.9.

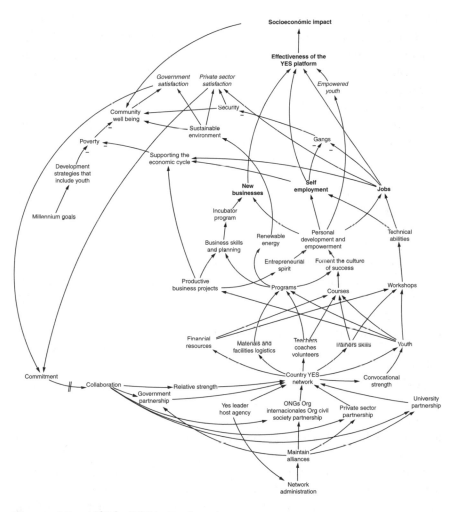

Figure 4.9   MfC for YES Latin America

Each stakeholder can have more than one "satisfier" – something that will keep it engaged in the network. The research showed that in this case government satisfaction comes from developing a sustainable environment and supporting the economy, poverty reduction, and increased community well-being. Private-sector satisfaction comes from creating a sustainable environment, developing qualified job candidates, and increasing security for themselves by reducing the number of youth involved in gangs (Peru and Panama have specific programs directed to youth in gangs).

One of the main network satisfiers is empowerment of youth. Having the relevant skills is necessary, but believing in oneself is just as important. Examples of how to read the causality in Figure 4.9:

- If the number of self-employed stays the same and the number of jobs of youth involved in gangs increases, the number of youth involved in gangs decreases. If the number of jobs stays the same and the self-employment of youth involved in gangs goes up, the youth involved in gangs decreases.
- If the number of youth in gangs decreases, security increases.
- If security increases, private businesses' satisfaction increases and community well-being also increases.
- If number of jobs, self-employment, or new businesses increases, the support for the economic cycle increases, reducing poverty.
- If poverty decreases, community well-being increases and satisfaction with government increases.

In all the cases the opposite applies.

Figure 4.9 is one of numerous maps developed to help YES participants understand strategic relationships and high leverage actions. The project produced several significant insights into the life cycle and survivability of YES that are more broadly useful for GANs. Working on their own to improve youth employment, stakeholders have limited impact. Working as a GAN effectively will increase this impact, because the collaboration brings forward each group's opportunities, possibilities, and strengths.

A GAN is very hard to develop without a sense of cohesiveness among the stakeholders. Understanding what each stakeholder needs from, and offers to, the network is fundamental to the impact and sustainability of the network itself. Taking a systemic approach is a powerful way to make explicit these needs and contributions.

Using MfC as a systemic mapping tool allows GAN leaders to integrate the local actions they perform within the context of the region and see how the region's work connects to the global goal of YES. It was both inspiring and clarifying for the leaders to see how they contribute to the whole.

Most importantly, a few leaders shifted their thinking from "what can they give me" to "how can what I do make them successful as well?" This significantly improved the possibilities for more powerful partnerships.

This shift in thinking is also the first step in addressing the long-term sustainability of the network. As the leaders shift to more of a win-win mindset, the probability that the stakeholders will want to more fully participate increases. This will bring more resources to the network, increasing the success and impact of the network. In fact, this reinforcing engine defines the network, what it can accomplish, and the impact it can create over time.

Explaining complexity

Table 4.1 summarizes comparatively these ways of seeing the whole. Another way of comparing them is through the concept of "complexity" that I introduced in Chapter 2. There it is described as having five components for GANs. These mapping tools help illuminate the complexity to make it discussable and understand impacts of actions. Bringing back in dimensions of complexity, we see that mapping can help in the following ways summarized in Table 4.2.

Table 4.1 A comparison of the mapping approaches for building comprehensive engagement strategies

	Visual output	Goal	Use	Limitations
Semantic clouds	• Words that are sized in relationship to their frequency of use	• Learn what words and phrases are most commonly used	• Defining the words to use in an activity	• Must be repeated in different languages • Even in one language there may be variation in use by geography, discipline, etc.
Issue crawls	• Map of URL connections	• Identify organizations in an issue arena • Identify sub-groups, central organizations, bridging organizations in virtual space	• Identifying key stakeholder and influencers in an issue area • Getting a general sense of relationships within the system	• Only good if issue arena organizations have good web-sites • Usually good for global arenas • Remember: virtual reality does not equal reality

Table 4.1 (Continued)

	Visual output	Goal	Use	Limitations
Systems archetypes	• Diagrams of the system's dynamics in terms of 10 archetypes	• Understand basic driving forces and feedback loops with respect to an issue	• Identifying high-leverage interventions • Identifying unintended consequences	• Time delays may vary significantly • Strength of different forces may vary significantly • Requires behavioral to validate
Concept mapping	• Maps of relationships between ideas, geographies or other variables of an issue	• Understand relationships between specific variables of an issue	• Strategic planning to influence specific variables	• Quite subjective and quality depends upon expertise
Geo mapping	• Maps of relationships between a geographic location and a specific variable	• Understand geographic variation of an activity or variable	• Develop geographic-based plans	• Maps require coordination between large and diverse databases or in-put sources
Social networks analysis	• Map of links between individuals, parts of an organization or organizations	• Identify work flows, alliances, who is central • Understand the network structure of the system	Strengthen a network by: • Addressing lack of connections • Addressing bottlenecks • Reducing duplication/ redundancy	• Must have good starting list of people/ organizations • In ONA/IONA data is gathered from individuals, but applied to organizations
Value networks analysis	• Maps of value creation process • List of roles in the network • Definition of value outputs	Understand how issues can be addressed in terms of: • Formal and informal exchanges between organizations	• Initiating a network • Strengthening a network by supporting specific roles, relationships, or interactions • Reducing duplication/ redundancy	• Challenging to identify "boundaries" and "roles" in a network for manageable analysis • Institutional models and mindsets get in the way

		Roles and interactions between them	Shifting from organization-based to role-based network development	Maps can initially appear complicated so output needs to be managed carefully for communication
Managing for clarity analysis	• Maps of people's mental models of how the system works (individual or combined) in terms of stakeholders, actions and strategic resources	• Understand how all the stakeholders interact to create the system (network) • Create a common vision among the stakeholders • Identify the strategic leverage points in order to increase impact	• Developing a strategic plan (global and local) • Creating a systemic understanding of the network • Creating a common language to promote sharing and learning among all the countries including all the stakeholders • Understanding how to measure impact and what limits it	• Creating and combining the maps requires significant expertise • Maps can initially appear complicated

Table 4.2 Visual analytic methods and complexity

	Focus	Spatial	Knowledge	Cultural	Change
Semantic clouds	Words			+	
Issue crawl	Stakeholders and relationships in a system	+	+	+	+
Systems archetypes	System feedback loops		+		++
Concept mapping	Concepts	+	I	+	+
Geo mapping	Geography, events, data	++	+	+	+
Social network analysis	Structure of relationships	+	+	+	++
Value network analysis	Value creation among relationships	++	++	+	++
Managing for clarity analysis	Mental models and leverage points for value creation	++	++	+	++

(+ indicates of some value, ++ indicates of great value for GANs)

1. *Spatial: Global–regional–local*
   Geo mapping is the most obvious approach to clarify spatial complexity. With *MfC* the integrated map of regions shows how the local network, the regional network, and the global network interact to achieve the global goal. It also shows how the local actions affect the regional and global outcomes across the network. VNA can describe these differences in terms of local-to-global roles. Issue crawls and SNA nodes can be coded to indicate specific regions. Concept mapping can be designed around the specific concept of spatial. In all of these methods specific regions can be mapped for comparison between regions.

2. *Knowledge: From data gatherers to those putting wisdom-in-action*
   Issue crawls present the simplest analysis of URL dynamics, and SNA describes social relationships that can be coded for different activities as can geo mapping with geographic relationships. VNA and MfC are particularly useful for GANs because they help participants arise above their individual organizational perspectives, and to really get into the network world of roles, exchanges, resources, and mental models. The real-time nature of geo mapping also makes it an attractive tool. Concept mapping can be designed around the specific concept of different dynamics.

3. *Cultural: Crossing differences of language, beliefs, values, sectors*
   SNA can be useful for understanding this form of complexity if the nodes are coded for cultural characteristics; this can reveal important patterns. Such coding with VNA can identify strengths and weaknesses associated with distinct cultural characteristics in terms of roles and exchanges.

   SNA, VNA, and MfC support deepening appreciation of cultural differences and how to work with them, if they are developed in a participatory way. They generate a common language and meaning of key elements, ideas, shared by the stakeholders of the network. They create an objective platform to talk about emotionally charged issues among the stakeholders.

   Semantic clouds help with identifying varying uses of words and associated concepts, although it is obviously restricted to a single language at a time. Concept mapping can be designed around the specific concept of different cultural attributes. Geo mapping can relate culture and specific locations.

4. *Change: Supporting reform, reformation, and transformation*
   The Systems Archetype mapping perhaps most clearly focuses upon clarifying how actions interact over times, with feedback loops. This

mapping approach describes underlying dynamics, however, rather than telling you anything about the strength of them. Nevertheless, it helps identify critical leverage points.

Other mapping approaches describe current reality based upon data from a system, rather than simply through archetypes. All of the mapping processes, if repeated periodically, will give a good descriptive understanding of how a system is changing. One famous example of SNA in the media arena showed Google as a peripheral player at the beginning of the millennium, and a few years later it was central. Mapping in general is a good way to help a GAN ensure that its actions are not based upon an old understanding about relationships, roles, and structures.

Additionally, with SNA, VNA, and MfC, participants can deepen understanding about the number of nodes in paths and the time it takes to move through them, to develop more expedient paths. Systems Archetypes uses a specific symbol to indicate time delays. In these methodologies, a shared understanding by the stakeholders of the feedback loops helps them grasp the sustainability of the network by linking today's actions to long-term network results. Concept mapping can be designed around the specific concept of time delays.

5. *Relational: Not described, since it is a combination of the other types of complexity.*

There are certainly other forms of visual diagnostics that can be very helpful. More traditional ones include mind-mapping which is often used in group planning settings, and mapping of issues using systems archetypes.

These methods can also be combined to great effect. The Global Finance Initiative made use of issue crawls to obtain an initial understanding of the field, then undertook VNA and SNA to deepen the analysis. Given the growth in capacity to collectively analyze information, we can anticipate further creative developments.

Notes

1. Senge, P. M. (1990). The Fifth Discipline: The Art and Practice of the Learning Organization. New York, Doubleday.
2. Ritchie-Dunham, J. (2008). "A Collaborative-Systemic Strategy Addressing the Dynamics of Poverty in Guatemala: Converting Seeming Impossibilities into Strategic Probabilities". Alleviating Poverty through Business Strategy. New York, NY, USA, Palgrave Macmillan.

3. Senge, P. M. (1990). Op.cit; Senge, P., et al. (1994). The Fifth Discipline Fieldbook. New York, NY, Currency Doubleday.

4. Kim, D. (1992). The Toolbox Reprint Series: Systems Archetypes I. Waltham, MA, Pegasus Communications, Inc.

5. Braun, W. (2002). "The Systems Archetypes." Retrieved April 8, 2010, from www.uni-klu.ac.at/~gossimit/pap/sd/wb_sysarch.pdf.

6. PIIM. "Millennium Development Goals Monitor." Retrieved April 8, 2010, from http://piim.newschool.edu/development/millennium-development-goals-monitor.

7. Allee, V. (2008). "Value Network Analysis and Value Conversion of Tangible and Intangible Assets." Journal of Intellectual Capital 9(1): 5–24; Allee, V. and O. Schwabe (2009). Measuring the Impact of Research Networks in the EU: Value Networks and Intellectual Capital Formation. Haarlem, The Netherlands, European Conference on Intellectual Capital.

8. Ritichie-Dunham, J. and H. Rabbino (2001). Managing from Clarity: Identifying, Aligning and Leveraging Strategic Resources. Chichester, UK, John Wiley & Sons, Ltd.

CHAPTER 5

Mastering change

GANs (Global Action Networks) are about global change with the vision of a flourishing world for all. International Bridges to Justice aims to end torture in the twenty-first century; the Global Compact aims to give life to 10 UN principles throughout the world; The Climate Group is about setting the world economy on the path to a low-carbon, prosperous future. These are colloquially referred to as "BHAGs" – big, hairy, audacious goals. To realize such goals, you had better have a clear change strategy, understand the assumptions behind your actions, access the skills and tools to support their development, and possess a good understanding of change processes.

Some people working in GANs may not think of their work as "change." For example, people working in the Global Fund to Fight AIDS might think of their work as financing; people in the Global Water Partnership (GWP) might think of it as building infrastructure to deliver water. However, this work is about realizing change to improve lives. Like other GANs, the Global Fund and GWP are the product of two change pressures. One is pressure to respond to changing realities that produce new opportunities and challenges. This includes globalization of the economy, new possibilities with communication technology, and increasing environmental stress. The other pressure for change is a pull to further develop values, beliefs, and timeless aspirations in the context of these shifting realities. This includes enhancing quality of life, equity, peace, and participation in decisions that affect us.

Writing about historic global change efforts, Oran Young points to two basic change strategies: collective action and social practices.[1] His "collective action" approach reflects the tradition of international treaties and conventions. In legal terms it can be thought of as a constitutional law approach: get the government powers in the room and write the rules that reflect the best theoretical thinking and what can be hammered out in compromise. (I'll refer to this as the "constitutional" tradition because social practice is also developed through collective action.) This reflects some core assumptions, including:

- National governments can determine what is best
- Negotiations as a process can produce effective results
- Experts are key in defining what is good
- Theory and rational thinking can drive action
- Enforcement/compliance will follow agreement

In Young's view the constitutional tradition at the global level is proving a failure, particularly in the post-Cold War world. Kyoto and Copenhagen are climate change examples; continuing wars are security examples; a world in which an estimated 1.02 billion people are undernourished is a poverty example.[2]

Consequently the social practices approach is gaining traction. Legally the social practices strategy is closest to common law approaches. It is a "norms-based" peer-pressure and voluntary approach drawing from tradition and experience. This approach reflects a different set of core assumptions, including:

- Stakeholders should be directly involved in defining what is best
- Negotiations should be supplemented with dialogue among stakeholders to transcend diverse beliefs, values, and perspectives
- All stakeholders (not just "experts") bring expertise in defining what is good
- Experience should drive action
- Participation in decision-making is key for generating compliance

GANs are clearly in the social practices camp, although some may have constitutional change strategies too. You can hear those attracted to GANs say "Let's just get out and *try* something, and not spend all our time talking about theory and the dotting of 'i's in an agreement that will never be followed anyways." Similarly, they emphasize their voluntary nature in comparison to regulation and laws.

The assumptions underlying GANs' particular change strategy are found in the seven strategic characteristics that define them. Their change strategy integrates the following assumptions:

1) Global and multi-level: National governments have a role in change, and issues are not spread uniformly around the world. However, effectively addressing the issue requires a global approach to both connect

people who are already beginning to think and act in new ways that change the way people and organizations think and act. The strategy must transcend national boundaries, and it requires "glocal" action: from local to global and vice versa without one being more important than the other.

2) Diversity-embracing: We are all in this together, and we all have a piece of the solution and responsibility to create a flourishing future. How to work together is not always obvious, and there are many challenges of coordinating, navigating, and communicating across diverse perspectives. However, we must start from a position of mutual respect and be open to listening.

3) Entrepreneurial action learning: To create change requires learning and sharing new ways of being and acting, individually and as a society; addressing the global challenges requires developing new knowledge and relationships to apply it effectively. This must be done through empowering people to act entrepreneurially in service of the big change goal.

4) Inter-organizational networks: Neither markets nor bureaucracies on their own provide the core principles, values, or capacity to generate the type of change at the scale needed. We need viral change that has coherence (direction) but is not centrally directed, and that can move rapidly across traditional organizing boundaries. To realize scale, organizations and other networks are key.

5) Systemic change: There is nevertheless a need for systemic change agents to "steward" the development of the networks and the global change processes. To address their particular issue requires the right mix of resources, skills, and relationships where collectively these properties reside. GANs as change agent networks must be knowledgeable about the issue itself, and particularly skillful in guiding the change processes.

6) Public good: To realize the change requires the ability to act with concern beyond one's own welfare, and focus upon a greater good. That does not mean forsaking your own or your organization's well-being, but it does mean developing it in a way that honors the greater good.

7) Voluntary leadership: The GANs provide a space for exploration and experimentation, and this cannot be forced upon people or organizations. It requires a willingness to be open and vulnerable to failures and criticism.

GANs wrap these strategic elements around a particular issue such as poverty, water, peace, torture, and sustainable food systems. And they steward a process of exploration and development of both practical solutions and movement building as core activities of their change strategy.

The Global Fund provides financing, but it does so specifically through multi-stakeholder Country Coordinating Mechanisms. The GWP builds infrastructure by creating coalitions of diverse stakeholders. They choose this strategy because they believe that building relationships between the stakeholders is key to realize their objectives.

Many GANs explain their change strategy in terms of the "tipping point" theory popularized by Malcolm Gladwell. They believe that once they have a critical mass of organizations reflecting their own beliefs and values, everyone will be obliged to accept them and they will become dominant. The way Gladwell writes about tipping points emphasizes the importance of GANs' network strategy to make this theory a reality. Gladwell compares change to "epidemics," because:

> ... epidemics behave in a very unusual and counterintuitive way. Think, for a moment, about an epidemic of measles in a kindergarten class. One child brings in the virus. It spreads to every other child in the class in a matter of days. And then, within a week or so, it completely dies out and none of the children will ever get measles again. That's typical behavior for epidemics: they can blow up and then die out really quickly, and even the smallest change – like one child with a virus – can get them started. My argument is that it is also the way that change often happens in the rest of the world. Things can happen all at once, and little changes can make a huge difference.[3]

It's the invention of the virus in the form of such things as effective participatory practices and transparency and a route for dissemination at a global level that the GANs are working on. This takes more time than the epidemic metaphor suggests, but it can be much quicker than other strategies.

What is "Change"

We are swimming in a world of "change," and like the concept of trust discussed earlier, distinguishing between different types of change is useful. This helps set reasonable goals, identify appropriate actions, and ensure the presence of skills that are necessary to support it. Over the past couple of decades, we have seen tremendous advances in understanding how to develop large change of the type that GANs aspire for.

Change can be described as being of three types. Moving from the most challenging to the easiest, these types are transformation, reform, and incremental. GANs are distinguished by aiming for transformational change, but are also involved with the other two types.

The distinctions build off of distinctions made in learning processes between single-, double-, and triple-loop *learning*.[4] Learning is thought of as the process of gaining new capabilities, and change results from the application of the capabilities. With single-loop learning the key question is "Are we doing things right?"; with double-loop it is "Are we doing the right things?"; and with triple-loop it is "How do we know what is best?" Table 5.1 summarizes the three types of change.

Table 5.1   Types of change

Type of change	Incremental – changing quantities	Reform – changing the way parts interact in a system	Transformation – reconceiving the system
Focus	Changing ways of acting and behaving	Changing ways of thinking	Changing ways of perceiving
Core questions	How can we do more of the same	What rules should we create	How do I make sense of this
	Are we doing things right	What are my mental models and assumptions	What is the purpose
			How do we know what is best
		Are we doing the right things? What is best practice	
Learning loops	Single loop	Second loop	Triple loop
Type of action	Enacting/applying known approaches/ scripts/solutions	Reflection and learning, critical analysis	Unlearning and relearning
When to use	For simple issues with causal order	For complicated non programmable issues	To innovate and create previously unimagined possibilities
	For routine, repetitive, predictable issues	When new solutions have been agreed upon	When no "solution" is apparent
	When the "answer" is known	When a problem is well-defined	When breakthrough thinking is needed
Purpose	To improve performance (behavior and activities) to implement defined solutions	To understand and change the system and its parts	To redefine/reinvent/ reconceive "the system", its purpose, and relationships

Table 5.1   (Continued)

Participation	Current actors addressing the problem	Stakeholders of the currently defined system	An exploratory microcosm of participants in the evolving understanding of "the system"
Power and relationships	Confirms existing rules. Preserves the established power structure and relationships among actors in the system	Opens rules to revision. Suspends established power relationships; promotes authentic interactions; creates a space for genuine change in the system	Opens issues to creating new ways of thinking and action about what sustains the system and what can emerge. Promotes fundamental shifts in power relationships and structures with emerging system awareness and identity
General dynamic	Implementing the predictable/ projectable	Defining and negotiating the projectable	Emerging the previously unimagined
Skills/ methods	Project management	Naming, framing, negotiating roles, and strategies	Co-authoring/narrative dialogue/revisioning tools, deepening awareness of world views
Personal role	I am acting on the problem	Others are the problem	I am part of the problem, "we" are in this together

Transformation

The "huge difference" of Gladwell is related to the paradigm shifts of Kuhn. When Thomas Kuhn wrote his seminal 1962 book on paradigm shifts, *The Structure of Scientific Revolutions*, he was writing about the physical sciences. He describes how changes occur in explanations (theories), about how the world works, and what is possible. For him a paradigm consists of definitions of *what* an analysis should observe, the kinds of questions that should be asked, how the questioning should be developed, and how the results should be interpreted.[5]

A classic example of such a paradigm shift is the change from conceiving the world as flat and the earth at the center of the universe to conceiving the world as round with the sun at the center of a solar system that is just one system within the universe. In this case:

- analysis shifted to observable data as opposed to reflective thinking and reading;

- questioning shifted to *why* does the ship disappear over the horizon bottom first rather than just disappear as a speck;
- the question was framed as "cause–effect": what possible causes could result in the observed effect; and
- the interpretation went beyond conventional thinking to question a fundamental premise (assumption).

Transformation involves a similar process. A wonderful example is with Sam Daley-Harris' frustration over the way traditional organizations ignore and marginalize data that do not conform to what they believe is possible. "There're these figures," says Sam, Director of the Microcredit Campaign Summit, "... Yunus Mohammed (Grameen Bank, Nobel Prize Winner), Ingrid Munro (Kenyan microcredit innovator)... and they (people in power) write off these people who break rules as 'special cases'... they dismiss it or marginalize it. If I walk into a USAID or World Bank office and said 'Ingrid in Kenya is making microloans successfully to former thieves, prostitutes, gang members'... what would they do with that information? Why didn't they look at Grameen Bank 25, 15 years ago? Why isn't that happening in Kenya? Because it breaks their pre-conceived conventional wisdoms of what is possible... it can't be replicated, it's a special case." Sam and the USAID/World Bank are looking with different paradigms.

Transformational change involves significant change in relationships and power structures. GANs typically arise out of questions requiring this type of change. The Sustainable Food Lab (SFL), for example, began with questions about how to transform the agriculture and food system into a sustainable one. Given GANs' change strategy, these types of questions are typically the subject of "whole system" gatherings (in other change strategies, they might be the subject of a clique of revolutionaries). For the SFL this meant large companies, small farmers groups, government agencies, and environmental organizations. Its process was unusually disciplined, drawing from the latest knowledge about how to address big problems.

This initial work over several months developed a vision of a sustainable agriculture future. It did this through workshops and other activities, initially with:

> ... the *diverging* phase – that of exploring the varied perspectives and priorities within the team in order to understand the complexity of current reality in the food system. Subsequent workshops ... focus(ed) on the *emerging* phase – that of seeing what sense can be made of the complexity of the system.[6]

Stakeholders collectively defined their vision of a sustainable agriculture system as one:

> ... in which the fertility of our soil is maintained and improved; the availability and quality of water are protected and enhanced; our biodiversity is protected; farmers, farm workers, and all other actors in value chains have livable incomes; the food we eat is affordable and promotes our health; sustainable businesses can thrive; and the flow of energy and the discharge of waste, including greenhouse gas emissions, are within the capacity of the earth to absorb forever.[7]

This envisions a transformational type of change, because it aims to redirect the agriculture system and change its fundamental orientations and core relationships. The vision describes a system where soil fertility, water, biodiversity, stakeholders, the food, and other components are re-oriented toward sustainability. The relationships between the stakeholders are re-oriented toward mutual concern, rather than the current approach where stakeholders are treated as independent and responsible for themselves. Overall, there is a reorientation toward structured inter-dependence.

This type of change presents a societal learning and change challenge. We are talking very big change, of course. It is comparable to the shift with the industrial revolution and the rise of the welfare state. When people experienced those changes, they experienced fundamental shifts in their lives and their life expectations. There were shifts in what was possible because of changes in technology, the types of organizations, and in the way the organizations interacted. I call this scale of change "societal learning and change" because just as when individuals learn to do things they could not do before, so with societal change entire societies learn how to do new things. It also emphasizes the importance of "learning processes." I've written another book about this, so I will only briefly explain it here.[8] You also might want to refer to the great work of Otto Scharmer and Nicanor Perlas in a similar vein.[9]

Table 5.2 says that the SFL challenge is to realize change in terms of four levels: individual, organizational, sectoral, and societal. Americans tend to think that if you get the right person, anything is possible (hence the fixation with who is President rather than the institutions of government). Europeans tend to focus on institutions and structures, with the argument that if you get them right then you can realize the change you are looking for (hence a focus upon the structure of the European Union, which is in many ways leaderless). Corporate social responsibility (CSR) critics often

Table 5.2 The societal learning and change matrix

Societal	Political Systems	Economic Systems	Social Systems
Sectoral	The State Sector	The Market Sector	The Social Sector
Organizational	Government agencies	Businesses	Community-based Orgs.
Individual	Mentally centered	Physically centered	Emotionally centered

say that individual organizations cannot successfully adopt CSR strategies because of market pressures. The whole market sector has to adopt them. Of course for the type of change GANs are working on, all of these are true and change must occur at all levels. In Table 5.2 the message is that change must occur at all four levels.

To the right of the levels are three columns that refer to the three systems that collectively make up society. Each of these systems has a distinct "organizing logic," which means each has different goals, values, and ways of organizing itself. For example, the political system focuses on questions of order and legality through citizens and/or voters (at least in our dominant version of legitimate government); the economic system focuses on questions of wealth generation and profitability through owners; and the social system focuses on questions of community health and justice through members.

The level that needs most explaining is the individual one. Work by Sandra Seagal and many educators classify individuals as being dominantly one of three types of learners:

- The mentally centered learners deal with abstractions and concepts (like the table!); they tend to dominate government organizations which are charged with developing laws and enforcing them by deciding whether people are acting inside or outside of "the rules."
- The physically centered learners (kinesthetic) learn by seeing, touching, and feeling – they are the "seeing-is-believing" people who tend to dominate business which focuses on physical, quantifiable outcomes.
- The emotionally centered learners are those who know reality when they feel it in their hearts, and when they are emotionally moved. These people tend to dominate community-based organizations (a category similar to non-profits/NGOs) that work on issues of spirit, justice and long-term sustainability.[10]

One insight that arises out of this is that the differences between business, government, and civil society arise from inherent differences in individuals, and the way they make sense of the world and learn.

Therefore, embracing diversity should include embracing these different ways of making sense of the world.[11]

Today we tend to think of these three sectors as distinct, and a lot of tension arises between them since their ways of seeing the world are so different. Sweden has integrated Seagal's insights into its education system, to reduce this type of tensions; Singapore has similarly integrated it into their police training, to support police (who tend to be rules-oriented) to interact successfully with others; and Intel Corporation has worked with her extensively to enhance team-work. Going back to the SFL example, its transformational vision requires working with these differences and weaving them together in new ways.

Most GANs do not have as disciplined processes for approaching the transformational challenge, as SFL had. Perhaps at the other end of the spectrum is International Bridges for Justice (IBJ), which is also very successful. IBJ works to end torture in the twenty-first century. Its founding is a bit unusual because it was so entrepreneurially driven at a local level. Rather than starting as a global or even regional group of stakeholders, IBJ started with an individual's drive to do something very directly in a specific location.

IBJ Founder and CEO Karen Tse explains that she's not focused upon the political prisoners who are tortured that Amnesty International attends to, but upon 90 percent of people who are tortured and are not political prisoners. IBJ's focus is on people who are just regular citizens and common criminals who are tortured because that is the way things are done.

Realizing IBJ's vision involves a basic power shift, particularly in favor of people who are imprisoned. It requires reform in traditional relationships, attitudes, and formal procedures to recognize the importance and legitimacy of the issue.

IBJ started out in China – not exactly the most obvious location to start – with the dynamic vision of Karen who is an American "outsider," but ethnically Chinese (which makes a difference). In the context of the Chinese situation in 2001, she was looking for transformation: to redirect the system and change fundamental orientations and core relationships. In this case, "the system" was made up of the judicial, legal, penal, security, and educational sub-systems.

The government was not "opposed" to ending torture, although ending it was not a top priority. Karen started out the same way most GANs start: by talking to stakeholders (the "exploration" stage). In this case, she built a partnership with the National Legal Aid of China to build connections with police, torture victims, legal scholars, judges, and others. In the societal learning and change language, she sought out emotionally and mentally centered people; physically centered business people were not key. She discovered a number of people who resonated with her goals, but no one really had an idea about how to realize them.

So Karen listened into the issue and the way it played out for different stakeholders. She practiced some fact-oriented listening to get a better understanding of the dimensions and characteristics of the problem, such as how widespread it was, who was likely to be a victim, and the details of situations when it happened. This is where traditional research can be helpful.

Karen is an emotional learner, and she practiced empathic listening – not judging, but inquiry about various perspectives of how and why torture occurs. And she looked for people with ideas about how it could be different, and energy and standing to help realize the difference.

Harkening back to the community-organizing dynamic described as core in the GAN development process, Karen then created events where these people could come together. With great skill, she created events of a couple of days where people would open up with their experiences and visions that produced an understanding how they were all parts of a greater system. This was generative listening. By bringing in the "whole," they could see how it could be different and create a presencing space (described in Chapter 3) to picture a torture-free world and what actions/tools could move in that direction.

Reform

This type of change is much more familiar. For example, often people refer to "reform of x industry." They mean that the formal rules that guide its operations should change. In fact, it is one reason many social change activists identify a successful change campaign with "advocacy" as a tool to change laws and policies.

To move into this stage the SFL began prototyping with action experiments and pilots that reflected their vision for sustainable agriculture. This experience aims to develop new procedures, formal relationships, and ways of behaving to reflect the values and beliefs of the vision.

For example, one SFL project is developing new business models to connect small-scale farmers and food companies "... that distribute risks and rewards more evenly across the supply chain, improve the flow of market information, and increase access to credit and technical assistance."[12] These qualities of the business model arise from the vision and new insights about interdependence. They challenge assumptions of the traditional business model of company plantations by identifying new relationships, rules, and processes.

IBJ followed a different set of activities, but was also prototyping to identify new rules and processes, and build new relationships. Karen's conversations led to an ongoing series of ideas and interventions. The first challenge, as is typical with GANs, was to make the issue a legitimate one for the broader public to talk about, and to generate awareness. One action to help this was a "big poster campaign" (a Chinese education tradition) with posters placed in police stations, courts, and jails to promote people's rights such as access to a lawyer (yes, these rights do technically exist in China, but no one has ever "given life" to them).

The prototyping experiments identify new rules to follow. This requires changing formal rules such as laws and policies, and informal ones such as behaviors and ways of interacting. From these experiences a new model is developed.

Incremental

The change challenge then passes into the domain of scaling up. This is change with widespread replication and adaptation of the models, and adoption of the reformed rules, processes, beliefs, and values. This might seem like the easy part, but history is littered with proven pilots that have never become influential. On the global scale that GANs are working, scaling up change is an enormous and important challenge.

SFL's strategy at this stage is product- and organization-focused, through the product-line. For example, SFL participants Rainforest Alliance and Unilever are joining together to produce a Lipton tea bearing the Rainforest logo. Lipton markets about 12 percent of all tea sold world-wide. Separately, Unilever committed to use exclusively palm oil certified by Roundtable on Sustainable Palm Oil for its beauty products by 2015.

IBJ's scaling up is geographic, by activity and by stakeholder group. Since 2003, IBJ has partnered with the Beijing University School of Law and the All-China Lawyers' Association's Constitutional and Human Rights Law Committee to launch extensive legal rights awareness campaigns on December 4th of each year. In 2010, the legal education campaigns were aimed at informing the most vulnerable groups in society of their procedural rights in criminal cases. The primary focus was on permanent rural residents, returning migrant workers, and their children.

In partnership with local law firms and law students, staff from IBJ's headquarters in Beijing facilitated a series of different events in 12 locations all over China. Through the successful events of the December 4th Rule of Law Day, IBJ's China offices continue to establish partnership with local universities and law firms in order to spread awareness about the legal rights all over China.

IBJ is also working in other countries where it must again go through the cycle of generating vision and tools appropriate for the particular culture and capacities of those countries. By 2010 IBJ had 18 country networks.

This is the stage when the "tipping point" theory comes to be tested. GANs theorize that they can produce new behaviors with individuals and new processes with organizations through informal carrots and sticks. For example, when a sufficient number of businesses in an industry become committed to the transformed strategies, the laggards will be forced to adopt the new standards. This will occur because they will not be considered "legitimate" and will be forced to operate in a Mafia-like manner, where they are denied access to financing and markets.

Four change strategies

People easily get into arguments about "correct strategies" to realize change. Often with a little bit of dialogue, they discover that they are actually talking about complementary strategies. Then, they start to understand the limitation of their own advocated strategy, and that it cannot succeed on its own. These types of insights spurred Ken Wilber to popularize an *integral* approach to support a comprehensive and integrated view of the world. They provide a framework to approach the comprehensive change challenge presented in the societal learning and change matrix of Table 5.2.

In audacious titles and substantive books, *A Brief History of Everything* and *A Theory of Everything*, Ken developed "a model that would unite all the known laws of the universe into one all-embracing theory that would literally explain everything in existence." He was driven by the questions about what would move us to a world that has the benefits of modernity such as increased freedoms and longevity, and address the substantial problems of modernity such as environmental degradation and inequality.

A key product of this work is what is now referred to as the "four-quadrant" diagram.[13] Very simply put, this arose from looking at all the great writers and theorists in spiritual (Christ, Ghandi, etc.), developmental (the core Chapter 3 concept with stages and levels), and other scientific, cultural, and thought traditions. The four quadrants in Table 5.3 were developed in a review of theories of Change.

Table 5.3   Four change strategies

	Interior	Exterior
Individual	**1. Spiritual-Psychological:** *Concerned with changing one's own sense of being.* Broad change theory: *It's all a question of individual perceptions and capacity.* Focus: • Deepening self-awareness • Developing one's knowledge, skills, competencies • Describing one's assumptions, values, mindsets, beliefs Methods: • Meditation • Personal reflection and inquiry • Personal development of mastery through courses and apprenticeships	**2. Inter-Personal:** *Concerned with changing one's own behaviors in interactions with others.* Broad change theory: *It's all a question of how individuals inter-act.* Focus: • Showing trust, respect, mutual understanding • Shifting behaviors to demonstrate interdependence • Reaching conciliation of inter-personal differences Methods: • Diversity training • Learning journeys into others' worlds • Group encounters/retreats of exploration • Mediation/negotiations training
Collective	**3. Social and Cultural:** *Concerned with collective values of fairness and justice.* Broad change theory: *It's all a question of collective values and beliefs.* Focus: • Collective goals and aspirations • Underlying values and beliefs • Implicit "rules" and assumptions • Discourse, language Methods: • Collective goal-setting and strategy creation • Developing value statements and processes for actualization • On-going media programs	**4. Structural and Systemic:** *Concerned with governance, decision-making processes and institutions.* Broad change theory: *It's all a question of processes, institutions and power.* Focus: • Policies, legislation • Institutions, procedures • Allocation of resources Methods: • Building political structures, agreements, frameworks, systems • New accounting/reporting/measurement systems

Source: Developed with particular influence of Fitzduff, M. and I. Jean (Forthcoming). *Current Challenges to the Field of Peacebuilding Work* (Advanced draft). Washington, DC, USA, U.S. Institute of Peace Press; Thomas, P. (2008). "Creating Generative Dialogic Learning Processes." *GC Community Quarterly Newsletter* October: 5–6. http://www.gc-community.net; Ritchie-Dunham, J. (2007). *The End of Poverty – The Beginning of Self-determination: An Integral Systemic Exploration of Self-determination in Guatemala*. Unpublished manuscript. http://instituteforstrategicclarity.org, Institute for Strategic Clarity. Accessed August 25, 2010.

This table suggests that a successful strategy must address four change challenges. Quadrant 1 deals with intention, personal identity, and ways of perceiving, Quadrant 2 with behavior and how it is developed, Quadrant 3 with culture, beliefs, and values, and Quadrant 4 with the structures and processes of social systems.

In order for an issue to change in the way GANs aspire, there must be action in all four Quadrants. That does not mean that the GAN itself has to lead the activity. However, to realize the change it is working for, it or its participants must undertake strategic interventions to ensure change is proceeding in all the Quadrants. Lack of change in one of the Quadrants will hold back development in the others.

Observations

Observation 1: The importance of dialogue

Of course some change strategies focus on constitutional change app-roaches or violent interventions and revolutions. With GANs' social practices strategy, dialogue is a critical element in the change processes. Both IBJ and SFL began with a very intense series of dialogues and conversations grounded in mutual respect, understanding, and common visions that are critical for the whole change process. Through talking people create and re-create our social worlds. This type of talk is indeed a type of action in itself.

Tim Bittiger, Regional Director of the Extractive Industries Trans-parency Initiative (EITI), comments: "EITI offers a platform for dia-logue to discuss transparency issues. We (the secretariat) are a ser-vice provider, guardians of methodology, organize board meetings, work with partners to provide technical assistance." All this support involves "dialogue."

GANs create rich and dense connections between people and organ-izations as a key part of their change strategy. They are bridge-building, community developers and network weavers. So GANs should become very sophisticated about dialogue approaches that make collective sense of reality and taking action.

Bettye Pruitt, some other colleagues, and I spent some time looking into how dialogue can be understood and what GANs are doing in their actual change processes. Following is a long excerpt from our report.

"We use the Four Fields of Conversation diagram presented in Figure 5.1 to help us think and talk about dialogue. In this framework, developed by Otto Scharmer, the four fields of conversation move from

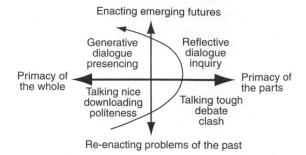

Figure 5.1   Four fields of conversation

Source: Scharmer, C. O. (2001). "Self-transcending Knowledge: Sensing and Organizing Around Emerging Opportunities." *Journal of Knowledge Management* 5(2): 137–150.

the least authentic and open, in the lower left-hand quadrant, counterclockwise to the most authentic, open, and creative in the upper left.[14]

We find this framework valuable because it allows us to make distinctions among processes that might be officially labeled dialogues, but in reality might have very different qualities of interaction. And it enables us to see more clearly how other interactions not formally considered dialogues – with people sitting in a room talking – might become more dialogic.

- **Talking nice:** This quadrant represents the most common form of conversation and communication. Scharmer defines this kind of interaction as "rule repeating." We say what we're expected to say in a specific situation: "how are you? I am fine."[15] The kind of listening that corresponds to this is not listening at all, but just playing the tape in our heads.

Box 5.1: Reflective dialogue

I was with a group called . . . Women in Security Conflict. We [agreed we had to] look at breaking the silence on the conflict in Kashmir. These were groups of women who always continued to blame each other, each other's community for their predicament. For example, the Muslim women in the valley blamed the Hindu community for what had happened to them. The Hindus who fled the valley blamed the Muslims for having driven them out of their homes and for ethnic cleansing and so on.

But when they came together in a safe place, which was [away] from their immediate environment, and they began to hear each other's narratives and pain, they realized their pain does not cancel out somebody else's pain. In other words, they both are going through a certain level of deprivation . . .

Now, at that moment, something happened where the women who were listening to each other's narratives . . . their whole body language changed, and a couple of them shed tears when they listened to what had happened to what were their erstwhile adversaries. And they found that there was a commonality of human experience. I think that was a very moving turning point . . . [Where] they never used to make eye contact with each other [they] began to acknowledge each others' presence. And so the "othering" process which had translated into body language and the kind of guarded adjectives that were being [used], all that began to melt. I won't say they hugged each other and embraced each other, but the walls of antipathy [came down].

Source: Meenakshi Gupinath, interview with Katrin Kaeufer, January 2005.

- **Talking tough:** The rule-repeating game of talking nice might be interrupted when the conversation moves into a debate. In debate we say what we're really thinking, so, in that sense, it is progress toward greater authenticity. It creates energy in the conversational field, though it doesn't really produce anything new. A debate is about making a point and winning. We listen to what confirms or disconfirms our point of view.
- **Reflective dialogue:** Often, however, debate can lead to reflective dialogue, since it allows its participants to be authentic and to confront reality. In a reflective dialogue, as participants in the conversation, we begin to see the other person's perspective. We might not necessarily agree with what the other person has to say, but we begin to understand where he or she is coming from. At the same time, in a reflective dialogue we begin to reflect on our own perspectives. We start observing ourselves while we are talking and listening. And our listening begins to be empathetic – we are not just listening to others' ideas to decide whether we agree or not, but also to try to understand where they are coming from. In his work on dialogue, Bill Isaacs identifies four capacities people exhibit when they engage in this kind of conversation: *voicing* – speaking the truth of one's own perspective; *listening* without resistance; *respecting* – demonstrating awareness of the impossibility of fully understanding others' positions; and *suspending* – letting go of assumptions, judgments, certainty.[16]

Box 5.2: Generative dialogue

Ochaeta [director of the Guatemalan Archdiocesan Human Rights Office, which was documenting the atrocities of the civil war] said he had a story that he wanted to tell. . . . [He] had gone to a Mayan village to witness the exhumation of a mass grave – one of many – from a massacre. When the earth had been removed, he noticed a number of small bones. He asked the forensics team if people had had their bones broken during the massacre. No, the grave contained the corpses of women who had been pregnant. The small bones belonged to their fetuses.

When Ochaeta finished telling his story, the team was completely silent. . . . I looked around the circle and caught the eye of an old man, who simply nodded at me slowly. The silence lasted a long time, perhaps five minutes. Then it ended and we took a break. . . . In interviews years later, many members of the team referred to it. In the words of one member:

"The group gained the possibility of speaking frankly. Things could be said without upsetting the other party. I believe this helped to create a favorable atmosphere in which to express, if not the truth, certainly each person's truth. . . . In the end, and particularly after listening to Ochaeta's story, I understood and felt in my heart all that had happened. And there was a feeling that we must struggle to prevent this from happening again."

Source: Kahane, A. (2004). *Solving Tough Problems: An Open Way of Talking, Listening, and Creating New Realities*. San Francisco, CA, USA, Berrett-Kohler, 116–117.

- **Generative dialogue:** In a generative dialogue our perception as participants shifts again. This time it moves from seeing the other person's perspective toward seeing the "whole." John Paul Lederach calls this shift into awareness of the whole the emergence of "moral imagination."[17] The interaction becomes more intense, the boundaries between participants become blurred, our perception of time slows down. This deeper form of dialogue is described as "presencing," which is a creative experience of bringing forth that sense of the whole that is trying to come forward.[18] Our definition of "generative dialogue" is grounded in our understanding of this quadrant of the conversation matrix: *generative dialogue is conversation that brings forth creative energy and collective intelligence out of a personal sense of connection to the whole.*

Thinking in terms of the quality of conversation enables a broader framing of dialogue, one that embraces the quality of *any* conversation – not just those that are formally organized as dialogues. The examples we provide here deal with violent conflict and post-conflict situations. Yet a great deal of investigation of dialogue has taken place in work settings. There the illustrations of dialogue experiences describe the space that opens up when business executives admit to each other they don't have answers to the questions before them, or when doctors and nurses begin to talk openly about the emotional burdens of working with the sick and dying and through that conversation start to help their hospitals make better decisions about the purchase and use of technology. These are the kind of spaces out of which innovations emerge".[19]

Observation 2: Continuing change strategy questions

There are significant questions about GANs' change strategy that still need answering. Elements are still not proven, and require more focused effort to adequately address. These include:

How exactly can governments be best engaged globally to effectively interact with the GANs and play governments' constitutional change role?

Governments are active participants in some GANs, but even those GANs focus on a social action strategy. At some point this has to interact and generate a constitutional change strategy. The reform stage in particular emphasizes the importance of governments in re-writing the rules. Many GANs, particularly the certification ones like the Forest Stewardship Council (FSC), purposely do not include government in their memberships because they fear this will both reduce their innovative capacity and scare off companies that would see governments' presence as leading to regulation. Are these concerns still legitimate, given GANs' experience and at least some governments' increased appreciation of the voluntary nature of GANs' work? If they remain legitimate, what is the longer-term strategy vis-à-vis the constitutional change actions?

How do GANs actually realize ongoing shifts in individuals' beliefs and values to realize global scale change?

We have a range of examples of how individuals' beliefs and values can shift, but how can this be done in an ongoing way as new individuals and organizations join? Is there some way to speed this up at scale? The SFL approach, for example, emphasizes the importance of small multi-day retreats that seem to be beyond the ability to apply with large numbers of people. But is it even necessary to apply it to large numbers of people? Can a tiny leadership group shift the systems on its own?

(How) can GANs influence organizations to change their processes, poli-cies, and relationships, and what does a sufficiently changed organization "look like"?

If a GAN vision requires that an organization transform, how does a GAN interact with the organization to realize this change? How might a GAN itself change to support organizations' transformation? Often organizations have "representatives" active in GANs, but expecting the individuals to realize the scale of change necessary seems unreasonable. *What role can they have in realizing the change? What other ways can GANs interact to realize the needed impact? And what do the transformed organizations actually look like?*

Is the "tipping point" a valid theory? How can GANs realize the change in a sufficient number of organizations? What is a sufficient number?

The tipping point theory is based on a couple of premises that appear problematic. One is that individual organizations or some group of them can adopt transformational approaches. But will they simply be squashed out of their niches by other organizations that continue to act in the tra-ditional ways? The experience of organizations adopting CSR standards suggests that even modest variations from tradition can be squeezed out when markets turn down.

What percentage of adopters will actually "tip" a system into the new processes, values, and relationships? Is it within the reach of GANs' strategy as a coalition of willing leaders, or will a greater number of participants in a GAN be required than the GAN can attract?

The tipping point might also require that a very substantial num-ber of organizations adopt a transformational approach. Even small groups of renegades can easily destroy public common goods, for example.

This again raises the question of government, and its role in formalizing new standards and the transformational approaches.

How can the limits to GANs' change strategy be addressed?

Of course there are limits to where and when GANs' approach can be used. If the Chinese government chose to actively oppose Karen (IBJ), a whole different strategy would be necessary and the array of possibilities and tools would change. Arab countries have proven particularly difficult challenges for GANs, because governments are so dominant and other organizations so weak that multi-stakeholder dialogue strategies don't work. This reflects different cultural approaches. What should GANs do in these situations?

Observation 3: Additional observations

Review of GANs experiences produces other observations:

- The transformation activities often need repeating with new stakeholders as they are brought into the network. They need to go through the shift in insight and relationship with purpose.
- GANs need to develop ceremonies and cycles of renewal of the shift in purpose and insight. People experience it, go back to their traditional work, and the connection naturally fades. This is particularly true at the (board) leadership level; staff can "live" the change process, but board members live in a very different world.
- Some GANs chose to focus upon only one or two of these types of change. For example, as a 2-year project the World Commission on Dams essentially focused on transformation and reform by devising new rules and procedures without any real prototyping. At the mission level the SFL is really about reform, with the mission "to accelerate the shift of sustainable food from niche to mainstream." Similarly, the Global Reporting Initiative (GRI) is focused upon reform by creating a new reporting framework and prototyping it, as opposed to scaling up which it hopes will happen through its certifiers.

    Will Martin, Chair of the Marine Stewardship Council (MSC), comments: "Some of the NGOs are coming to a more collaborative type of approach, where they work with the fishery and I think that's a future trend. The effectiveness of the old approaches is quite low. The application of a command and control management system for fisheries is archaic in many ways, and the NGOs have seen their role to improve and tighten and really work at the legal structure, the command-and-control structure. They're constantly criticizing the bad practices, but that has been ineffective." But are these complementary strategies?
- Most GANs involved in certification and assessment processes do not have a consistent social practices strategy. They are multi-stakeholder at the global and often some sub-global level (such as national). But most often neither directly nor through the processes they promote (such as certification) do they stimulate formation of local multi-stakeholder structures that can create and sustain the change processes. For example, the MSC approaches certification as a technical exercise.

Most often people like auditors act as certifiers who simply gather information from stakeholders. They do nothing to stimulate collective stakeholder dialogue about managing resources, nor is there any expectation that the stakeholders form a collective group to plan and manage issues as they arise between certifications.

• Sometimes, such as with cell phones, a physical technology can be much more than a quick fix without recognition of such. Cell phones have revolutionized relationships between small farmers and markets by making market information easily available and cutting out the middle men.

Processes for change

The last 20 years has seen wonderful progress in developing change tools, frameworks, and processes that apply them. This includes everything from skillful facilitation of multi-stakeholder meetings, to developing multi-stakeholder communities, to large system strategic planning and visioning. These new tools can vastly improve the effectiveness of GANs' work, but in general GANs still make little use of them – something that we can remedy.

One such example of recent progress is the Engagement Streams Framework of the (US) National Coalition on Dialogue and Deliberation (NCDD). It summarizes 19 leading methodologies for dialogue and deliberation in charts "designed to help people decide which dialogue and deliberation methods are the best fit for their circumstances."[20] They are categorized by four purposes: Exploration, Conflict Transformation, Decision Making, and Collaborative Action. Table 5.4 provides examples.

Some basic guidelines with these change methodologies:

• Generate dialogue: Figure 5.1 describes four ways of interacting verbally. These all have their time, but the daily language of GANs is "dialogue" which David Bohm describes as "a stream of meaning flowing among and through us and between us."[21]
• Create engagement: The community-building imperative of GANs means that engagement is highly valued. There should be lots of smaller group work where everyone can participate.
• Bring in the "whole system": GANs are diversity embracing, and their processes should include all stakeholders in a system to build social

capital. After all, it is all about system-building. So think "whole system," although there are important times to support meetings of individual stakeholder groups, as well.

- Everyone is "an expert": Everyone has a story to tell and some thoughts about an issue, although some are shier and less experienced than others. But the processes encourage everyone sharing. Expert speakers are rarely used, except to spur a more central activity.
- Appeal to physically, mentally, and emotionally centered learners. Move around! Draw! Tell stories! Mix up the modes of expression; validate them all.
- Pay attention to the setting: People will do more creative work in a more creative setting. Let there be light! And favor rounds and squares for discussion; minimize the front-of-the-room versus the rows of chairs set-up.

Another challenge to change processes is the tendency to be insufficiently comprehensive about what has to change, and to make assessments and plans without considering the full scope of the change challenge. This is

Table 5.4 Characteristics of well-known dialogue & deliberation processes

Methodology NAME & focus	Size of group	Session	Participant selection	Description
WORLD CAFE Exploration	Up to hundreds in 1 room at tables of four	Single event ranging from 90 minutes to 3 days	Often held at conferences, involving all attendees; otherwise, invitations boost representativeness	World Cafés enable groups of people to participate together in evolving rounds of dialogue with three or four others while at the same time remaining part of a single, larger, connected conversation. Small, intimate conversations link and build on each other as people move between groups, cross-pollinate ideas, and discover new insights into questions or issues that really matter in their life, work, or community. (www.theworldcafe.com)

Table 5.4 (Continued)

Methodology NAME & focus	Size of group	Session	Participant selection	Description
CONSENSUS CONFERENCE Decision-making	Large group	2 weekends for participants to prepare, 2–4 day conference	Random selection	Consensus Conferences, developed in Denmark, typically involves a group of citizens with varied backgrounds who meet to discuss issues of a scientific or technical nature. The conference has two stages: the first involves small group meetings with experts to discuss the issues and work toward consensus. The second stage assembles experts, media, and the public where the conference's main observations and conclusions are presented. (www.thataway.org/46192a)
FUTURE SEARCH Collaborative Action, also Conflict Transformation	60–80 people	3 days	All inclusive (attempts to bring all involved)	Future Search is an interactive planning process which helps a group of people discover a set of shared values or themes (common ground) and agree on a plan of action for implementing them. (www.futuresearch.net)
APPRECIATIVE INQUIRY Exploration Collaborative Action	20–2000	From 1-hour interviews to 4–6-day summits	Internal and external stakeholders	Appreciative Inquiry is a change method that encourages stakeholders to explore the best of the past and present in their organizations and communities. AI involves, in a central way, the art and practice of asking questions that strengthen a system's capacity to apprehend, anticipate, and heighten positive potential. (www.appreciativeinquiry.cwru.edu)

Source: NCDD (circa 2007). *NCDD's Engagement Streams Framework, National Coalition on Dialogue and Deliberation*; excerpt of 4 out of 19.

important because even if a GAN is successful in three aspects of change, weakness in a fourth aspect may lead to failure.

The societal learning and change matrix in Table 5.2 is one approach to being comprehensive. Another is Table 5.5, and was applied in a change process of The Access Initiative (TAI). The goal was to assess how TAI is doing in its work to give life to Principle 10 of the Rio Declaration to make environmental decision-making participatory and information accessible. The principle tool of TAI is an assessment of government performance with respect to its Principle 10 commitment.

Again building off Ken Wilber's model as for Table 5.3, there are four dimensions of change in TAI's approach as presented in the four quadrants in Table 5.5. For example, for TAI to be successful requires changes in self-awareness, knowledge, skills, competencies, assumptions, mindsets, and beliefs. People agreed that TAI is really focused upon making change to structures and systems, that other changes are necessary, and that some of those other changes are occurring, but only as by-products rather than through intentionality.

Table 5.5   Four dimensions of change

Individual	Relationships
• Self-awareness	• Trust, respect, recognition
• Knowledge, skills, competencies	• Awareness of interdependence
• Assumptions, mindsets, beliefs	• Reconciliation/conflict transformation
Example:	*Example:*
• *Creating of self-awareness among citizens for asking for information (shifting to being confident, responsible citizens not 'underlings')*	• *Mutual cooperation between NGOs*
	• *Higher level of cooperation between NGOs and government institutions*
Culture	**Structures/Systems**
• Underlying values and beliefs	• Policies, legislation
• Implicit "rules"	• Institutions, procedures
• Discourse, language	• Allocation of resources
Example:	*Example:*
Strong media campaign against polluters	• *Pressure to the Ministry for releasing information and data; awareness that they could be asked*
	• *Forming of intersectoral group in Ministry for support*
	• *Changes in legislation (e.g. significantly increased fines for polluters)*

Source: Adapted from Generative Change Community. (2009). *The Access Initiative – Re-envisioning Process Dialogue with TAI Macedonia*. Washington, DC, USA, Unpublished internal report for The Access Initiative.

This analysis reconnected TAI's assessment tool to its change goal, and provided the opportunity to think more broadly beyond that tool about how to achieve change in the four dimensions.

A change process design example

If you were given 10 million euros and 3–5 years, how would you go about "changing the role of the financial system to better serve economic, social and environmental objectives"? In 2009, the EU asked that question and said it was willing to provide the resources. It provided an opportunity to put together a leading change strategy. I worked to develop this with a consortium of more than 20 European universities under the leadership of Maurizio Zollo Director of the Center for Research on Organization and Management at Bocconi University in Milan.

The project goal is a transformational one. Over a 5-year period the project could generate a collective vision and also begin reform activities to develop prototypes.

One exciting aspect about the EU Call was that it clearly wanted what I'd call a societal learning and change strategy: one where financial system stakeholders work together to (1) gain important new knowledge and perspectives to change the way they think about the financial system, and (2) develop new social ties that provide for ongoing development of new ideas, strategies, structures, and processes with regard to the financial system.

In other words, the goal of the Call was not simply to produce new reports, books, and ideas. It wanted the new knowledge "held" by stakeholders and that they have the vision and relationships to further it.

The proposal to the EU was titled RE-designing Financial ORganizations and Markets (REFORM). It proposed conventional research by an inter-university faculty to investigate from a multi-disciplinary perspective the historic financial system dynamics with comprehensive analysis of the reasons for the financial crisis. Conventional research is important to build a sound strategy and ensure legitimacy. It is also important for building consensus about current reality. But as a change project, the emphasis was on an action research strategy. This research approach is distinguished by participation of stakeholders in the research issue arena, reflexivity (ongoing adjustment in response to what is being learned), an orientation toward taking action, and a goal of realizing impacts through the participation.[22]

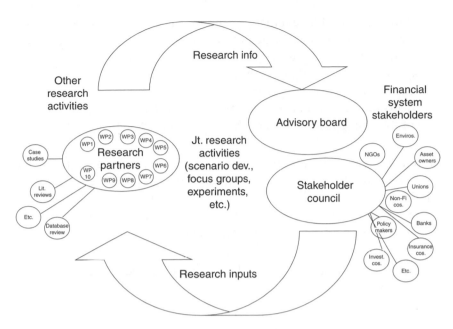

Figure 5.2 REFORM participants and flow of activities

In this case, the action research structure is displayed in Figure 5.2.
The action research activities were:

Mapping social structures and developing a holistic computer model. This would simulate cross-system (finance–environment–social–economic–political) and cross-level (local-to-global) interdependences. This contrasts with the narrow product and firm-level simulations used by finance that contributed to the financial crisis. This activity is an important component of the late transformation activity of defining some potential prototypes and the reform change activities of actually testing the prototypes to develop new models of rules and relationships.

Engaging stakeholders. This is the major place where the dialogue methodologies would be used. REFORM proposed forming a stakeholder council to include financiers, policy makers, regulators and social-, labor-, consumer-, and environmental-activists working on finance issues. With the researchers, the Councillors would co-lead the project and engage their respective constituencies. This would be supported by an innovative social media strategy.

Scenario-building. Through stakeholder engagement with small focus groups around the world and larger European ones, REFORM would develop plausible alternative futures. This is a key part of the transformational change activities, but the plan included a move into reform activities by testing options with stakeholders.

Experimenting. Working with financial firms and other stakeholders, REFORM proposed testing new approaches to such things as decision-making and product development. This would also make use of the dialogue tools, and be the core reform change activities.

REFORM listed anticipated impacts for each stakeholder group. For *Financiers and the Finance Industry* it said: "Those who have led commercial finance have not had the persuasive frameworks or the analytical tools to support the products and strategies that reflect an integrative financial system. This project aims to build their capacity for this by:

Deepening understanding of which of their choices contributed to the financial crisis;

Building a vision through the scenario development of how they can be successful in an integrative financial system;

Providing a modeling tool that integrates risk from a whole-systems perspective that can support their decision-making;

Strengthening ties with other stakeholder groups and understanding of their perspectives."[23]

Impacts for other stakeholder groups similarly emphasized enhanced knowledge and development of new ties across traditional divides that would allow stakeholders to continue the development. By this time, the stakeholders should have formed their own structures and formal processes to support the long-term work of integrating social, environmental, and economic concerns into the logic of the financial system.

More on processes

I've only presented illustrative examples to emphasize the range of knowledge and tools that are available. There are many other processes and methodologies, and they can be creatively integrated. Some good resources include:

Bojer, M. M., et al. (2006). *Mapping Dialogue: A Research Project Profiling Dialogue Tools and Processes for Social Change*. Johannesburg, South Africa. Pioneers of Change Associates.

Brown, J. (2005). *The World Cafe: Shaping Our Futures Through Conversations That Matter*. San Francisco, CA, USA, Berrett-Koehler.

Bunker, B. and B. Alban (1997). *Large Group Interventions: Engaging the Whole System for Rapid Change*. San Francisco, CA, USA, Jossey-Bass.

Bunker, B. B. (2006). *The Handbook of Large Group Methods: Creating Systemic Change in Organizations and Communities*. San Francisco, CA, USA, Jossey-Bass.

Kahane, A. (2010). *The Power of Love: A Theory and Practice of Social Change*. San Francisco, CA, USA, Berrett-Koehler.

Pruitt, B. and P. Thomas (2007). *Democratic Dialogue – A Handbook for Practitioners*. New York, USA, United Nations Development Programme.

Ramirez, R., et al. (2008). *Business Planning in Turbulent Times: New Methods for Applying Scenarios*. London, UK, Earthscan.

Scharmer, C. O. (2007). *Theory U: Leading from the Future as it Emerges*. Boston, MA, USA, Society for Organizational Learning.

Van der Heijden, K. (2005). *Scenarios: The Art of Strategic Conversation*. Chichester, UK, Wiley.

Weisbord, M. and S. Janoff (2010). *Future Search: Getting the Whole System in the Room for Vision, Commitment, and Action*. San Francisco, CA, Berrett-Koehler.

Notes

1. Young, O. R. (ed.) (1999). *The Effectiveness of International Environmental Regimes*. Cambridge, MA, Massachusetts Institute of Technology Press.
2. FAO (2009). *State of Food Insecurity*. Rome, Italy, Food and Agriculture Organisation.
3. Gladwell, M. (2010). "What is the Tipping Point?" Retrieved March 16, from http://www.gladwell.com/tippingpoint/index.html.
4. Bateson, G. (1972). *Steps to an Ecology of Mind*. San Francisco, Chandler Publishing Company; Argyris, C. and D. Schon (1978). *Organizational Learning: A Theory of Action Perspective*. Reading, MA, Addison-Wesley Publishing; Senge, P. M. (1990). *The Fifth Discipline: The Art and Practice of the Learning Organization*. New York, Doubleday; Flood, R. L. and N. R. A. Romm (1996). *Diversity Management – Triple Loop Learning*. Chichester, UK, John Wiley & Sons.
5. Kuhn, T. (1962). *The Structure of Scientific Revolutions*. Chicago, IL, The University of Chicago Press.

6. Sweitzer, S. (2004). *Foundation Workshop June 1–3, 2004 Learning History,* Sustainable Food Laboratory.
7. SFL. (2010a). "Home Page." Retrieved March 22, 2010, from http://www. sustainablefoodlab.org/.
8. Waddell, S. (2005). *Societal Learning and Change: How Governments, Business and Civil Society are Creating Solutions to Complex Multi-Stakeholder Problems.* Sheffield, UK, Greenleaf Publishing.
9. Scharmer, C. O. (2009). *Theory U: Leading from the Future as it Emerges.* San Francisco, CA, USA, Berrett-Koehler; Perlas, N. (2000). *Shaping Globalization: Civil Society, Cultural Power and Threefolding.* Quezon City, Philippines, Center for Alternative Development Initiatives.
10. Seagal, S. and D. Horne (2000). *Human Dynamics: A New Framework for Understanding People and Realizing the Potneital in Our Organizations.* Waltham, MA USA, Pegasus Communications.
11. Waddell, S. (2007). "Realising Global Change: Developing the Tools, Building the Infrastructure." *Journal of Corporate Citizenship* Special Issue(26): 69–84.
12. SFL. (2010b). "Projects." Retrieved March 22, 2010, from http://www.sustainable foodlab.org/initiatives/.
13. Wilber, K. (1996). *A Brief History of Everything.* Dublin, Ireland, Gill & Macmillan Ltd; Wilber, K. (2000). *A Theory of Everything: An Integral Vision for Business, Politics, Science and Spirituality.* Boston, MA, USA, Shambhala Publications.
14. Scharmer, C. O. (2001). "Self-transcending Knowledge: Sensing and Organizing Around Emerging Opportunities." *Journal of Knowledge Management* 5(2): 137–150.
15. Scharmer, C. O. (2007). *Theory U: Leading from the Future as it Emerges.* Boston, MA, USA, Society for Organizational Learning.
16. Isaacs, W. (1999). *Dialogue and the Art of Thinking Together.* New York, NY, Currency Doubleday.
17. Lederach, J. P. (2005). *The Moral Imagination: The Art and Soul of Building Peace.* New York, NY, USA, Oxford University Press.
18. Jaworski, J., et al. (2004). *Presence: Human Purpose and the Field of the Future.* Cambridge, MA, USA, Society for Organizational Learning; Scharmer, C. O. (2007). Op.cit.
19. Pruitt, B. and S. Waddell (2005). "Dialogic Approaches to Global Challenges: Moving from 'Dialogue Fatigue' to Dialogic Change Processes". *Generative Dialogue Project*, Generative Dialogue Project.
20. NCDD (circa 2007). *NCDD's Engagement Streams Framework, National Coalition on Dialogue and Deliberation.*
21. Bohm, D. (1992). "On Dialogue." *Noetic Sciences Review* 23: 16–18.
22. Reason, P. and H. Bradbury (2001). "Introduction: Inquiry and Participation in Search of a World Worthy of Human Aspiration". *The Handbook of Action Research.* P. Reason and H. Bradbury. Newbury Park, CA, Sage Publications: 1–14.
23. Zollo, M. (2010). *RE-designing Financial ORganizations and Markets* (REFORM). Milan, Italy, University of Bocconi.

CHAPTER 6

Formalizing the connections

How are GANs (Global Action Networks) governed? What is their decision-making structure? These are common questions. The answers, as the chapter on development stages suggests, change as a GAN develops. However, they tend to follow some patterns that are worth describing to get a sense of the range of answers being explored at this moment of GANs' development as a new organizational form.

But best is to start again with GANs' goals, to re-emphasize that structure should support and sequentially follow development of goals, strategies, and experiments. GANs have two levels of outcomes, which is an ongoing tension for their structure. One is a collectively defined goal that all participating organizations can buy into. It derives from the fundamental rationale for founding a GAN – the need to bring together distinctive competencies and resources on a global scale. This is a goal that may be called a system-organizing goal, such as the Mission for Global Water Challenge (GWC):

> ...to create a global movement to meet the urgent need for safe water and sanitation by spurring collective awareness and investment in innovation by corporate, public, and nongovernmental actors. Our challenge is to provide tools and education to empower people to find their own solutions.

The corporation Coca Cola participates in the GWC not only to *meet the urgent need for safe water and sanitation,* but to realize the goal in such a way that the profit goals for Coca Cola will also be supported. Success in a GAN is determined by *collective commitment to both the over-arching goal, and to the support stakeholders provide each other to reach at least some of their individual objectives.* This emphasizes the importance of clearly articulating these two different sets of goals and ensuring reciprocal and collective commitment to them. However, both individual level as well as collective goals can shift (and probably should if the GAN is achieving transformational change) over time.

This produces an overall tension that was described by one staff lead of a GAN:

> Very few (Board members) actually want to do something...they aren't terribly motivated. Not even furthering the network that they're part of. It's "We're here to defend our interests."

Although this may be stated in an extreme way, it reveals the value of defining both goals as being legitimate and necessary in order to avoid undermining the overarching goal. Harkening back to the chapter on GANs as a change strategy, the goal is to actually change the way Coca Cola thinks about its profit-making activities. This requires integrating the transformation processes described earlier, into the life cycle of the Board.

Another core tension is one between expertise and legitimacy of representation of a core stakeholder group. Although there can sometimes happily be overlap in both of these, often there is conflict. That is to say that someone may be an influential and necessary voice to include in decision-making, but their life experience and training do not provide them with the ability to understand some issues.

I noticed this first at a relatively young age when working in the finance arena and was myself on a Board. There was continual deference to people with "expertise" in the arena, although the critical questions were about "who" would benefit from certain decisions. When people in position of power feel lacking in expertise, they are easily intimidated by those with it. But of course, the opposite can happen when someone with insufficient understanding will simply take a stubborn position, "dig their heels in" and refuse to support reasonable action.

This dynamic also can lead staff to get reports from relatively uninformed sources, but which have legitimizing imprimaturs and brands. Often this results in requesting advice from a brand consulting firm, when it really has no understanding about the dynamics of the GAN (and in the background hands off the work to a junior just out of university), rather than a small consultancy or academic that could provide much more informed advice.

In general, GANs strongly favor ensuring voice of stakeholder group and geography, rather than particular competencies. It is common to have no one with particular legal or financial skills on the board of a GAN in contrast with many other organizations.

Other structural and process issues arise over being a movement, administratively/scientifically accurate, and managerially effective. These are three perspectives that arise out of the logics of civil society versus governments/academia versus business. The fact is, the GAN must integrate these and divine a structure and processes to support this.

An effective GAN will not make decisions as efficiently or quickly as a business, because it has a participatory logic (it values participation). However, the participatory processes must be managed efficiently both for its own sake and to maintain business support. GANs often are engaged in certification processes and assessments, but they must avoid being transfixed by refinement and scientific accuracy, which can easily lead to inappropriate resource allocation. The goal is not scientific accuracy; it is change and generation of discussion to change behavior. TI (Transparency International) pointedly calls its index a Corruption *Perceptions* Index to reflect its methodology and that it is not interested in a highly scientific index but one to support its focus upon realizing change.

Here then is a summary of some of the tensions that play out with particular force in structural design of GANs, although they are present in all organizations:

- between the goals of the parts versus the whole;
- between voice/interests of the powerful and those of the marginalized;
- between ensuring legitimate voice and expertise/wisdom; and
- between movement, administrative/scientific accuracy, and efficiency.

Of course no structural design can fully address these. There will inevitably be clashes and questioned judgment calls and controversies. Handling these emphasizes the importance of ensuring the structure supports enormous trust. Handling them also emphasizes the importance of skillfully applying the change processes of the previous chapter internally, such as with periodic moments of taking members (and Boards) back to the moments of presencing to renew connection with the generative motivation for the GAN.

Design principles

Principles are a great way to help guide structural development. When you have a question about whether to do X or Y, you can always review the direction in response to them. And when you are assessing strategy as a whole, it is a good idea to review them by turning back to the principles and ask if they are reflected in decisions about structure and decision-making.

Developing long lists of principles is not of much help, however. A long list confuses, and quite possibly suggests conflicting outcomes since it often indicates the principles are not well thought out. Dee Hock stewarded development of the concept of the "chaordic" organization and its associated principles that are a good guide for GANs.[1] "Chaord" is a word derived from *chao*s and *ord*er, and the organizing approach combines elements of both. The six design principles are

1) *Multi-centric and distributive*: Principles of subsidiarity are emphasized, where decisions and activities are at the level that is the closest possible to those being affected and engaged. This supports independence and non-centralized structures. It means that those developing the network locally have authority to make decisions within broad guidelines.
2) *Participant-owned and owner-governed*: Members govern themselves, collectively "own" their joint production (most often knowledge products) and the parts of the network in which they participate.
3) *Self-organizing and self-evolving*: Participation is always voluntary. Participants can form a new organizational unit around cores such as a project, question, or geography within the common purpose and principles.
4) *Diverse and adaptive*: The structure facilitates innovation, experimentation, and adaptation to diverse settings around a common purpose.
5) *Tied by purpose and principles*: Numerous independent organizations are joined by common purpose and principles, to provide easy linkage to existing organizations.
6) *Enabling*: Participants provide the motivating force; chaordic organizations do not "push", but rather educe.[1]
   I would add a seventh principle that I find is part of Hock's thinking but not made explicit:
7) *Reflecting principles of fractals and the concept of DNA*: Each subgroup contains the same core structures as other groups. This is particularly important for connections to be made easily between groups. It means that core concepts of "membership" and how to compose a Board or leadership group are similar throughout the network.

---

[1] "Educe" comes from the same root as *educate*. Whereas inducing involves inserting into, educe focuses upon drawing out.

Structural decisions can be assessed by more operational goals including the need to:

- Build legitimacy, connections, and trust with specific groups
- Include diverse perspectives to devise actions that work for all groups
- Mobilize and scale action
- Ensure financing
- Access expertise and knowledge
- Manage efficiently

Of course GANs cannot immediately reflect these principles and goals on a global level. However, they can be used with the question: is the proposed change in our network structure aligned with these?

Maintaining coherence and effectiveness requires flexibility and ongoing attention. It has played out in the Forest Stewardship Council (FSC) with some difficulty. Globally, the FSC is organized into "Chambers" around three key stakeholder groups: business, environmentalists, and social/community development NGOs. This division reflects the dynamic of FSC's founding, when there was huge division between these groups. But a mark of FSC's success is that the divisions have been reduced. Nevertheless, FSC Executive Director Andre de Freitas points out development is uneven:

> Good participation from all the three FSC Chambers is essential to our legitimacy. The Social Chamber is usually the least organized and would benefit from more active participation. Some new members could bring new perspectives.

The definition of "Chambers" arises from the goal to have forestry that is sustainable from a social, economic, and environmental perspective. Nevertheless, this can give rise to feelings on behalf of business that there is a two-to-one power relationship, with two groups of NGOs versus one group of business.

In addition, there is no government presence (perhaps in part due to distrust of governments because of their desire to control). However, in most countries government owns most forests, and everywhere it at least regulates them; in addition, governments have enormous purchasing power that could be harnessed to buy only FSC-certified products and promote the FSC as a brand. In terms of policy, governments are enormously influential as well; in Bolivia, the government integrated the FSC standards as policy. FSC at the global level today retains as its DNA the original three chambers of its founding, but is considering bringing in government more formally as an Advisory Group, as the Global Reporting Initiative (GRI) has done.

Unlike most GANs of its age (founded in 1993), FSC does not have a formalized structure of geographic units. It has over 50 National Initiatives, however, that have grown up on their own with a wide diversity of arrangements. (Their role in FSC's structure is now being formalized.) They did not necessarily reflect the global structure, but reflected its principle to ensure representation of key stakeholder group. For example, the Canadians include a chamber for First Nations people (aboriginals, "Indians") who have an important role in forests. (In 2010, FSC was reviewing the issue of geographic units.)

Core structural components

Membership

The basic common element behind the concept of "membership" is the expression of formal commitment to the GAN. Usually this is by a written commitment to a set of goals or principles. For some like the Principles for Responsible Investment (PRI) and the Global Compact, building commitment to principles is the core work of the GAN. The initial obligation is committing in writing to the principles, reporting on their application, and committing to participation in activities. The words "membership" and "signatory" are sometimes used interchangeably.

GANs are by definition inter-organizational networks where individuals as members do not have a role. However, there are some exceptions. TI still has a small number of individual members as its historic legacy, and anyone who registers with the GRI can be a member. The International Union for Conservation of Nature (IUCN) accepts individuals as members of six Commissions organized around specific topics.

Some GANs are very open networks, and aim to maximize membership numbers with very few hurdles. In some cases the network is quite closed in terms of power-sharing: in the Global Water Partnership (GWP) the only ones who can appoint the Steering Committee (Board) are 11 founding governments and UN agencies (the Sponsoring Partners). In others, there is no difference between the voting members and the Board such as with the Global Alliance for Improved Nutrition (GAIN).

Table 6.1 Aspects of "Members"

Citizen	Participant	Co-owner	Customer
Who is seen as a potential participant/member?	Who is active in realizing the goals?	Who makes the decisions/ has formal authority	Who is paying for the work?

A couple of years ago I had conversations with several global, multi-stakeholder networks to better understand these issues. The same word is used in very different ways, and confusion between distinct concepts was creating confusion among network participants. Table 6.1 is a product of the conversations, and suggests that networks should distinguish between four roles. For both the network and its stakeholders, decisions to fit into one category versus the other are wrapped up with important strategic decisions.

The networks generally have a broad approach to who can become a participant: anyone who is a stakeholder in their issue or wants to become one. This is equivalent to the concept of "citizen" as someone who has rights, but does not necessarily exercise them.

Co-owners have some specified decision-making rights, typically around voting in Board or other elections, standing for election, or voting on policy issues. Being a co-owner is usually associated with signing on to a set of principles at a minimum.

Occasionally certain categories of organizations are not citizens, although they are stakeholders. For the Tobacco-Free Initiative, a decision was made to prohibit tobacco companies from participating since the Initiative's goals and those of the companies were perceived as antithetical.

Some stakeholders are happy to simply be a citizen, take advantage of the work of the networks, but not become active – referred to economically as a "free-rider." This is particularly true for networks that produce new learning or policy change, such as The Climate Group when it brings together cities and other stakeholders to develop innovations around LED lighting – of course the networks are usually pleased to have their learning adopted, but free-riders make networks' business model problematic.

A stakeholder might be a "citizen," but make a strategic decision to actively oppose a network. One example is with forest companies that have formed the Sustainable Forestry Initiative in opposition to the FSC's multi-stakeholder certification.

Other stakeholders might strategically choose to be participants, but not be a co-owner. Greenpeace is a strong campaigner on fishery issues and participates in the Marine Stewardship Council (MSC) assessments to determine whether a fishery is sustainable. However, it does not sit on MSC's Stakeholder Council, because it prefers the added independence of action that can come with the role of "participant" versus "co-owner."

For many networks, certain categories are allowed to participate, but not be co-owners. IUCN allows some businesses as participants, but they are pointedly not allowed to be co-owners. Governments cannot become members of the GRI (although it has developed a Governmental Advisory Group), out of fear that its voluntary nature would be seen as an avenue to mandatory rules that would diminish GRI's ability to attract corporate members.

In contrast, in terms of the table, governments are co-owners in the Kimberley Process (KP) to stop the flow of conflict diamonds. However, the Process refers to them as "Participants"; active business and NGO stakeholders are referred to as "Observers" but are participants in terms of the Table. Participants and Observers meet in Plenary annually.

Not uncommonly, organizations are referred to as "members" officially, but have no formal decision-making power. In fact, they are simply participants. The Microcredit Summit Campaign refers to "members" as those who have done a variety of things, the most notable reporting for 3 years on their activity to support the Campaign's goals. However, the Campaign is legally a program of an NGO called Results Education Fund whose Board has legal authority (is the owner). The Campaign Executive Committee consists of people who have agreed to be such at the request of staff, but its meetings are sporadic and advisory.

The Global Compact also uses "member" for participants. The Compact is technically an agent of the UN. The PRI is designed for control by Asset Owners who are a specific category of signatories; the two other PRI signatory categories are participants only (Investment Managers, Professional Service Partners).

TI is another model, with National Chapters being Co-Owners. Representatives from its National Chapters elect people to the TI Board.

The fourth concept that often gets mixed with "membership" is really a financing strategy. Some networks require that members pay dues. However, often this obligation is restricted to, or higher for, for-profit companies. The Fair Labor Association (FLA), for example, has a sliding scale based upon the size of the company and with a minimum payment of US$5,000. The rationale for selecting only companies to pay is that they actually derive financial benefit for participation whereas for the NGOs participation is a net cost.

Member groupings globally

As diversity-embracing entities that are global, GANs often formalize groupings of members to ensure they have diverse voices and representation. In many cases participants are divided into categories on the basis of (1) stakeholder group and/or (2) geography. Typically participants select which stakeholder group they want to be placed in. The Microcredit Summit Campaign has 15 "Councils," the MSC has 8 "issue groups" in two categories, the World Water Council has five "colleges," and the FSC has Economic, Social, and Environmental Chambers. Certainly the latter represents a more manageable number of divisions, although all spring from a theory about distinct views that must be included and resources/expertise/support tapped to realize the goals.

National and regional groupings are common; TI has National Chapters; the GWP has Regional Water Partnerships and Country Water Partnerships that are autonomous "participants," with their own statutes and governing Boards. The Global Fund to Fight AIDS, Tuberculosis, and Malaria has Country Coordinating Mechanisms that are a partnership composed of all key stakeholders. They are responsible for submitting funding proposals to the Global Fund, nominating the entities accountable for administering the funding, and overseeing grant implementation. The CCM preferably is an already-existing body, but a country can instead decide to create a new entity to serve as CCM.

The Access Initiative (TAI) began with projects in several countries, to develop assessments of those countries' implementation of Principle 10 of the Rio Declaration. Teams were formed in the project countries of local NGOs. The original thought was to find one NGO to sponsor the project, but research revealed that single organizations did not possess the three types of needed expertise: environmental, participatory, and legal expertise. Therefore coalitions of three NGOs formed to develop working relationships with governments to realize implementation of Principle 10. With some variations, this has continued not just because of the need for skills but because the "dynamics of three" proved conducive to collective decision-making: it supported broader ownership of the GAN locally, while avoiding the divisiveness that often arises with partnerships of two.

The sub-groupings can become quite complex. The GRI's Stakeholder Council with up to 60 people (individuals and organizations) is elected to ensure specific numbers divided into four stakeholder groups, each with representation from five geographic groupings.

The geographic divisions tend to be more problematic for some. The Global Partnership for the Prevention of Armed Conflict's (GPPAC) Executive Director Peter van Tuijl explains how they started out with a UN-type geographic administrative model to develop 15 regions defined by country groupings. "We now make a distinction when we talk about regions-as-a-political process that is much more fluid, and regions-as-administrative-units for activities, funds dispersal, etc." By a political process he points out that the conflicts GPPAC works with are often sub-region and often trans-boundary which emphasizes the need for "networking" as an active verb. "There are different parts of networking going on that are relevant for different conflicts . . . they all need different configurations of players. So let's be positive about that, relate to these formations and include them if appropriate in the (Board) and work themes."

If a GAN has a national-level entity, it usually reflects the structure of the global entity in terms of stakeholder groupings. Some, like TI, have considerable variance.

The UN global compact: A particularly unusual case

The Global Compact is a multi-stakeholder network "of" the UN. "We knew it was important to leverage the good parts of the UN – the ideas of peace, development and human rights – and yet avoid falling into the trap of the machinery," says Compact Executive Head Georg Kell. "But how to do it, we didn't know. It evolved over the years."

The goal is to realize integration of 10 Principles into the workings of the private sector. Today the Compact has the UN's public advocacy and executive branch support through the role of the Secretary General (SG) as Chair of its Board; it has the UN's legislative support of the General Assembly (GA) and protection from undue individual country influence through a resolution of support the GA passes every 2 years; and it has access to the vast UN system at the national and global levels through an Inter-Agency Working Group that includes the UNEP, the UNDP, and other UN agencies.

In consultation with those in the Compact network the SG appoints "around twenty members, drawn from four constituency groups – business, civil society, labor and the United Nations (the Secretary-General and the Executive Director serve ex-officio). The appointments aim to ensure "a fair geographic distribution . . . reflecting a balance between the distribution of participants in the Global Compact and the relative size and impact of the business community across the world."

Committees

GANs usually have Finance, Executive, and other committees commonly associated with organizations. Many of the GANs are engaged with issues and strategies that require a high degree of technical expertise in order to ensure quality, trust, and effectiveness. For some, these are formally represented in structures. The Global Fund to Fight AIDS, Tuberculosis, and Malaria Technical Review Panel is appointed by the Fund's Board. The MSC has a Technical Advisory Board that has a seat on the main Board.

For the certification GANs, there is also often some subdivision for certifiers and the accreditation process. Sometimes this is just a training program. The MSC and FSC have jointly developed Accreditation Services International (ASI) as a legally separate entity to undertake these activities.

The IUCN has a particularly interesting structure that aims to mobilize particular individual interests and priorities. The six Commissions unite 10,000 volunteer experts from a range of disciplines. They assess the state of the world's natural resources and provide the Union with know-how and policy advice on conservation issues.

The Stop TB participants have coalesced into Working Groups to accelerate progress in seven specific areas including TB/HIV, New TB Drugs, New TB Vaccines, New TB Diagnostics, and Advocacy, Communications, and Social Mobilization.

Boards and councils

Governing Boards and Councils are usually established through direct votes by co-owners at large or a grouping of them. Most include "seats" for specific stakeholder groups to ensure voice from a specific constituency (geographic or interest) rather than ensure particular expertise. The Global Fund Board has 20 voting and 6 non-voting members with a rather complex formula of 7 developing (implementer) countries, 8 donors and 5 civil society and private sector. The concept of "constituency" is then applied:

> Eight donor seats are comprised of either a single country or a group of like-minded or geographically linked countries who have combined to form a constituency. The implementer countries are defined by the seven regional groupings of the World Health Organization (WHO) with one additional seat for Africa. The three civil society, one

private sector and one private foundations seats are allocated according to nominations from within representative groupings of the various stakeholder organizations.[2]

With open membership and large numbers of voters, the categories can get quite complex. The IUCN Council is voted in by its co-owners and includes:

- the Chairs of IUCN's six Commissions (groups of participants who elect to become co-owners of a Commission that is organized around a specific topic or activity);
- three Regional Councillors from each of IUCN's eight Statutory Regions;
- a representative of IUCN's Host Country – the Swiss Confederation; and
- five additional Councillors chosen by Council on the basis of diverse qualifications, interests, and skills.

The GRI has a complex two-tier governance structure. Its Stakeholder Council (SC) consists of up to 60 people who are elected by Organizational Stakeholders and individual members. There is a prescribed number of seats on the Council for each of four constituency groups (business 22, NGOs 16, Mediating Institutions (consultants, academics) 16, Labor 6). For the Board elections a Nominating Committee comprising both Board and SC members makes recommendations to the SC that then votes. Additionally, there are provisions to ensure representation from five geographic groupings.

   In most cases, the by-laws of a GAN are silent about rules for sub-groupings of stakeholders who elect Board members. The FLA specifies different procedures for different "caucuses":

> The Board of Directors of the Association shall consist of six industry representatives, six Labor/NGO representatives, six university representatives and a Chair. The industry Board Members shall be selected by the Industry Caucus. The Labor/NGO Board Members shall be selected by a majority of the then-serving Labor/NGO Board Members. The College or University Affiliate Board Members shall be chosen by the University Advisory Council.[3]

Regardless of the mechanisms, Ger Berkamp, of the World Water Council, sees two different ways of thinking about the role of Boards.

For some working in a Board is about having competent people and delivering value added. Another model is a Board as a much more political entity where you need to get elected with real campaigns. With such a Board, you see other mechanisms being used to become and function as a Board member. These do not necessarily have to do with whether the people are competent in a particular area of expertise central to the organization's mission.

In this respect it is important to understand what motivates people to get elected and work on a Board. For some this has a lot do with positioning of (a Board member's) organization. By being on the Board you are seen to be an important member of the water sector internationally. The degree to which Board members actively engage varies from individual to individual. Some only concentrate on their presence others go way beyond that and really engage.

Rather than a "constructed" Board, in the World Water Council there are real elections with campaigns, and there is a lot of political deal-making to get on the Board.

The role of Chair, likewise, has two different approaches. One sees the Chair as someone who brings people together, summarizes, synthesizes, and comes up with collective decision; others see the Chair as more king-like with a lot of power with little notion of a collective, and making a collective decision. The focus is less about building support for a decision, than making a decision and then treating the Board vote as a formality. The first approach reflects core GAN needs.

GAN-wide meetings

Global face-to-face meetings, for at least co-owners and usually others, become a regular occurrence in Stage 3. These can be enormously costly and complex events that combine an education, networking, accountability, reporting, and voting function. For IUCN these attract 4,000 people and are held every 4 years; FSC has General Assemblies every 3 years; TI's are annual; GRI has an annual Stakeholder Council meeting, when the Board presents a report as an accountability measure.

Rather than an annual meeting, FLA has three Board meetings a year, each in a different geographic location, that are open to members. It is not uncommon to have 60 companies come; at a China meeting there were 120 NGOs.

Generally speaking, the GANs adopt traditions from government and NGOs to plan, set policy, and vote. The FSC's triannual General Assemblies involve complex procedures where the three chambers act like three houses of representatives. Each develops motions and then tries to get other chambers to support them in the General Assembly.

There are good reasons to question the way these meetings are organized. First, they are based upon traditions that appear to be proving increasingly unsuccessful, judging from declining voter turnout in traditional democracies and increasing criticism of their legislatures as dysfunctional. The FSC process, for example, tends to highlight divisions and points of difference in a negotiations-type setting that easily can result in time spent on minutia and alignments being made that have negative outcomes for minorities.

Second, there are enormously exciting and apparently more effective and engaging collective planning and decision-making processes that have been developed over the past couple of decades (again referenced in the chapter on change). If these meetings were organized in the "whole systems planning" mode, there would be intensely participatory work and development of plans at the face-to-face meetings. People would leave with a deep understanding of the plans, their next steps in realizing them, and networked closely to people who can help realize them.

Third, new communications technologies present new possibilities that still have to be tapped. I was involved with a very interesting virtual voting and discussion process with the Global Knowledge Partnership that produced a new Board and plan. There are enormous social media possibilities that should be aggressively explored and whose importance is just now being recognized.

Fourth, the "one big meeting" idea is really drawn from much more geographically constrained traditions. The GANs' global complexion raises a lot of questions about the accessibility, cost, and size of such events.

Legal structure

GANs are global, cross-sectoral, and networks. Legal incorporation procedures are national and subnational; they demand that an organization identify if it is a government agency, NGO, or business. When people talk about networks' legal status, they tend to speak about hierarchical ones with subsidiaries, or ones under some type of relatively tight control like franchise; perhaps the best analogue for a GAN is the cooperative as legal form (although I have never heard of one selecting it, I suppose probably because they do not work well globally).

So GANs' development is constrained by the lack of an appropriate legal form. In the meantime they are a square peg in a round hole. Almost always the Secretariat chooses to become an NGO, as do other nodes when they become sufficiently large. Sometimes a GAN obtains Intergovernmental Organization status, as the GWP has. This affords some benefits, such as being able to hire without reference to local work permits.

Emerging models

There are many ways that the structural models might be grouped: by geographic treatment, role of stakeholders, and funding mechanisms being some examples. However, given the emphasis I give to GANs as multi-stakeholder processes, perhaps the most relevant distinctions are with their attitude towards "co-ownership."

From this perspective, three different generalized models emerge. Particularly useful is to understand why the different models are developed. Although design decisions are influenced by philosophy and ideology, to be successful the GANs must align their structure to their strategy with their particular issue. Therefore, the issue and strategies themselves are probably larger forces, with philosophy/ideology guiding decisions within the array of what will be successful.

This takes us back to Chapter 2, Table 2.3, What GANs Do that describes GANs as performing six functions *vis-à-vis* their issue. Are there particular structures that appear to be used more often by GANs that have one dominant function? Here are some of the generalized suggestions that emerge from current experience:

- *All want increased participation*, but there are differences in the bar for admittance. For example, the Microcredit Summit Campaign simply requires that organizations describe how they will contribute to the Campaign goals. Companies joining the FLAs are subject to Independent External Monitoring and measures to ensure compliance.

  For GANs focused upon the function of *Learning, Research and Capacity Development,* relatively modest-sized networks in terms of participants appear desirable. This would include the labor-focused GANs such as Social Accountability International (SAI), Ethical Trading Initiative, and FLA that are really focused upon specific companies/plants/supply chains in the global economy.

  For *System Organizing* GANs – Microcredit Summit Campaign, the World Water Council (WWC), and TI are perhaps the outstanding examples where this is a dominant function – getting a large number of participants *is* important. The WWC does this through its focus upon associations of organizations for members; TI with growth in participation in the National Chapters and Local Action Centers.

- Some GANs *translate participation into co-ownership*: if you participate, you get the right to vote. This notably includes the *measuring and certifying* GANs. This logically follows from their work that requires participants to change their actions, and they are more likely to do this if they are co-owners.
- Some GANs *separate participation and co-ownership*. These come in a few types:

  - The PRI put a specific stakeholder group in charge, but the goal is to grow this number significantly. For the Global Compact the UN is owner. TAI separates membership for NGOs from governments that it encourages as participants.

    For PRI, this is tenable because the Asset Owners who are in charge actually hire the other two categories. For TAI, the NGOs have legitimacy as constituents of the governments and the governments have formally committed to Principle 10 of the Earth Charter. In both these cases, the GANs have a dominant *Advocating* function where one group of stakeholders is urging on others, although TAI's particular tool is assessments.

    For the Global Compact the strategy is viable because of the attraction of the UN as a sponsor and legitimizer. Moreover, although the Compact's multi-stakeholder Board is not technically "in control," it has very significant influence. The Compact is dominantly an *Advocating* GAN as it promotes the 10 UN principles; it is also a *Learning, Research and Capacity Development* GAN as, like the certifying GANs, it creates knowledge about how to operationalize the principles. (It is also verging toward *Assessment* as it develops pressure tactics to encourage reporting on application of the principles.)

  - GANs that have some aspect of closed ownership include *Financing* ones like the GWP (closed globally, multi-stakeholder locally) and the Global Alliance for Improved Nutrition. In these cases, specific funders or "sponsoring organizations" are allocated Board seats. Undoubtedly this comes from views about trust, money, power, control, and accountability that lead to discomfort with open ownership.

Table 6.2 Connection between what GANs do and structure

Function	Large number of participants?	Co-ownership	Goal
Shared visioning	See below	See below	Creating events and interactions that generate shared understanding and vision
System organizing	Important	Participants	Bringing together an emerging global system of diverse stakeholders to generate coherence in strategies
Learning, research, cap. dev.	Less important	Participants	Developing and disseminating new knowledge and tools with research, piloting new approaches, and training
Measuring/ certifying	Important	Participants	Developing indices, assessments, and/or certification processes
Financing	Important	Restricted to insiders	Combining forces to aggregate their impact and create a more efficient funding vehicle than any one could do on its own
Advocating	Important	Restricted by stakeholder group	Mobilizing voice and increasing pressure upon specific stakeholders who are blocking (actively or inactively) change

These findings are summarized in Table 6.2. Perhaps it's the anomalies that are most interesting. Is there some factor that has not been considered? Or are the conclusions wrong?

The *Shared Visioning* function is perhaps the most complicated. Generally GANs treat this as a task to be completed by a relatively small group, tools are to be developed, and these tools are to be applied in a rather mechanistic and hierarchical manner. If application of the tools generates a new vision, great. Certainly the tools can be used by those who are not really interested in vision development, these people exist in significant number, and their using the tools will give life to the vision.

However, this raises some basic strategic and philosophical questions about how GANs think of shared visioning. It is hard to believe that it is ever really "done." Are not more sophisticated cycles of renewal needed that incorporate experiences? Would we not be better off if the creation of global conversations about the issue is seen as an ongoing activity, rather than simply a possible by-product of other activities? Certainly social media technologies vastly expand the possibilities for this, and some of the GANs are indeed starting to develop this.

Initially a shared visioning process usually is sponsored by a trusted organization, but it must quickly engage participants so they at least feel like "co-owners" or they will not feel it is safe or worthwhile place to participate. Perhaps TI, moving into Stage 4 as described in Chapter 3, is most actively exploring what it means to have an ongoing shared visioning process with a very large number of co-owners.

The Microcredit Summit Campaign is an anomaly, given its tight control by the NGO Results Education Fund in the face of its system organizing focus. The Campaign is experiencing problems, and this might be a source of them. From a development stage viewpoint, it is a case of arrested development where it cannot really move to Stage 4 until it really changes its control structure.

Youth Enterprise and Sustainability (YES) that focuses upon youth employment is perhaps suffering from a similar challenge. It is really a learning and capacity development GAN. It is perhaps the archetypical example of a "self-organizing" GAN with a very opaque control structure but the Secretariat is almost non-existent. Its country networks breed with the entrepreneurial energy of youth and local action. Is this a new model of GAN emerging, or will it find its development severely restricted without greater formalization?

The financing GANs deserve more discussion. Their structure supports a traditional power relationship with money. Moreover, they are based in a North–South (developed–developing) country dynamic where the North is again associated with the ultimate power-holder. Will they evolve into a more "shared-power" model? Two trends suggest that this might be so. One is that the South continues to gain in power, seen notably with the emergence of the G-20 to replace the G-8 as an important forum for discussion about international finance issues. Another is that the whole "donor agency" and "development" logic seems to be weakening in the face of an increased need for truly global public goods development strategies. Those who worry about the product of more open elections might take comfort in the quality of Boards of other GANs like TI.

All of this discussion of structure gives further support to the idea that we are still in a relatively early stage of GANs' development. First of all, considering their shared seven characteristics, there is a considerable variety. Second, there seems to be at least some significant lack of alignment between structures and strategies/values.

Third, there still seems to be not altogether useful appropriation of the experience of other sectors. Notably, the concept of "Secretariat" is still powerful; decision-making processes draw from political traditions that arose in the eighteenth and nineteenth centuries.

Fourth and perhaps the most important, the technologies and knowledge that can help the networks develop more rapidly are not being accessed, but the technologies are still in rapid development. I am always reminded of the work of Verna Allee developing "roles and exchanges" as core network development concepts, rather than "organizations" and "people" (see Chapter 4). The social technologies of organizing and change processes and the physical technologies such as social media suggest that structural options will continue developing rapidly.

Notes

1. Hock, D. (1999). *Birth of the Chaordic Organization*. San Francisco, CA, Berrett-Koehler.
2. Global Fund (Undated). *Guidelines on Constituency Processes*. Geneva, Switzerland, Global Fund to Fight AIDS, Tuberculosis and Malaria, p. 3
3. FLA (2009). *Charter Document*. Washington, DC, USA, Fair Labor Association, p. 5.

CHAPTER 7

Growing the competencies required for success

I once listened to a network leader describe her frustration with a year-long initiative to bring another group of organizations into her established network. There had been seven meetings, and she felt there was little progress. As we talked, I brought up the topic of competencies to investigate particular approaches, skills, and tools that she might use. I referred to a model of eight different competencies that I have identified as key to networks' success. The model proved a great diagnostic tool. By the end of the conversation we had identified four particular competencies key to her initiative:

- communications,
- leadership,
- network development, and
- change.

Analyzing her situation in this way helped pull apart a confusion of issues, and identify strategies and tools to address her situation. In particular, it suggested the need for:

- incorporating the change competency and
- her network to renew its vision.

The work of GANs (Global Action Networks) requires three types of skills, abilities, and expertise. Particularly in their early days they lead with physical or substantive *issue* expertise such as expertise in some aspect of water, forestry, labor, conflict prevention, or youth employment. In early days, a GANs' leaders are usually seen as experts in the issue. This is important to ensure the GAN is grounded in its issue and to build legitimacy of the GAN with key stakeholders.

A second type of expertise is *tool* expertise. There are certain activities that GANs elect to realize their vision. These are associated with Table 2.3, What GANs do, and include such tools as certification, resource management, index development, and financing.

But as GANs develop, these types of expertise become less central. GANs do not aim to develop leading substantive issue expertise – that is the work of universities, think tanks, and consultancies that participate in GANs. And after applying tool expertise to create a financing or certification system, simple expansion in detail and maintenance are required. GANs just need to make sure that they have these types of expertise in their network to maintain legitimacy, relevance, and an appropriate level of quality. They usually have a place for issue and tool expertise, such as with a Technical Committee.

As GANs develop, a third type of expertise becomes increasingly important. It is *change process* expertise in applying the tool to the issue arena to enhance social, economic, and environmental outcomes in the issue field using the tools. The type of change process expertise that GANs need is driven by their particular theory of change that, as Chapter 5 explained, is a multi-stakeholder one. The work of developing (1) change through (2) multi-stakeholder processes is what defines the complexion and array of the competencies that GANs need for success. A different complexion of similar competencies is often needed in other types of organizations.

To understand how this change process work distinguishes GANs, consider the tool of "certification and standards." The International Organization for Standardization (ISO) also produces standards that are used in certification. ISO is a business–government network. ISO has an important "system organizing" role. But it is not a GAN. Its goal is not about change, but rather summarizing current standards and ensuring there is some international uniformity and way of translating standards between countries. ISO emphasizes tool expertise rather than change process expertise. It does not have triple loop change as part of its fundamental purpose – transformational change that includes change in power relationships.

GANs involved with measurement and certification, on the other hand, take a position of leadership by gathering stakeholders who want to *significantly advance the standards in terms of their social, environmental, and economic impact.* Advancing practice for this triple-bottom-line impact is distinctive in GANs across issues. GANs' belief that the certification should be done by embracing diversity and voluntarily gives additional wrinkles to the particular competencies that they have to both develop and integrate for success.

Being clear about these competencies is important for several reasons. As demonstrated in the opening example, they provide a framework for identifying the skills and tools necessary to successfully approach a specific opportunity or challenge. In more traditional management thinking, they connect to operational decisions and priority setting in a number of ways, including:

- Recruitment
- Learning and development
- Performance measurement
- Reorganization and team building
- Career development
- Promotion and succession planning[1]

As we shall see, perhaps the most important implication of the competencies is for the way GANs actually organize themselves.

Core competencies

"Competencies" is a concept usually applied to individuals – what does an individual have to be really good at, to successfully fulfill a role? A competency is usually described in terms of three qualities:

- Knowledge: Through education and experience we gain knowledge about facts and understanding about how something works.
- Skills: This is associated with talent and application of knowledge in an effective way. It can be *vis-à-vis* a technical skill such as use of a software, or an interpersonal skill as in "diplomatic skills."
- Attributes/behavioral qualities: These are about actions in specific situations. Thoughtfulness, reactionary, inventive, and personable are all examples.

The concept of competencies is equally valuable applied to networks and the question: what do GANs have to be able to do really well to realize success? The framework presented in Figure 7.1 aims to be a comprehensive definition of the competencies necessary for a network to be effective. It is sometimes referred to as the "flower" or "petal" diagram – a description more obvious when presented with each competency being a different color. The figure arises from working with network participants and outside experts such as academics and consultants. Experts tend to focus upon

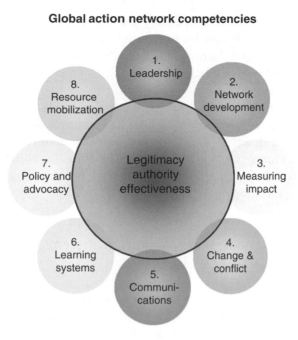

Figure 7.1 Competencies

one of the competencies; when this comprehensive model is presented, they commonly say "Yes, but competency X is the really critical one." In fact, they all have to be developed for a network to be effective. At different periods a GAN may focus on developing only one or two, but true success will only come with development of all.

These competencies are, of course, only distinct conceptually – they interact, and the way they interact is also important. For example, leadership must be skillful at addressing change; people working on learning must also have a strategy to measure their impact.

Although these competencies may appear to be similar to those for traditional organizations, mimicking those organizations' traditions, and basing the competency development upon their knowledge, skills, and attributes can be very problematic. Leadership in a network setting, for example, is very distinct from that in a hierarchical organization. We are still at early stages of understanding how these competencies play out for networks, but following is a sketch based upon best knowledge to date.

Of course each of these competencies connects to a vast literature and set of opinions. I will simply sketch some of the thinking on each that I've found helpful; a proper review of this deserves a book of its own.

I begin discussion of each competency with an overview of the quality of knowledge, and then follow by suggesting three or four important skills and attributes. The goal is to give a taste of the distinctiveness of these competencies for GANs to support their development, and to propose a framework for further discussion and work.

When thinking about these competencies, remember that GANs are complex systems as described in Chapter 2. You might want to refer back to Table 2.4 that describes the difference between traditional approaches and those for complex adaptive systems. The shifts in the table describe differences between competencies that may have the same name in a traditional organization, and those for GANs.

Competency 1. Leadership – Realizing coherent entrepreneurial activity at all levels

Heroic and hierarchical models of leadership do not work for networks. Dispersed, visionary, collaborative, and entrepreneurial qualities and skills must be nurtured amongst network members and staff for networks to realize their promise. How can these skills be nurtured and developed with the diverse stakeholders and experts that networks engage? What are cultural challenges of leaders in a global world that values diversity, and how can the challenges be addressed? How can ambiguity, dilemmas, and paradoxes inherent in much of networks' work be addressed while maintaining visionary direction?

These sorts of question have been at the heart of an innovative Boston College leadership program called Leadership for Change that I had the fortune to initiate. The decade with a wonderful faculty and my decade of work with GANs have made an enormous contribution to my own appreciation of a new approach to leadership that is particularly relevant to GANs.

Leadership knowledge

Grady McGonagill and Claire Reinhelt of the Leadership Learning Community are researchers on leadership.

They write: The following perspectives illustrate the redefinition of leadership to emphasize the importance of shared, collective leadership:

- Leadership is an activity, not a role. It can be enacted by anyone in a system, independent of their role.[2]

- "Heroic" leadership leads to "over-management," defense of turf rather than concern with shared goals, and weak teamwork and coordination; by contrast, shared "post-heroic leadership" releases the potential power of everyone.[3]
- Leadership arises within communities of practice whenever people work together and make meaning of their experiences and when people participate in collaborative forms of action across the dividing lines of perspective, values, beliefs, and cultures.[4]

In a 2010 Bertelsmann Foundation report Grady and Peter Pruyn built upon work by Claire and summarized the knowledge relevant to leadership for GANs. To give greater definition to "collective leadership," they created a matrix that emphasizes distinct capacities are needed at different "levels" of the system and different levels of capacity development.

This matrix is reproduced in Table 7.1 with a row and column shaded to indicate the parts particularly relevant to GANs. Of course GANs have to have capacity in the other boxes as well, but the ones shaded are where GANs should focus on excelling. The bottom row refers to the issue arena that the GAN is working in.

The table helps GANs ask themselves how they are doing with respect to the shaded leadership development challenges in particular, and then set strategies for addressing them. Currently most GANs are "doing" the shaded activities, but without a capacity development strategy to make sure they excel at them.

Another wonderful thing about the matrix is that it suggests interventions that GANs have been working on, but without being as explicit about how their work is distinctive. It emphasizes that "leadership" is not just a characteristic possessed by individuals, but that the GAN itself has leadership and a role in developing leadership.

Some top leadership skills

Probably no skill is as central to networks as the ability to connect. For GANs, this means connecting between individuals and organizations with diverse cultures and ways of perceiving the world. Managing Director for Transparency International (TI) describes this on a very personal level that he experienced when he was in prison in South Africa for his opposition to apartheid. He was 18, and facing the prospect of being raped.

> I don't think you can engage violence with someone you truly love ... and so I ask "what does this mean?" That if there's a true bond

Table 7.1   Leadership knowledge framework

Level of system targeted		Goal of development effort				
		Individual capacity	*Team capacity*	*Organizational capacity*	*Network capacity*	*Systems capacity*
	Individuals	1. Develop capacity of individuals for self-awareness, ongoing learning, and exercising initiative	2. Develop capacity of individuals to work together in groups and lead teams	3. Develop capacity of individuals to understand and lead organizations	4. Develop capacity of individuals to cultivate and leverage peer relationships	5. Develop capacity of individuals to see the big picture, understand root causes, and influence systems
	Teams	6. Develop capacity of teams to develop and elicit the full potential of all team members	7. Develop capacity of teams to define and attain purposes	8. Develop capacity of teams to enhance organizational performance	9. Develop capacity of teams to align their goals and activities across boundaries	10. Develop capacity of teams to prototype systems change
	Organizations	11. Develop capacity of organizations to support staff, volunteer, and board member development	12. Develop capacity of organizations to support effective teamwork	13. Develop capacity of organizations to foster internal collaboration to effectively adapt to challenges	14. Develop capacity of organizations to collaborate with one another	15. Develop capacity of organizational coalitions to lead systemic change
	Communities	16. Develop capacity of communities to support reflective learning and engagement of community members	17. Develop capacity of communities to foster and support inclusive group initiatives	18. Develop capacity of communities to sustain organizations that promote community well-being	19. Develop capacity of communities to learn together and align efforts towards common goals	20. Develop capacity of communities to advocate systems change
	Fields of policy and practice	21. Develop capacity of fields to cultivate innovative thought leaders and practitioners	22. Develop capacity of fields to organize around shared interests and goals	23. Develop capacity of fields to organize and disseminate knowledge and field best practices	24. Develop capacity of fields to find synergies across institutional silos and disciplinary boundaries	25. Develop capacity of fields to generate policy solutions and transform institutional practices and culture

Source: McGonagill, G. and P. W. Pruyn (2010). "Leadership Development in the U.S.: Principles and Patterns of Best Practice". *Bertelsmann Stiftung Leadership Series.* S. Vopel. Berlin, Germany, Bertelsmann Stiftung, p. 113.

with these people, I won't get raped . . . so I'll have to really work to act on this bond.

You can't act out that you have a bond with somebody . . . if you think that they're a total jerk, racist, then this will fail. I had to overcome something within myself. You have to seek out the common humanity with someone who you dislike, you might disrespect and have very negative feelings towards . . . you can't "act out" that you have positive feelings. You need to truly believe it. For me that was my own biggest achievement because I had to overcome all my own prejudices. The process to social justice is in many ways more challenging to overcoming your own prejudices than the big social justice issues you fight on a big stage.

This might seem very distant from the tension that comes with connecting between organizational sectors (government–business–civil society). However, many of the same leadership challenges arise. There is strong tendency to exaggerate, create stereo-types, and even vilify others in contrast to one's own position and organization. One powerful intellectual insight that has helped me overcome this arises from my work on identifying distinct attributes of these organizational sectors. When I matched this to the work of Sandra Seagal,[5] on individual learning styles, I understood that the sectors tend to be aggregations of different learning styles – kinesthetically centered and physical for business, mentally centered for government and emotionally centered for civil society (see Chapter 5). This insight provides an invaluable way for people to understand their differences so they can meaningfully work together.

Some top leadership skills

- Connecting
- Stewarding
- Handling paradox and ambiguity
- Inspiring

Connecting means GANs must be able to see, encompass, and reflect diverse perspectives. If they are seen simply as a civil society organization, they will lose their capacity to make connections across sectoral divides. If they are seen simply as a collection of donors, they will be restricted to very utilitarian connections that will dissolve when money disappears. GANs must pay great attention to their formal governance structures to facilitate connecting to them, to ensure connecting is an ongoing activity and that people see their own views integrated into GANs' work.

One concept that supports this approach to leadership is stewarding and "stewardship," a term that Peter Block advocated to replace "leadership." His 1993 book provoked controversy when it was published. Peter writes:

> Stewardship focuses our attention on aspects of our workplaces that have been most difficult to change, namely the distribution of power, purpose, and rewards.... Stewardship is to hold something in trust for another. Stewardship is...the choice to preside over the orderly distribution of power. This means giving people at the bottom and the boundaries of the organization choice over how to serve a customer, a citizen, a community. It is the willingness to be accountable for the well-being of the larger organization by operating in services, rather than in control, of those around us. Stated simply, it is accountability without control or compliance.[6]

For Peter, the concept of "authentic service" is key. He associates it with a balance of power, primary commitment to the larger community, collective definition of culture, and equitable rewards. Ania Grobicki, Global Water Partnership (GWP) Executive Secretary, reflects this in response to key qualities she'd look for in someone to replace her: "The desire to serve ... to want really to serve people and lead the organization to achieve our vision and mission through service." Similarly, Marcos Espinal of the Executive Secretary Stop TB Partnership says: "I always define myself as the servant of the partners .... to convene, the credit goes to the partners. When I hire, I say 'you will suffer because the credit won't go to the staff, but to the partners.' " Stewarding contrasts nicely with the dominant "operating logics" of sector organizations. *Administering* of rules and laws dominates government; *managing* to goals dominates business; and *co-developing* with lots of community input is the dominant logic for civil society.

The scale of global networks, their ambitiousness in terms of vision, and their diversity-embracing quality all bring out the need to skillfully handle paradox and ambiguity. In some ways, paradox is at the heart of GANs work: creating outcomes that make sense for diverse stakeholders. How can a direction be rewarding for business and government and civil society? The ambiguity is about living with uncertainty, and yet taking action. Rarely is there truly "a right answer" when working with diverse stakeholders. There are better and worse ones from different perspectives. Leadership in part is about *emerging* decisions that are guided by a clear vision of what is important.

For example, I have seen tensions of ambiguity with the concept of "transparency." Usually business and government have a much more restrained interpretation of what this means, in comparison to civil society. Everyone supports being transparent, but there are different views about how much to share and when. Should differences within a support team be part of an online discussion? When does information become distracting and confusing as opposed to edifying and helpful? What role should leadership have in shaping data and information into knowledge?

GANs are dealing with big issues, and the leadership skill of inspiring is important to generate the energy and enthusiasm to keep moving ahead. This is done in part by continually bringing participants back to the vision that they are working for. We need better ceremonies and etiquettes to support these reconnections. They need greater formalization and integration into the working of GANs – while avoiding a cult-like approach and maintaining an open, questioning one.

Many think of ceremonies as bad and inauthentic. However, to infuse leadership we need to have moments, such as with face-to-face meetings, when we actually pause to renew and hold up visions. This both inspires and reinforces the need to make decisions and take actions that are accountable to, and reflective of, the vision.

In the Boston College program, I always aimed to develop these leadership skills to contribute to deepening capacity to understand how our actions can affect people and events. This is associated with the concept of the "butterfly effect," so-called because of the idea that a butterfly flapping its wings can influence events far away. It is also associated with the capacity to understand how our actions can influence options years in the future. This is related to the Iroquois concept of the seventh generation, the idea that decisions should be considered for their impact on the seventh generation.

Some top leadership attributes

Peter Senge is commonly rated among the top management consultants in the US and globally. When I showed him the flower diagram of competencies, he nodded and said "But you know leadership is the key." For him leadership relates to being *systems intelligent* (SI) – something that many would associate with being wise.

For me the fundamentals start with a set of deep capacities with which few in leadership positions today could claim to have developed: systems intelligence, building partnership across boundaries, and openness of mind, heart, and will. To develop such capacities requires a lifelong commitment to grow as a human being in ways not well understood in contemporary culture. Yet, in other ways, these are the foundations for leadership that have been understood for a very long time.[7]

Some top leadership attributes

- Systems Intelligent
- Leaderful
- Trustworthy
- Entrepreneurial

By SI, Peter means the ability to see systems as described in Chapter 2, and the relationships and inter-dependencies in them. He draws upon his experience in developing the Sustainable Food Lab (SFL) to illustrate his meaning.

Before the members of the Food Lab could work together effectively, they needed to share understanding of the systemic forces driving the "race to the bottom" and how they were all part of creating these forces: as companies pursuing business-as-usual business models with little regard for the effects on farming families and communities or on environmental systems, as farmers unable to moderate pressures for continual production growth, and all of us as consumers whenever we buy food at the cheapest price with little thought as to where the food comes from.[8]

By "building partnerships across boundaries," Peter is referring to the diversity-embracing quality of GANs. By "openness" he means the ability to be challenged and discover new approaches, and learn from others.

Referring to SI as an attribute emphasizes that it pervades the whole being of successful GANs, rather than a skill that can be applied to certain issues. It is a mindset. Explaining SI for individuals, Hamalainen and Sarrinen write that it is "... intelligent behavior in the context of complex systems involving interaction and feedback. A person acting with systems intelligence engages successfully and productively with the holistic feedback mechanisms of her environment. She experiences herself as part of an interdependent environment, aware of the influence of the whole upon herself as well as her own influence upon the whole. With this heightened awareness, she is able to act intelligently."[9]

Joe Raelin, like Grady and Claire, sees a new paradigm of leadership emerging. His concept of "leaderful" was developed in part through his participation in the group of wonderful faculty who put together the Boston College Leadership for Change program. It is a complementary description leadership that can take GANs to their ultimate purpose.

> In the Twenty-First-Century organization, we need to establish communities where everyone shares the experience of serving as a leader, not sequentially, but concurrently and collectively. In other words, leaders co-exist at the same time and all together. In addition, we expect each member of a community to make a unique contribution to the growth of that community, both independently and interdependently with other. In this sense, our leaders are inherently collaborative, which in turn they derive from their compassion toward other human beings. Their well-developed sense of self permits them to develop a deep consideration of others.[10]

Raelin associates leaderfulness with four shifts in behavior. With *concurrent* leadership, there can be more than one leader operating within a community at the same time. With *collective* leadership, people assume responsibility as a whole. *Collaborative* leadership is particularly relevant to change, since it means people work together to learn diverse views, identify paths to change, and implement them together. In contrast to the tradition of leaders who dispassionately make the tough decisions for the enterprise, Raelin sees *compassion* as a key quality in avoiding self-centered control. The dignity of each person is preserved regardless of one's background, status, or point of view.

Also key to networks success is being trustworthy. As mentioned in Chapter 2, this means trust of *intent*: that you and I share a goal. Then there is trust in *competence:* that you and I are actually capable of doing what we say we will do. And third is trust of *understanding:* that you and I have shared understanding of the words and language and commitments.[11] These three forms of trust are important for individuals, working groups, Secretariats, and the whole network of GANs. It is critical to reputation, and without high reputation GANs cannot succeed.

As voluntary associations GANs rely on peer pressure, persuasion of logic, and moral assertion of what's right and just. In this situation, an inspirational vision is paramount. People and organizations undoubtedly have utilitarian goals when they participate in GANs. Without regularly asserting an inspiring vision, these goals will take over.

"Entrepreneurial" is a popular word today, and its definition has been widened with the concept of "social entrepreneurship." Ashoka, the pre-eminent global supporter of social entrepreneurs, describes them this way:

> Social entrepreneurs are individuals with innovative solutions to society's most pressing social problems. They are ambitious and persistent, tackling major social issues and offering new ideas for wide-scale change.
>
> Rather than leaving societal needs to the government or business sectors, social entrepreneurs find what is not working and solve the problem by changing the system, spreading the solution, and persuading entire societies to take new leaps.
>
> Social entrepreneurs often seem to be possessed by their ideas, committing their lives to changing the direction of their field. They are both visionaries and ultimate realists, concerned with the practical implementation of their vision above all else.[12]

GANs must be vehicles for nurturing, stewarding, and supporting this type of energy and drive. The contrasting image is a bureaucracy that is focused upon application of rules and processes that suppress and frustrate social entrepreneurs, or a managerial one that pursues profit objectives with negligible consideration for other impacts.

Competency 2. Network development – Aligning effective strategies, patterns, and structures

This is the competency that most people automatically associate with networks. It refers to activities of strategy, structure, and governance. Developing these activities for networks is distinguished by the importance of participation and systems thinking. I refer to this with the simple term "Network Development," to reflect the job titles most often associated with the competency.

Network development knowledge

The way a network is organized should reflect its strategy and encourage both effectiveness and accountability. Networks have developed a range of approaches to the governance, planning, and structural challenges. These approaches take a GAN through stages of development. Chapter 3 really investigated these challenges and the knowledge necessary to address them, summarized in Figure 7.2.

Network development skills

Let's return to the issue of global finance, the Global Finance Initiative (GFI), and the vision of a global financial system that integrates social, environmental, and economic concerns. This is a huge topic. Systems thinking makes the scale manageable. Unlike traditional science, which focuses upon the parts, systems thinking understands the parts and their relationships to make the whole. For example, systems thinking helps identify sub-systems of global finance such as ones of global public policy

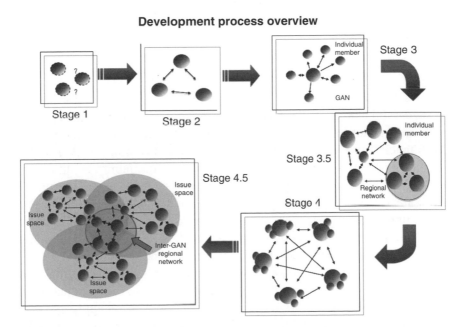

Figure 7.2   Network development knowledge framework

organizations, national counterparts, environmental stakeholders, and others. Systems thinking helps identify patterns of interactions and strategic leverage points where the interactions can most easily be influenced. The underlying principles of the system that are leading to crises and opportunities are revealed.

"Mental models" and underlying assumptions are associated with these principles. The assumptions are usually so ingrained in our thinking that they are not even recognized. Often they are highly limiting and problematic. For example, the common mental model with finance is that democratization of financial institutions will lead to destabilization and enhance short-term thinking; voters will not be able to understand the complexities of finance, they will chose immediate benefits over investment, and there will be wild swings in direction as Boards with different philosophies are elected.

Some top network development skills

- Systems thinking
- Community development/network weaving
- Strategizing
- Empowering

In fact, there is a very long and robust history of credit unions that are as successful as banks, that challenges this type of thinking. Each person with an account has one vote. In Canada these are a very large part of the financial system. I was personally involved in running (successfully) for the Board of Directors at the world's largest community credit union, VanCity in Vancouver. People actively campaign and it is a major media event since VanCity is the largest locally owned financial institution. The credit union's success presents a good illustration how different people will have different assumptions, mental models, and system principles, based upon their experiences, beliefs, values, and education.

These principles are associated with Peter Senge's systems intelligence. They explain not just the current relationships, but also the ones that need development to realize the vision. Through this type of approach with the GFI, we were able to identify that one major problem is a lack of interaction between those in the environmental and social development communities, with key global public policy organizations.

This gap in relationships is referred to by network analyst Ron Burt as "structural holes."[13] These are like dead zones, where there is not even antagonism – there is nothing. Network development is about eliminating these. Today the terms "boundary spanning" and "network weaving" are often used for this work.[14] Historically it is called "community development work." For GANs the community is global. For global finance, these holes are one of the systemic properties that are giving rise to poor social–environmental–economic impact outcomes. In fact, the GFI system analysis describes global finance as actually very insular and self-serving.

To change this situation requires a community-development strategy. One essential quality of such strategies is that they build relationships and a sense of common purpose. Where people previously felt isolated and in conflict, a GAN develops connections and movement in a common direction (coherence).

Community development provides forums and empowers people to speak and interact in new ways to develop alternative futures. This intimately concerns re-defining "system" boundaries – for finance, this means who is in and who is out in terms of financial system decision-making. In the GFI we identified three traditional insider stakeholder groups as G-7 policy makers (including Ministers of Finance), G-7 regulators like central banks and commercial financial institutions like banks, investment firms, and insurance companies. We also identified traditional "outsider" groups, which are stakeholders who have an interest in, and are affected by, the financial system. This included asset owners (such a pension fund investors), civil society organizations (NGOs concerned with social and economic impacts), non-financial businesses, labor unions, critical academics, and non-G7 (now G-20) governments.

The GFI community development strategy then focused upon strengthening and weaving together networks of the outsider stakeholders as a first step, and as a second step bringing together the insider and outsider stakeholders. The first step is important to empower the outsiders. Obviously, this process underlines the fact that community development is a medium- and long-term activity that is central to GANs work. It also emphasizes the importance of being able to think strategically about large, complex systems.

Network development attributes

Developing networks requires understanding stakeholders' needs, aspirations, and challenges to be able to appropriately respond to them. Bringing together the outsider finance stakeholders requires understanding a disem-powered outsider mentality and operating style, in contrast to the powerful insider interests.

Some top network development attributes

- Empathetic
- Trustworthy
- Visionary
- Entrepreneurial

However, to bridge the gap between them requires being sympathetic to all groups. Although compassion – one of the four Cs of "leaderful" – is usually associated with the underdog, it is an important quality to associate with the powerful, as well. Often in organizing business – civil society col-laborations, I have heard business people describe CSOs as more powerful than they are, much to the astonishment of the Civil Society Organizations (CSOs). From the business side, often there is a much more natural alliance between CSOs and governments; business feels side-swiped by CSO campaigns that put it in a reactive position.

In fact, this is where understanding the distinctive competencies of the sectors is particularly useful. CSOs' power is related to their ability to mobilize people, and businesses' is related to ability to mobilize capital. These two types of power are very different.

There is a sequence in the importance of the Network Development attributes for GANs:

- first is developing empathy and understanding of diverse perspectives;
- second is development of trust among the stakeholders to deepen connections;
- this in turn leads to exchanges and gatherings across the differences that produce a vision that connects the stakeholders;
- then comes the entrepreneurial action to give life to the vision.

This work requires understanding how the different parties can ben-efit from building relationships and increasing their interdependence. Table 7.2 aims to get at this understanding for business–government–civil society. It presents some generic mutual gains. Creating a table like this with case-specific gains is a good way to guide Network Development. The vision (developed through the Change competency) should unify the

Table 7.2 Potential mutual gain outcomes of business–government–civil society organization relationships

Government	Business	CSOs
• provide ways to increase effectiveness of public service provision *and* accountability (if right system created!) • reduce direct involvement in rule enforcement while increasing its effectiveness • improve welfare • provide legal infrastructure	• expand markets • ensure supplies • develop new products • lower production and delivery costs • expand investments • improve human resources • build support for local activity • improve quality, regularity	• increase access of the poor to goods and services • provide new economic opportunities • improve basic medical, education, and health • reduce environmental impact • strengthen local cultures • social cohesion

Source: Waddell, S. (2005). *Societal Learning and Change: How Governments, Business and Civil Society are Creating Solutions to Complex Multi-Stakeholder Problems*. Sheffield, UK, Greenleaf Publishing.

stakeholders and transcend their individual positions in a description the stakeholders finding compelling and that they would not be able to realize individually. However, the operational reality is that there must be much more operational and prosaic wins for participants to build the network. A network will not hold together simply around some long-term idea; participants will simply become inactive and leave if they do not obtain more immediate and concrete benefits in terms of their diverse needs.

Competency 3. Measuring impact – providing continuous feedback to improve effectiveness and support

A colleague at the GWP once described to me their dilemma with measuring impact. He explained that a goal is to enhance education, with the understanding that provision of safe and secure drinking water is one of the most important contributors to health of all time. With safe drinking water, the children will be healthier and be able to attend school more regularly. But wait! The GWP does not provide safe drinking water, nor does it even create safe drinking water infrastructure. Through organizing partners and provision of some technical resources, GWP supports others to implement good practices for the sustainable management of their water resources.

And the GWP vision is *a water secure world*. Its mission is *to support the sustainable development and management of water resources at all levels*. Certainly these make no mention of education! It is a fine vision and mission, but they do not get at the "healthy and happy people" end outcomes the GWP is actually aiming for.

This dilemma also showed up in some work I did with The Access Initiative (TAI). I noticed that some TAI participants were anxious about the rigor and quality of their assessment tool. But the goal of TAI is not to have a high quality tool – it is to give life to Principle 10 of the Rio Declaration. So any energy and resources applied to improving the tool can only be justified if their application is the best use of those resources in terms of the bigger change goal. But becoming distracted with perfecting the tool is easy, given the complexity of the work.

Measuring impact knowledge

There are many different ways to approach impact measurement, but using the wrong methods can actually undermine a change network's efforts. The value of appropriate impact measurement is that it not only helps explain to funders the return on their investment, but it also is an important tool for priority-setting, decision-making, and managing.

At a March 2007 meeting, GAN representatives were asked about the qualities that they perceived as important for a good impact measurement system. Among the top qualities were simple, flexible, adaptable, a coherent system, participatory, integrating qualitative and quantitative, credibility, and generative of learning. Some of this contrasts with traditional evaluation approaches that come from an industrial "input/output" model. They are either *formative* evaluation that gets a production or program model ready (working out the bugs) or *summative* evaluations at the end of a project to assess "did it work?" These use frameworks like SMART (Specific, Measurable, Achievable, Relevant, Time-bound). The evaluator is typically thought of as outside of the project being evaluated, and as a dis-interested observer and analyst who delivers periodic reports.

These two approaches alone are insufficient for networks. That is because:

- Methods for evaluating simple tasks cannot address the complications of the interaction in network participants' relationships.
- There is not one, but an emergent number of possible pathways that require exploration and development to address issues such as ending

corruption, creating sustainable forestry, and integrating triple-bottom-line imperatives into corporations.

- Change networks' visions require a long time to realize. With all the change in their operating environments over that time, adaptive strategies are required, although simple ones can be good for relatively short-term sub-initiatives.
- Change networks usually do not aim to "take credit" for the actual valued outcomes (such as healthy, happy people). They aim for a backseat in favor of their participants' being recognized for their work. This makes attribution, a cornerstone of traditional impact measurement, highly problematic.

Referring back to the distinctions between simple, complicated, and complex activities described in Chapter 2, traditional evaluation approaches are appropriate for *simple* tasks where there is standardization and a single set of objectives. In networks, different objectives that are valued by different stakeholders which requires measurement methods that can address *complicated* activities. However, GANs are distinguished by an over-arching mission that requires *complex* activities. Therefore, although they need impact measurement methods that will address all three activities, GANs' measurement umbrella method must accommodate complexity.

Good questions and learning are foundations that unite all the evaluation approaches. As described in Chapter 5, the work of GANs embraces three types of change that are distinguished by the types of questions they ask and the type of learning required. Simple activities are associated with incremental change and single-loop learning that asks questions within the established policies, structures, and goal (e.g. are we doing well at providing people fish to eat?); complicated activities, change-as-reform, and double-loop learning that asks questions about the policies, structures, and goals (e.g. should we instead be teaching how to fish for people to feed themselves?); and complex activities dealing with transformation and triple-loop learning that asks questions about how we think about an issue (e.g. how do we understand the eco-systems-fish-consumption relationships?).

One leading entrepreneur in this field is Michael Quinn Patton who has created the concept of "developmental evaluation." He writes:

> Developmental evaluation supports innovation *development* to guide adaptation to emergent and dynamic realities in complex environments.... Informed by systems thinking and sensitive to complex

nonlinear dynamics, developmental evaluation supports social innovation and adaptive management. Evaluation processes include asking evaluative questions, applying evaluation logic, and gathering real-time data to inform ongoing decision making and adaptations. As in action research strategies, the evaluator is part of the development team from beginning to end, rather than someone who comes in at the end to simply do a *post facto* analysis.[15]

Another colleague, Sanjeev Khagram, has been puzzling about this situation for some time with the Impacts Community of Practice sponsored through iScale. While working with GANs and others he has developed an approach that he calls impact planning, assessment, reporting, and learning systems (IPARLS). He explains:

> IPARLS can provide and translate credible evidence to key stakeholders including policymakers and citizens in real time in appropriate ways for effective utilization. IPARLS integrates various activities such as monitoring and evaluation and impact evaluation for a range of purposes from adaptive management to demonstrating results to fostering accountability. The evidence generated by impact evaluations is much more likely to be credible and utilized when they are embedded in IPARLS.[16]

IPARLS links the measuring impact to several competencies, such as learning systems and communications. He continues to emphasize IPARLS' integrative nature. "An IPARL system includes:

(1) A theory of change
(2) A theory or multiple theories of action
(3) An integrated assessment approach
(4) A set of public and donor reporting mechanisms
(5) A range of constituency voice processes
(6) A focus on continuous learning"[17]

This constitutes a good list of the range of knowledge that an impact system for networks must comprise. These components are summarized in Figure 7.3, with the Dewey/Kolb learning cycle being central. This approach is quite different from traditional measurement and evaluation approaches. It emphasizes an underlying theoretical base to give rigor, and describes evaluation as integrating several activities, fully engaging stakeholders, and reframing evaluation as a learning process.

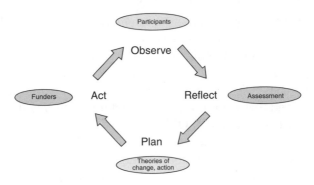

Figure 7.3 Measuring impact knowledge framework PARLS components

Measuring impact skills

The need for measuring and evaluating skills is obvious, and this includes, for example, the ability to address issues of validity and establishing data-gathering systems. But the IPARLS approach suggests some particular types of skills necessary within this broad description. Learning is brought to the fore.

Some top measuring impact skills

- Measuring and evaluating
- Action learning
- Analyzing large complex systems

To understand the needed skills, some specific approaches can be referenced. One approach developed by the International Development Research Centre (of Canada: IDRC) is called Outcome Mapping (OM). Applied to GANs, it focuses upon the creation of feedback systems both to respondents and to those who want to know how the network is doing. (The sub-title to Outcome Mapping is *Building Learning and Reflection into Development Programs*.) The developers of OM explain that:

> The originality of the methodology is its shift away from assessing the products of a program (e.g., policy relevance, poverty alleviation, reduced conflict) to focus on changes in behaviours, relationships, actions, and/or activities of the people and organizations with whom a development program works directly.[18]

The focus of OM is upon learning and changes in behavior. This arises from the observation that the aspired changes usually occur at a significant time after an action or program, and that the outcomes might be different than expected. One core concept is "boundary partners": for GANs, this means participants. OM recognizes that a GAN is only one actor in realizing change, and that there is a complicated interaction with participants in realizing change. Therefore, OM does not aim to attribute an outcome to the GAN action, but to understand the contributions the GAN makes to an outcome as well as its boundary partners.

OM assesses strategies, issues, or relationships. There is a three-stage cycle to design an OM plan, usually conducted in a workshop with participants:

1) Intentional Design: This aims to ensure there is consensus about the definition of the "macro level changes," by answering Why? Who? What? How?
2) Outcome and Performance Monitoring: Its learning emphasis means OM is based on principles of participation. The OM process itself is designed to support development of the outcomes. A disciplined process of participant record-keeping and observation is key.
3) Evaluation Planning: An evaluation plan identifies the main actions to be taken to apply the OM framework.

Process and outcome evaluation are integrated by collecting observations about process implementation and results being achieved by participants.

Another approach to measuring impact created with the leadership of David Bonbright and Keystone is developed around the concept of *constituency voice*. As the name suggests, it focuses upon identifying stakeholders and asking them questions to assess the change strategy. As with OM, it therefore emphasizes participation. The participation can be through a variety of methods, such as focus groups, surveys, and interviews. Its core activity, therefore, is to establish effective feedback mechanisms and ways to use the data.

One application collected constituents' perceptions of the impacts of the Campaign to End Pediatric HIV/AIDS (CEPA). It created the following over 6 months:

1) Design and implementation of a global-level baseline survey based on CEPA's theory of change;
2) Design of the country-level baseline survey;
3) Implementation of the country-level baseline survey

This would lead to subsequent additional feedback surveys of both global and specific national constituents to test changes compared to the baselines.

These approaches emphasize the importance of a clearly identified theory of change and being able to work with stakeholders to collaboratively develop and implement the measurement approach. In this way, the knowledge is "socially embedded," since those who are being assessed are active co-participants in the process. This is a key quality of action learning.

A third approach, like the first two, takes a systems approach. However, it is quite different in other ways. Jim Ritchie Dunham and the Institute for Strategic Clarity have been developing an approach with a *Systemic Leverage Index*. The approach is founded in systems thinking and complex systems. It considers how different groups and organizations are trying to achieve their own goals and produce a larger collective goal. There are four guiding questions:

1. Thinking at the level of the whole system, is there a set of the overall measures of the impact this network is trying to have?
2. Do the different groups (environmental, social, economic, North, South, different parts of the supply chain, etc.) that contribute to the whole have different value sets? Is it clear how the contributions of these different groups combine? If I'm an environmental group, what do I do every day, what do I want, and what do I want to do to the larger goal?
3. What happens when the individual decisions of these groups start to influence each other? For example, the actions of one party in the supply chain start to influence other parties in the supply chain?
4. What specific interventions is the GAN making within the system? Is it getting high leverage impact from its resources and its specific interventions, and how much are they helping us to our larger impact goal?

This approach produces an index of the "health" of the system at key points within it, from the perspective of different stakeholder groups and levels (local–global). This could be, for example, indexes with respect to each of these four questions.

Measuring impact attributes

Measuring impact with GANs must be attentive to detail, but not meticulous about it. The issues that GANs are dealing with are so large,

there are so many variables, and so many unknowns that impact measurement systems will only provide information about direction and not
precise quantitative analysis.

Some top measuring impact attributes

- Attentive to detail (but not meticulous)
- Diversity embracing
- Inquisitive
- Theory-based

These methodologies help explain why the measuring impact competency of GANs must be diversity embracing. The approach must be
able to work with a great range of stakeholders in a very personal way.
The stakeholders have very different power roles in the larger system the
GAN aims to influence. The Constituency Voice approach emphasizes
this most. The OM approach deals with behaviors, which are very heavily
influenced by culture and therefore requires great diversity sensitivity.

The Systemic Leverage Approach most categorically emphasizes the
quality of being systematic. The measuring impact approach must consider not just different individuals' positions, but provide analysis at the
local-to-global levels.

Perhaps the core to any good impact measurement system is the quality of inquisitiveness. People must be curious about how they are doing,
and how they can do better. Reporting to donors can become perfunctory;
learning cannot.

One useful quality that this discussion about attributes and skills raises
again of IPARLS is its emphasis upon the need to integrate various
approaches in terms of methodologies. No one approach can do it all. But
as IPARLS also emphasizes, a sound measurement system begins with a
theory of change. A GAN must be clear about its strategy, to be able to
measure its success.

Competency 4. Conflict and change – Developing complex change skillfully

GANs' work requires addressing significant conflict arising from diverse
points of view, power differences and their core change mission. After

all, realizing change requires overcoming natural resistance, traditions, and entrenched interests. MSC Standards and Licensing Director Andrew Mallison describes theirs is "... a very conflicted space with diametrically opposed interests. Catchers want minimum costs, conservationists don't want any catch. Essentially we're in the middle. If we go to industry, then conservation groups are unhappy about certifying anyone.... if we make it too tough, it becomes too expensive (to commercially harvest)."

To approach their change work, GANs must be proficient at addressing problems from a whole-system perspective. This involves various types of change and change processes. It demands addressing critical questions such as: how can networks' change efforts engage the broad numbers of people, realize the depth of change, and sufficiently sustain the change process for the long periods that are necessary?

This is probably the competency that is most undervalued and under-recognized by GANs. They recognize, of course, that they are addressing global change issues. But in general they lack sophistication in development and application of the knowledge, skills, and attributes needed to excel.

Change knowledge

Chapter 5 reviewed the knowledge relevant to this competency. Table 7.3 summarizes key items. The knowledge covers the full spectrum of change processes, from incremental change to the most challenging type of transformational change with still-unimagined possibilities.

Some top change skills

A GAN's strategy represents a change process that the GAN is stewarding. The GAN is the forum for sustaining the change activities for the many years necessary to realize the vision. The activities must be grounded in a solid change strategy. Chapter 5 explained that there are essentially two different peaceful global change strategies: a constitutional one where all the governments get together to make agreements, with actual application of agreements being highly variable. The dominant GAN change strategy is a social practices one, which is multi-stakeholder and experiment-focused. The goal is to shift what is seen as "normal behavior" and standards. This is what GANs must be highly skilled at developing, and there is much to learn about how to do this. For example, the Forest Stewardship Council (FSC) aims to shift companies, communities, and

Table 7.3 Conflict and change knowledge framework

Type of change	Incremental ... changing quantities	Reform ... changing the way parts interact in a system	Transformation ... reconceiving the system
Focus	Changing ways of acting and behaving	Changing ways of thinking	Changing ways of perceiving
Core questions	How can we do more of the same? Are we doing things right?	What rules should we create? What are my mental models and assumptions? Are we doing the right things? What is the best practice?	How do I make sense of this? What is the purpose? How do we know what is best?
Learning loops	Single loop	Second loop	Triple loop
Type of action	Enacting/applying known approaches/ scripts/solutions	Reflection and learning, critical analysis	Unlearning and relearning
When to use	For simple issues with causal order For routine, repetitive, predictable issues, When the "answer" is known	For complex, non-programmable issues When new solutions have been agreed upon When a problem is well-defined	To innovate and create previously unimagined possibilities. When no "solution" is apparent? When breakthrough thinking is needed
Participation	Current actors addressing the problem	Stakeholders of the currently defined system	An exploratory microcosm of participants in the evolving understanding of "the system"
General dynamic	Implementing the predictable/ projectable	Defining and negotiating the projectable.	Emerging the previously unimagined
Skills/methods	Project management	Naming, framing, negotiating roles and strategies	Co-authoring/ narrative dialogue/ revisioning tools, deepening awareness of world views
Personal role	I am acting on the problem	Others are the problem	I am part of the problem, "we" are in this together

NGOs' behavior to integrate values, rules, and processes that will produce sustainable forestry practices.

The concept of "stewarding" often takes the form of creating other organizations to do some particular part of the change process. For example, the FSC has established Accreditation International to do the accreditation part of the work important to incremental change.

Some top change skills

- Stewarding change processes
- Systems Thinking
- Facilitating/Mediating/ Negotiating/Visioning

Of course there are many more variables than an X and Y, and they interact in complex ways. This again emphasizes the importance of systems thinking skills. This time their importance might be best illustrated by contrasting a systems thinking approach with another common approach to change: "root cause." That term suggests that some specific cause of the challenge being addressed can be identified and pulled out like a weed, leaving a garden to naturally flourish. There are no root causes for the issues that GANs address. This is why they are referred to as "complex." There is a great tangle of inter-acting sources. Chapter 4 presented systems archetypes and other methods for understanding these change challenges.

As described in Chapter 2, GANs are not only *networks*, but also *organizations* in the form of a Secretariat, and *partnerships* of organizations doing a specific sub-activity like applying certification to a particular forest. But GANs are trying to change behaviors of all the organizations in its issue *system* (such as forestry). This means that although the change process focuses upon changing "the system," a GAN is also deeply involved in changing its participants' behavior, and that as a GAN develops it must change its own behavior in response to success and to grow.

I find that often people in GANs become overly focused upon "changing the system," without sufficiently attending to the other places where an ongoing cycle of change is needed. For example, simply defining a vision, mission, and strategy once is not sufficient. As a GAN gains experience and success and the environment of its issue system change, the GAN's vision, mission, and strategy must be reassessed.

A great example of this is with the example that opened this chapter. The network felt that it had "done" its change work and visioning, and was approaching the question about how to engage (incorporate?) another group of stakeholders as a technical process. This situation often faces GANs as they expand into new geographic regions or sub-issues.

In fact, the network should undertake a revisioning change process with the other group of stakeholders, to engage them effectively. It is possible that the network would find its original vision and strategy re-affirmed and an incremental change approach to engage the new stakeholders would prove adequate. However, the network should hold itself open to changing its vision and strategy to transcend and incorporate new ideas from the new stakeholders. The new stakeholders need to go through the visioning process that others in the GAN have gone through.

This systems change process the GAN is stewarding requires skills in facilitation, negotiations, mediation, and visioning. These are often associated with face-to-face meeting skills. But the meetings are only one part of this activity. The teleconferences, research activities, local projects, online discussions, and other activities are all part of the change process. It is valuable to think of facilitation, negotiating, mediating, and visioning as encompassing all these different ways of interacting. For example, skillfully facilitating an online discussion is as important as – in fact likely of greater importance given the global nature of GANs – facilitating face-to-face meetings.

Some top change attributes

Change is a disconcerting and difficult process for most people and organizations. It is associated with confusion and uncertainty that give rise to fears. A GAN will be much more attractive if people see it as supportive and understanding of them as they go through the change.

Some top change attributes

- Supportive
- Patient
- Persistent

This brings back the leadership competencies of supporting ambiguity and paradox. Most people prefer situations that are "black and white." They have difficulty with the concept that people can have very different views, and yet both can be right. One way for a GAN to be supportive is to build capacity for ambiguity tolerance.

Holding to an appropriate pace of change means being both patient and persistent. In his work on personal mastery, Peter Senge has a wonderful image to portray the concept of "holding creative tension." He has a rubber band stretched tightly between two hands, one over top the other. The higher represents the goals, the lower one our existing state. Often during change processes the vision is lowered, instead of the existing state being raised. And often when the existing state is raised, the goals do not change. The role of the GAN is to ensure that there is creative tension, with the goals and the existing state both moving ahead.

Competency 5. Communications – Creating robust glocal conversations and connections

I remember satellite television feeds of the 1980s that connected citizens of the Soviet Union and the United States, to create citizen-to-citizen forums. They had a remarkable impact. For the first time citizens could see and talk with each other without intermediaries, although of course there was some "control." But Americans, for example, could see that Russians could dress stylishly and speak with their own voices persuasively about their lives and views.

Creating global conversations, a key activity of GANs, is greatly facilitated by new communications technologies. These are local–global (glocal), and within each level and across sub-interest groups. However, the surface of new potential is still just being scratched.

Communications knowledge

There are two types of communications knowledge that GANs must possess, represented in Figure 7.4. One is the traditional pre-Web 2.0/social media type. I was a Communications Director for the 1980s in this world when organizations told people things, without an interactive capacity. It includes the rapidly diminishing world of print, and static web-sites. It also includes broadcast media of traditional radio and television with reporters, journalists, and producers acting as intermediaries.

The other type of knowledge is the social media world. Figure 7.4 presents this in order of a community-building sequence that relates to initiating a GAN. Specific tools are good to help listen to understand what is happening in the issue arena of the GAN; others are good for engaging people once the lay of the land is determined; the social content

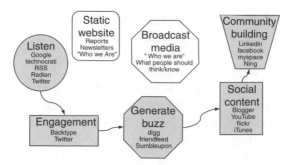

Figure 7.4 Communications knowledge framework

Source: Shaded components text: Kanter, B. (2010). "Nonprofit Social Media Strategy Map." Retrieved April 5, 2010, from http://bit.ly/9wM9y6.

and community building tools are useful even at earlier stages to link initiating participants.

Some top communications skills

Despite the big changes with Web 2.0 and the social media world, some core communications skills remain the same: listening, speaking, writing, and visualizing. However, increasingly important are two other skills. No longer is the focus upon *telling*. Rather, it is about creating conversations between diverse groups. Stimulating and sustaining conversations is an art for both traditional and social media worlds.

In the social media world, the emphasis is on creating robust, dynamic, and attractive community platforms. This de-emphasizes the traditional focus on providing content, in favor of provision of places for people to generate content. Also in the social media world, visual presentation takes on much greater importance.

Some top communications skills

- Listening, speaking, writing, visualizing
- Conversing
- Creating community platforms

One place that this all comes together is with Madmundo.tv, created by the Bridge Initiative in Paris. Patrice has created a marvelous way to create conversation through the Madmundo.tv platform. He begins with an issue and a person who is passionate about a question on the issue. He then supports development of a community conversation and story of the type that binds people across geographic distance.

One of his productions concerned AIDS with the Global Fund to Fight AIDS. A South African AIDS-infected child asked the question "Why must I die?" to G8 participants Gordon Brown (UK Finance Minister), Paul Wolfowitz (World Bank President), and Kofi Annan (UN Secretary General). The questions and responses were videoed and put on the web along with a written explanation. A conversation was then created with others who commented in writing or added their own videos on the web. Out of this, Patrice created a traditional TV presentation.

Some top communications attributes

This approach really emphasizes the value of creativity. The media can be combined in new and imaginative ways that are extremely powerful. The communications creativity of a GAN helps drive the attraction of being associated with it.

Some top communications attributes

- Creative
- Open
- Participatory
- Empathetic

The greatest difficulty for people from traditional organizational life is to let go of notions of control in this new communications world. The communications competency for networks is different from traditional organizations because there are no clear organizational boundaries. The story of the network is the story of its participants. If the network is healthy, there is a high degree of participation in community forums without an attempt to control the conversations. Again, the idea of stewarding them as leaderful co-participants is a good guiding image.

Of course there are certain versions of reality that a GAN will want to produce, but these should be driven by a high degree of participation. Cobus de Swardt of TI took great pleasure in the 2009 TI report. It was produced by the network, and the Secretariat only had a supporting role. It reads like the network's story, rather than an official version of institutional history that is commonly associated with annual reports.

People must be able to see themselves represented in the network's activities and conversations. Being empathetic of course means listening deeply; but it also means being comfortable with people with diverse views who participate in a GAN.

Competency 6. Learning systems: Transforming data to wisdom-in-action network-wide

I began this chapter by explaining that there are three types of competence that are important for GANs: issue, tool, and process competence. GAN participants and others need to deepen knowledge about the issue they are addressing, they must refine and develop new tools, and they must develop a highly effective learning strategy to realize this. The learning systems competency aims to support development of all three of these.

Usually people think of "learning" as something possessed and done by individuals. However, the concepts of the learning organization and societal learning are also relevant. The core goal here is to develop GANs as learning networks. Network learning occurs when: (a) learning is done in order to achieve a network's purposes; (b) learning is shared or distributed by people throughout the network; and (c) learning outcomes are institutionalized in the processes, systems, and structures of the network.[19]

Like the change competency, I find the learning systems competency is very underdeveloped in GANs. This isn't universal, of course. Paul Faeth, President of the Global Water Challenge (GWC) comments: "If we didn't do learning the rest (of the competencies) wouldn't matter." However, in 2007 in Kuala Lumpur we held a meeting of people from GANs who had some responsibility for "learning." Of first note, there were very few GANs that formally assigned the responsibility. Of second note, those who did come said their GAN spent minimal resources on learning. However, GANs typically spend enormous percentages of their staff and money on face-to-face meetings. But these are not thought of as "learning events." They exist as decision-making places and ones where information-sharing occurs with a very technical objective. Rarely are they also organized to build network and participant capacity as part of a well-defined learning strategy.

Learning systems knowledge

In 2003, the Severe Acute Respiratory Syndrome (SARS) virus quickly spread from a visiting international traveler in Hong Kong to the world. After describing this situation, Bill Snyder and Etienne Wenger, both known as gurus in the community of practice (CoP) world, ask: "How

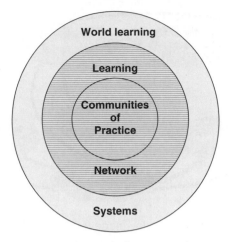

Figure 7.5   Learning systems knowledge framework 1

can we connect the power and accessibility of local civic engagement with active stewardship at national and international levels? What are the design criteria for such a system and what might it look like?"[20]

I find useful the concepts of "community of practice," "learning ecology," and a "world learning system" that are being developed by Bill and Etienne. (The end of Chapter 2 describes CoPs.) As three basic specifications for a world learning system of Figure 7.5, Bill and Etienne identify:

- *Action-learning capacity* to address problems while continuously reflecting on what approaches are working and why – and then using these insights to guide future actions.
- *Cross-boundary representation* that includes participants from all sectors – private, public, and nonprofit – and from a sufficient range of demographic constituencies and professional disciplines to match the complexity of factors and stakeholders driving the problem.
- *Cross-level linkages* that connect learning-system activities at local, national, and global levels – wherever civic problems and opportunities arise.[21]

These are so closely aligned with the work of a GAN that they can be taken as framing a GAN itself as a world learning system. Knowing how to create this is part of the core knowledge of the learning systems competency.

But the learning ecology concept is equally important. Think of all the possible types of activities when learning happens. These are not

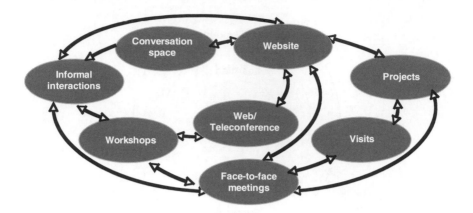

Figure 7.6   Learning systems knowledge framework 2 learning ecology

Source: Snyder, W. M. and X. d. S. Briggs (2003). Communities of Practice: A New Tool for Government Managers. Arlington, VA, USA, IBM Center for the Business of Government, pp. 13–16.

necessarily framed as "learning activities" – sometimes learning is not even the primary goal. However, they can be structured to support learning as an explicitly valued activity. These are virtual and face-to-face interactions that can be one-on-one, sub-group, or community-wide. Figure 7.6 describes this as an interacting set of activities that are framed as learning spaces.

The knowledge of the learning systems competency is about developing these activities and creating synergies and inter-actions with a rhythm and cycle that fits with people's other tasks. The secret of developing such robust systems is to connect people's other tasks with the learning activity, so it supports task completion rather than be experienced as something additional that is expected. In other words, the activities become institutionalized in the processes, systems, and structures of the network.

Using these three concepts can produce a learning network. Peter Senge's definition for a learning organization can be adapted to define this vision as networks:

> ... where people continually expand their capacity to create the results they truly desire, where new and expansive patterns of thinking are nurtured, where collective aspiration is set free, and where people are continually learning to see the whole together.[22]

These activities must address both explicit and tacit knowledge. Explicit knowledge can be written down and easily shared like facts and procedures. Formal education processes, databases, and books are great for sharing explicit knowledge. Tacit knowledge is knowledge that one has but cannot explain, and includes intuitions, values, artistry, and expertise. It is best developed through such activities as dialogue, mentoring, joint problem-solving, and informal exchanges.

However, still missing from this is reference to knowledge management that is a critical associated knowledge domain for the learning systems competency. This includes creating a system that is comprehensive, useful, and accessible. Colleague Thomas Kriese specializes in online communications and social media. He emphasizes the need to think of making documents traditionally kept on individuals' computers for oneself, as documents for a wider community. How these types of issues are handled is critical to supporting a robust learning ecology.

Also there is knowledge about learning technologies that support development of the learning ecology. There is almost no use by GANs of webinars, for example. And there are enormously exciting new platforms that support an individual's learning goals and connect to resources to realize them.

Learning systems skills

The learning ecology is a systems diagram, and a learning network must be competent at developing learning systems. This means understanding the learning needs, the range of activities where learning is or can be an objective, ensuring there is a learning design element when these activities occur, and fitting it within the larger learning ecology to link it as appropriate with other learning activities. Then pay attention to the rhythm of the whole, people's responses, and continually shift as appropriate in response to them and the network's shifting needs.

Some top learning systems skills

- Developing systems
- Learning
- Teaching
- Connecting

This systems development is best done in close connection to the goals and work of the network and its participants. For example, as GANs grow to new geographic regions and engage new participants, those new participants need to learn how to work in a diversity-embracing network.

This systems approach is nicely described by one study stating that "our experience shows that on-the-job training is most effective when it is reinforced through some sort of formal teaching and feedback loop. Although resistance to change is often viewed as a barrier to building new capabilities, almost as many respondents to this survey identified a lack of resources and an unclear vision as barriers."[23]

All of this involves learning and making tacit knowledge explicit. Tacit knowledge is the unspoken and unwritten knowledge represented in learning generated through actions and completion of tasks. In particular, we are talking about action learning (described in Measuring Impact competency) of the network about how to develop the GAN as a learning network. Creating learning processes for the learning itself is a great way to model learning as well.

Action learning is particularly appropriate in a network where knowledge is so "emergent" – GANs are often innovating and cannot find historic "answers" about how to proceed. Action learning provides real-time processes for feedback to quickly integrate the learnings into next steps, all in a peer learning environment. From this point of view, the Kimberley (conflict diamond) Process (KP), for example, is a series of experiments about how to control the flow of conflict diamonds, and weave those lessons into its global network.

A GAN also must be a skilled teacher. Teaching is a more formal exchange between someone who has knowledge and someone who does not. For GANs this skill is particularly important at founding stages, because people either resist, or there is not widespread understanding of, the issue the GAN is addressing or how the GAN is addressing it. For example, at the early stages Transparency had to teach people about corruption in order for resisting institutions like the World Bank to take it seriously. Today TI is still teaching, but now more about how to address corruption. This "teaching" activity has strong connections to the communications and advocacy competencies.

The teaching certainly also happens with more traditional workshops to build GAN participants' abilities. For example, the GRI organizes trainings about its reporting framework and to develop reporting skills and the ability of its stakeholders to work productively across their differences.

The learning occurs in a network way. That means that there is not a central disseminator of knowledge, but rather many depending on the topic. The network emphasizes capacity for connecting people who need to learn with people who have relevant knowledge. For example, in standards-setting networks there should be an easy way to connect experienced people to inexperienced people who are addressing conflicts between business and civil society over some particular standard.

Some top learning attributes

The downside of entrepreneurial often is the "just do it" attitude taken to an extreme. GAN staff are usually too busy "doing the doing." They put little time into looking for the latest knowledge to know whether what they are doing and how they are doing it represents the best strategy. This means lots of repetitive mistakes and repetitive lessons learned. I am still occasionally astonished when people in senior network positions excitedly share a new insight *they* have about networks with the assertion that it is new knowledge, when the insight has been well-documented for years. This also happens with learning professionals. I remember being at an FSC General Assembly when an academic who had just written a book about FSC started to make incredible claims about how unique the FSC was, in total ignorance of the bigger GAN community.

Some top learning systems attributes

- Learning culture
- Relevant
- Wise

All this underlines the importance of creating a learning culture. There is a humbleness associated with such a culture – there is an assumption that even if others do not know something you are trying to figure out, someone has raised the question before or has a piece of the puzzle. Creating a learning culture must start at the top with the most senior people. Often these people give strong double messages, saying that they really value learning, but then are too busy to ever engage in activities that have a strong process learning or even competency development goal.

Part of a learning culture is also being inquisitive. Rather than thinking of yourself (or your GAN) as being the expert and focusing upon telling people things, a learning culture emphasizes the importance of producing good questions and ways to carry on conversations and activities to address them. Often these are conversations over a year or more. With the learning ecology and systems developing skills in mind, these can be sustained when the question is important. In this situation, people who are formally responsible for learning are responsible for sustaining and stewarding the conversation.

Despite its generally positive connotations, learning is derisively referred to sometimes as "learning for learning's sake" or "academic." Ray Stata, the head of the American company Analog Devices, was asked "How do you distinguish between valid learning and specious learning?" He responded "One of the fundamentals is that valid learning does not occur unless you continuously go back to reality. All knowledge is objective in the sense that there must be some correspondence to reality."[24]

GANs' actions are certainly guided by theory – simply defined by the expectation that doing X will produce Y. However, they are fundamentally *action* oriented. The learning system, therefore, is an applied learning system. To be of use and have robust life, it must be relevant to the work of participants. This means that if someone is puzzling about how to develop a multi-stakeholder strategy in China given the dominant role of government, the learning ecology will produce activities to answer the question. Ideally the learning ecology is vibrant and the individuals asking the questions are familiar enough with the options that the learning ecology presents, to activate them.

One way to frame this competency is as the ability to transform data, to information, to knowledge, to action, and finally to wisdom-in-action, as described in Chapter 2. Certainly a robust learning system will not simply deal with data, information, and knowledge. It will deal with questions about the best way to apply these. Values and principles are reflected in people's actions and choices. Wisdom reflects the ability to make difficult choices (which may include no action) while understanding contexts and implications from a whole system awareness.

I see development of wisdom and its spread can be associated with the development of GANs themselves. In their Stage 4 development when they become highly decentralized with strong connections between GANs, a GAN must be able to transcend its own issue to strongly connect to others. For example, although the GWP is focused upon water, as it develops, the connections grow between them and those dealing with climate change, the natural environment, health, and poverty. If a GAN makes these types of connections too early in its development, however, it will lose its focus because its identity is too weak; if a GAN does not eventually develop these types of broader relationships, it will never enter Stage 4. Wisdom is exemplified in knowing when and how to make these choices. A learning system should reflect and support development of that type of wisdom.

Competency 7. Policy and advocacy – Generating tight connections between action and policy

Networks embody two approaches to policy and advocacy. The more traditional is advocating that others change, and urging others to adopt particular policies. Here the network power comes from combining organizations for size and power of voice. The second approach is to gather diverse stakeholders together as peers who recognize that new policies are needed, and to collectively develop them. Here networks act as laboratories where diversity produces innovative, whole-system approaches that can be quickly disseminated through the participating organizations. GANs emphasize the second approach.

Policy and advocacy knowledge

Wolfgang Reinicke, who introduced me to global multi-stakeholder networks, looks at them through a political science lens. He calls a similar group of networks Global Public Policy Networks: "... loose alliances of government agencies, international organizations, corporations, and elements of civil society such as nongovernmental organizations, professional associations, or religious groups that join together to achieve what none can accomplish on its own."[25] He emphasizes their contribution to resolving issues with producing global public policy and goods.

Working with Tariq Banuri (then with the Tellus and Stockholm Environmental Institutes), we built upon this work to produce Figure 7.7. It describes the traditional global public policy making process that produces international agreements and conventions such as the one establishing the Kyoto Accord and the Rio Declaration on Environment and Development produced at the 1992 UN conference. GANs' work can be framed as addressing weaknesses in this process. For example, TAI categorically focuses upon giving life to Principle 10 of the Rio Declaration, which was an empty commitment for most governments.

In the national policy-making cycle there are basically four activities. Citizens (1) express their opinions to their elected representatives, who (2) get together in legislatures to debate what should be done. Legislatures pass laws and regulations that the bureaucracy (3) then translates into programs carried out by multiple organizations to (4) educate, enforce, and take other supportive actions. If there is some controversy with this process, citizens are then able to go back to their elected representatives for changes.

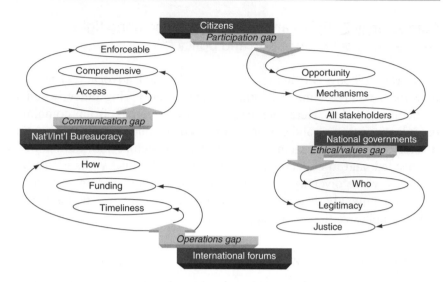

Figure 7.7 Policy and advocacy knowledge framework

Source: Waddell, S. J. (2003). "Global Action Networks: Building Global Public Policy Systems of Accountability." *AccountAbility Quarterly* 20: 19–26, p. 20.

At the global level the underlying institutions such as legislatures, political parties, courts, and regulatory structures are not present. Citizens have almost no options for connecting meaningfully with global decision-making processes, and this is referred to as the *participation gap*. Participants must perceive that what they are participating in is legitimate and incorporate their views. When this does not occur, an *ethical or values gap* arises. The difficulty of identifying and organizing an effective response to implement international agreements gives rise to the *operational gap*. The fourth gap, the *communications gap*, arises as the need to communicate to citizens the global public policy goals and the value of abiding by their norms and rules. This framework summarizes the policy and advocacy knowledge that GANs need.[26]

Some top policy and advocacy skills

As distinguished from mono-sectoral networks like trade associations and NGO coalitions, GANs have a collaborative learning strategy toward policy and advocacy. TAI has probably taken this work the furthest in terms of developing it as a core strategy. Essentially TAI creates learning projects with national governments. This requires the collaborative, peer-learning approach characterized by action learning.

Some top policy and advocacy skills

- Action learning
- Developing policy
- Connecting cross-sector

Of course the GANs must also have expertise in writing and developing policy as well. This includes familiarity with legislative processes and knowledge about when and how to exert pressure effectively. TAI has national coalitions of NGOs that typically include partners with expertise in this arena, and connections to legislators.

To be effective, all this can require fancy footwork in terms of creating cross-sector alliances with government. "TAI members recognize that governments are not monolithic; they are filled with allies and opponents," comments Joe Foti, TAI Associate.

This leads to a diversity of TAI strategies. One is that TAI gains government legitimacy and help because it receives funding from the government agencies such as the UK Foreign and Commonwealth Office. TAI country coalitions find that the national Ministry of Environment is usually interested in working with civil society, because the MoE is usually weak on finance, political power, and science, and *vis-à-vis* the Ministry of Finance. Judges in Argentina and the Ministry of Information in Mexico also have helpful roles.

In Thailand the TAI coalition includes an institute sponsored by the King of Thailand, which gives it legitimacy in government eyes. And in Africa, the TAI–Cameroon representative was asked to speak on the government's behalf at a UNEP Governing Council meeting when the discussion was about adopting the draft guidelines on implementation of P10.

Some top policy and advocacy attributes

For governments a basic question to any advocacy group is "who do you represent?" and "why should we listen to/work with you?" GANs must be seen as legitimate and valuable commentators on policy. This legitimacy is developed in a number of ways. TAI finds that the fact its local coalitions are members of a global network can greatly heighten legitimacy for the local networks *vis-à-vis* their national governments. There is also the question of who to have as members of the local coalitions themselves. They can bring legitimacy because of their history, expertise, constituency, or other qualities.

Some top policy and advocacy attributes

- Legitimate
- Authoritative
- Persuasive

For most GANs one of the most powerful assets is their ability to speak authoritatively on their issue. For TAI this is greatly enhanced by the scientific reputations of some of its national coalition NGOs, as well as the founding leadership of the World Resources Institute. GANs' development of new information and knowledge can also be packaged in particularly powerful ways. For example, most governments pay attention to TI's Transparency Perception Index.

In the end, all advocacy depends upon being persuasive in some form. This might occur because of the sheer size of the GANs' constituency, its insider political connections, its knowledge and information, or its ability to speak effectively. Often a quality of the GAN strategy is to play an "insider–outsider" strategy, by building strategic ties with insiders and providing insider partners an avenue to work outside as well.

Competency 8. Resource mobilization – Growing commitment to global public goods

I was leading a discussion of a half dozen leaders of GANs on the topic of competencies critical to success when we turned to the question of resource mobilization. I was surprised that none of the leaders thought of it as a major issue for them, in comparison to the other competencies.

"But what if you think about barriers to your network really *flourishing* and realizing its goals?" I asked. That moved the issue of financing to the top of the list of challenges.

Resource mobilizing strategies and needs vary greatly with development stages. At the beginning, one or two venture investors usually come forward plus a lot of community volunteer works. With success and growth, the challenge of creating a sustainable business model grows. GANs are still underappreciated and poorly understood, their needs are large, and the global public goods financing systems are weak.

Resource mobilization knowledge framework

Traditional business is funded by profits, government by taxes, and NGOs by donations. Networks are combining all these strategies to build an economic model appropriate for their multi-stakeholder quality. However, how to do this well is still not clear. Moreover, how to maneuver as global organizations in a world where most funding is at best regional also creates challenges.

By far the dominant financing framework is "development." Substantial global network funding comes through taxes with funding from donor agencies like USAID and DFID, and multilaterals like the World Bank. In this tradition, the richest nations have a moral obligation to distribute some of their wealth to poorer ones in the same sort of distributive rationale that drove development of the welfare state.

However, as Ernest Ligteringen who heads up the GRI commented to me, it is fitting a round peg in a square hole. GRI, for example, is not about developing poorer countries' capacity to apply the GRI framework. GRI is about the creation of a global public good for use globally: a sustainability reporting framework. Ironically for many GANs, this means that they are more active in the developing countries than in the richer ones.

This current state of affairs is highly problematic for three reasons. One is that it creates a two-tiered strategy and set of activities for creation of global public goods. It produces a real barrier to creation of truly global public goods. For example, the GWP is essentially a group of rich country funders financing work in other countries. However, water really needs a

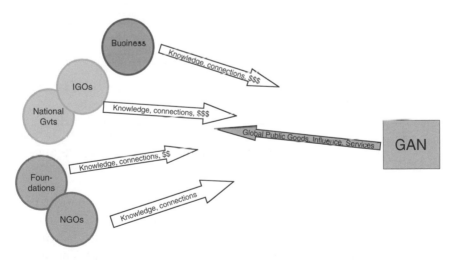

Figure 7.8   Resource mobilization knowledge framework

global strategy. Similarly, TAI finds working in Europe highly problematic because there is a separate European strategy referred to as the Aarhaus Protocol.

A second reason that "development" is an unsatisfactory approach is that it gives richer countries disproportionate power over other countries. There is an unhealthy funder–recipient dynamic that perpetuates concerns about colonialism, rather than a collective problem-solving dynamic.

But perhaps the most pressing problem is that the development framework simply perpetuates a philanthropic attitude to badly needed global public goods production. "Donor" countries are naturally miserly. The long-term – and only realistic medium-term solution as well – is that the development/donation framework be replaced by a global public goods one. The important work of global public good financing must be with categorical national tax transfers for that purpose, or a global tax. The Leading Group on Innovative Financing for Development is venturing into this arena.

Some top resource mobilization skills

Current business models for GANs are not obvious. When they get to Stages 3 and 4 they need to have at least $3 to $5 million in resources for just the Secretariat, and many times that for the network to flourish. Given their work, this is an incredibly small amount of money that they struggle mightily to get. The networks as a whole really need many times that amount to really rise to the challenges that they are addressing.

Some top resource mobilization skills

- Developing business models
- Translating needs into opportunities
- Managing finances

One of the more successful in raising funds is TI. Cobus de Swardt, TI Managing Director, explains they've evolved their business model.

> Our original operating model was everyone is responsible for their own funding so everyone (National Chapters operate in 102 countries) including the Secretariat raises their own funding independently of each other. Then there was the question of due diligence. This meant many of our chapters didn't get sufficient resources and they had to do the same thing 102 times (apply). So what we've changed is twofold.

Chapters remain responsible for raising their own funds, but the Secretariat will be responsible for maximizing the brand and the ability to look at economies of scale and the ability to do the same thing in many countries. So we now raise funds for one proposal for 25 countries. And that translates to economies of scale for donors, for chapters, for us. In the past, if something went wrong in a local chapter, the donor came to us although we had not impact on what went wrong. And what happens in any of the chapters affects our reputation.

Gathering finance information about networks is very complicated, since it requires defining what part of the network the data cover. As networks develop, most increasingly depend upon sub-parts (regional, particular program) raising their own funds. In May 2008, I surveyed 11 networks[1] ranging from 8 to 15 years of age with the initial question:

What was the total income (revenue) that came to/through the Secretariat for the most recent fiscal year including funds that may have gone to other parts of the network?

The response ranged from $500,000 to $11.4 million, with the average of $3.6 million.

But the finance question is also wrapped up in strategy. Being multi-stakeholder, the networks could be expected to have tax-based contributions from government, civil society-based funding from foundations, and revenue generation from services and fees.

Table 7.4 gives responses to the question:

Please indicate the approximate percent of funds that flow to/through the Secretariat that come from the following sources.

Most networks perceived potential conflicts of interest with business revenue generation. One way the Global Compact addresses this is with a foundation to receive business donations; the foundation does not fund core Secretariat costs, but only the broader network.

Strategy also raises Secretariat–network relationship questions. For TI the Secretariat role in putting together up to 30 National Chapters for joint funding proposals increased dramatically in 2010 from less than €1 million a year to more than €5 million.

---

[1] Building Partnerships for Development in Water and Sanitation, Global AIDS Alliance, Global Knowledge Partnership, GWP, GRI, International Federation of Organic Agriculture Movements (IFOAM), Mountain Forum, SFL, TAI, TI, Youth Enterprise and Sustainability (YES).

Table 7.4 Source of funds (%)

	IGOs	Nat Gvt Dev Orgs	Other Gvt	Fdns	Business	NGOs	Individuals	Other
1.	20	75	0	0	3	2		20
2.	0	0	0	80	0	18	2	0
3.	2	79	0	0	10	0	0	2
4.	0	100	0	0	0	0	0	0
5.	5	5	20	0	50	0	0	5
6.	0	0	20	30	5	0	0	0
7.	0	90	5	5	0	0	0	0
8.	0	0	0	50	25	5	0	0
9.	50	0	45	5	0	0	0	50
10.	1	82	1	9	5	0	0	1
11.	0	20	30	0	40	10	0	0
Ave.	7	41	11	16	13	3	0	9

Table 7.5 Reasons for funding (%)

	Donation	Institutional support	Network flow-through	Project	Member-ship fees	Goods and services	Endowment income	Sponsor-ships	Other
1.	3	25	0	72	0	0	0	0	0
2.	2	20	18	50	0	10	0	0	0
3.	0	17	53	21	9	0	0	0	0
4.	75	0	0	25	0	0	0	0	0
5.	0	38	0	37	0	20	0	0	5
6.	5	0	30	20	30	10	0	5	0
7.	75	5	0	10	0	10	0	0	0
8.	0	0	55	20	25	0	0	0	0
9.	0	25	63	2	0	10	0	0	0
10.	0	52	48	0	0	0	0	0	0
11.	0	0	0	100	0	0	0	0	0
Ave	15	17	24	32	6	5	0	0	0

Table 7.5 gives responses to the question:

Please indicate the approximate percent of the types of funding/reasons for funding.

These tables indicate great variety in business models. But the data are very unsatisfactory. We need a bigger database and more analysis with regard to relationship between business model and issues of strategy, stage of development, geographic reach, and Secretariat versus node costs.

An underlying challenge is clearly articulating needs of GAN participants and matching it in some way to the value of the work of GANs. Certainly this relates to the Measuring Impact competency, but it also raises the big issues about who should pay for what. These are still very difficult issues to discuss. Governments can easily shrug off requests because the businesses should pay, business can say government should pay, and NGOs say they are impoverished. By and large, with a very few exceptions like the Gates and Ford Foundations, private foundations do not support global public good production.

Another issue is the way funding is so clearly tied to tangible "issue" outputs. GANs are really process actors that affect issues and the ability to address them effectively. This means that funders are fundamentally "suspicious" of networks and prefer to finance "grass-roots" organizations. Moreover, funding is often restricted geographically. GANs work globally, but funding is often country- or at best region-specific.

One underlying rationale for this fragmented state of affairs is to enhance accountability. The financing GANs like the Global Fund to Fight AIDS in many ways are like investment fund managers, accountable to donors. The importance of their capacity to skillfully manage funds is particularly acute, and a crisis arose for the Global Fund around this very issue. Certainly these large financiers must pay particular attention to financial management, but the other GANs need to pay attention because of the importance of every dollar and euro. They are anorexic and cannot afford any problems due to financial mis-management.

Some top resource mobilization attributes

This state of affairs emphasizes the importance of being persuasive, transparent, and accountable. The GANs generally embrace these attributes, although they take resources to realize. "Making the business case" is a highly popular phrase that does not necessarily easily transfer into global public goods production financing. Paul Faeth, President of the GWC, points out he is competing for funding with issues like health care: "There isn't a lot of money that goes to drinking water/sanitation globally ... there're more people dying from poor drinking water than from malaria/measles. Talking about infrastructure and behavior change ... it's not as easy as giving a shot, nor as straight-forward as a (mosquito) bed-net ... it's very difficult."

Some top resource mobilization attributes

- Persuasive
- Transparent
- Accountable

Persuasion is generally practiced through specific anecdotes and stories, with generalized figures such as hectares of certified forests. These can leave a funder that has a particular geographic community interest cool to the idea of funding a *global* network.

This emphasizes the importance of GANs' local network partners. However, they often find themselves in a conflicting situation. Local partners' work with the GAN often is only a small part of their overall work, and often they want money from the same funders for other programs.

Transparency and accountability find important support with Internet technologies, and generally GANs provide data openly. However, sometimes they find themselves in competition with one another when they work in the same issue arena, which can create some tensions. Some corporations pay to both the Global Compact and to the GRI, for example. As well, the accountability issue can pose challenges because of the diversity and number of stakeholders that the GAN is accountable to. These stakeholders come from very different financial reporting traditions that can make reasonable standards a challenge given most GANs' modest size.

Power, politics, and the competencies

On separate occasions I spoke about the eight competencies with Ger Berkamp, Director General of the World Water Council (WWC), and Peter van Tuijl, Director of the Global Partnership for the Prevention of Armed Conflict (GPPAC). In both cases when the question arose about what may be missing in this framework, they brought up power and politics.

> "The political management of the network . . . it needs taken care of as a political process," said Ger.

> "Capacity to deal with power differences," said Peter. "It misses the political edge – for the network both internally and externally."

Daily both Ger and Peter deal with diverse demands and interests to move the network toward its vision. In their positions they have leadership responsibility with their Boards, major stakeholder groups, and particularly influential individuals.

With "politics and power" they are talking about the ability to mobilize support for and/or opposition to policies, values, and goals. Internally, they are talking about the ability to work with power differences inherent with the array of constituencies in a global multi-stakeholder network. Externally, they are talking about the ability of the network to influence organizations that are not active participants in the network.

However, in a network like WWC and GPPAC, there is a huge gray area of when the power and politics issue is internal and external. Even if an organization is a participant in the networks, the organization does not automatically agree with the network decisions, move to implement them, or even know how to implement them.

Sociologist Amatai Etzioni categorizes power into three types. As voluntary associations the networks have little *coercive* power generally associated with governments. They have little *remunerative* power generally associated with business – they simply don't have the financial or other resources to allocate. They must depend upon *normative* power: peer pressure, persuasion of logic, and moral assertion of what's right and just.[27]

However, others have coercive and remunerative power that they may apply to influence the direction of the network – either in support of the network's goals or to undermine them. This is always particularly worrisome *vis-à-vis* funders, but it can come from others as well. TI has faced the coercive power with intimidation by the Government of Sri Lanka against its chapter there.

Power and politics is a topic of the Leadership competency: how can individuals, groups, and the network share leadership to create a leaderful culture and way of working together? And how do we address powerplay leadership?

Power and politics is a topic for the Network Development competency where the question becomes how to create strategies, structures, and processes to manage power in the interests of the larger network. This involves ensuring and balancing diverse stakeholders' voice and influence.

Power and politics is also a big topic of the Change competency. Transformational change of the type that GANs aim for involves a fundamental change in power and political arrangements. The core work of GANs is to realize a "tipping point" where the values and standards promoted by the GAN become "the norm."

Of course there is lot of overlap among the competencies. Change, Network Development, and Leadership competencies are all needed to clarify, address, and create accountability for contributing to two sets of goals: those of individual participants (organizations, Board members) that are conditions for being active in the network and also those goals of the network to realize its vision.

Developing the expertise

One goal of the competencies framework is to suggest how to organize capacity-building programs for GANs. Business schools are organized around core functional divisions like Marketing and Finance; schools of government are organized around divisions reflected in Ministries such as justice (law), health, and international relations. For GANs, capacity-building programs might be developed around the competencies since they align with trends in the way GANs are actually organizing themselves.

However, capacity-building programs are only one element in developing the needed expertise. And in fact, traditional classroom-based education is not going to get GANs where they need to be with respect to the competencies, although it can have a modest role. Today we are well into development of the life-long learning world. Development of the competencies must be integrated into the daily work of GANs, so they do indeed become learning networks. Communities of Practice, learning ecology, and world learning systems provide powerful frameworks for developing GANs as learning networks.

Because the capacities have to be developed in very diverse settings, they cannot be prescribed as with traditional training programs. They must be co-developed and co-owned. Indeed, as suggested in the Learning Systems competency, capacity-development is not something done *for* others but *with* others. The capacity development itself must be experimental and responsive to changing needs.

Developing capacity depends upon numerous drivers. The traditional focus is upon such things as workshops and alignment of reward systems. However, one report lists 11 internal and 5 external drivers to consider.[28]

One of the drivers is formal structures, processes, and systems. GANs can further reinforce the development of these competencies by creating organizational units, titles and teams associated with them to focus the development of the capacity. GANs will often have something like a department for Network Development (seen with the Network Building Programme of the GPPAC, and titles such as TI's "Governance Manager"). GANs commonly have organizational units for communications, monitoring, and evaluation, something for resource mobilization, often for policy, and sometimes for learning. The Change competency that I find so important really deserves its own unit in my opinion, although I have never seen it. The Leadership competency is the one that does not call out for an organizational unit, although there are innumerable capacity-building programs with that focus.

There are three capacity-development strategies to consider. One is the more traditional "planned strategy." This approach involves targets and crafting achievements to clear objectives, with schedules of activities. It is particularly appropriate when there is clarity about needs and a relatively stable funding source.

The second approach is "incrementalism." This is about adaptability and taking advantage of opportunities as they arise within a program defined by more flexible guidelines rather than fixed targets. This is a good approach when there is greater instability in the general operating environment.

The third approach is "emergence." This is appropriate in a volatile environment. Capacity is developed out of relationships in doing the work. There are not clear objectives, but rather opportunities that are nurtured through information-, knowledge-, and skill-building relationships that grow organically.[29]

Of course in practice there is mingling of these three approaches. In my own experience, the biggest challenge to building these competencies is to create conscious valuing of their development with the necessary reflective spaces. People working in and with GANs are naturally very action-oriented, and they tend to work from the premise that "action = good". However, systems thinking tells us that often actions are counter-productive. Moreover, even when an action is productive, there is value in actually investigating the best tools, knowledge, and strategies for it. And after action, there is value in review and reflection about what was done and how it could be improved. Learning requires discipline!

Notes

1. Center for Corporate Citizenship (2009). *Leadership Competencies for Corporate Citizenship: Getting to the Roots of Success*. Boston, MA, USA, Boston College.
2. Heifetz, R. A. (1994). *Leadership without Easy Answers*. Cambridge, Mass., Belknap Press of Harvard University Press.
3. Bradford, D. L. and A. R. Cohen (1998). *Power Up: Transforming Organizations Through Shared Leadership*. New York, J. Wiley.
4. Drath, W. H. and C. J. Palus (1994). *Making Common Sense: Leadership as Meaning-Making in a Community of Practice*. Greensboro, N.C., Center for Creative Leadership; Drath, W. H. (2001). *The Deep Blue Sea: Rethinking The Source of Leadership*. San Francisco, Jossey-Bass; McGonagill, G. and C. Reinelt (Forthcoming). "Supporting Leadership Development in the Social Sector: How Foundations Can Make Strategic Investments". The Foundation Review.

5. Seagal, S. and D. Horne (2000). *Human Dynamics: A New Framework for Understanding People and Realizing the Potential in Our Organizations*. Waltham, MA USA, Pegasus Communications.

6. Block, P. (1993). *Stewardship: Choosing Service over Self-Interest*. San Francisco, CA, USA, Berrett-Koehler.

7. Senge, P. (2006). "Systems Citizenship: The Leadership Mandate for this Millennium." *Reflections: The SoL Journal on Knowledge, Learning, and Change* 7(3): 1–8.

8. Ibid., pp. 5–6.

9. Hämäläinen, R. P. and E. Saarinen (2007). "Systems Intelligence: A Key Competence for Organizational Life." *Reflections: The SoL Journal on Knowledge, Learning, and Change* 7(4): 17–28.

10. Raelin, J. (2003). *Creating Leaderful Organizations: How to Bring Out Leadership in Everyone*. San Francisco, CA, USA, Berrett-Koehler.

11. Luhmann, N. (1979). *Trust and Power*. Chichester, UK, Wiley.

12. Ashoka. (2010). "What is a Social Entrepreneur?" Retrieved April 2, 2010, from http://www.ashoka.org/social_entrepreneur.

13. Burt, R. (1992). *Structural Holes: The Social Structure of Competition*. Cambridge, MA, Harvard University Press.

14. Krebs, V. and J. Holley. (2002). "Building Smart Communities through Network Weaving." Retrieved April 2, 2010, from http://supportingadvancement. com/web_sightings/community_building/community_building.pdf; Plastrik, P. and M. Taylor. (2006). "NET GAINS: A Handbook for Network Builders Seeking Social Change." Retrieved April 2, 2010, from http://www.in4c.net/index.asp?lt=net_gains_ download.

15. Patton, M. Q. (2010). *Development Innovation: Applying Complexity Concepts to Enhance Innovation and Use*. New York, NY, USA, Guilford Press.

16. Khagram, S., et al. (2009). "Evidence for Development Effectiveness." *Journal of Development Effectiveness* 1(3): 247–270.

17. Ibid., p. 252.

18. IDRC. (2010). "Outcome Mapping." Retrieved April 5, 2010, from http://www.idrc. ca/en/ev-26586-201-1-DO_TOPIC.html.

19. Snyder, W. M. (1996). *Organization Learning and Performance: An Exploration of the Linkages Between Organization Learning, Knowledge, and Performance*. Dissertation, University of Southern California.

20. Snyder, W. M. and E. Wenger (2004). "Our World as a Learning System: A Communities-of-Practice Approach". *Creating a Learning Culture: Strategy, Technology, and Practice*. M. L. Conner and J. G. Clawson (eds). Cambridge, UK, The Press Syndicate of the University of Cambridge: 35–58.

21. Ibid., pp. 36–37.

22. Senge, P. M. (1990). *The Fifth Discipline: The Art and Practice of the Learning Organization*. New York, Doubleday.

23. Gryger, L., et al. (2010). "Building Organizational Capabilities: McKinsey Global Survey Results." *McKinsey Quarterly* https://www.mckinseyquarterly. com/Organization/Strategic_Organization/Building_organizational_capabilities_ McKinsey_Global_Survey_results_2540 Accessed March 10, 2010.

24. Senge, P. M. (1990). Op.cit.

25. Reinicke, W. (1999). "The Other World Wide Web: Global Public Policy Networks." *Foreign Policy* 117: 44–57.
26. Waddell, S. J. (2003). "Global Action Networks: Building Global Public Policy Systems of Accountability." *AccountAbility Quarterly* 20: 19–26.
27. Etzioni, A. (1961). A Comparative Analysis of Complex Organizations. New York, Free Press.
28. Baser, H. and P. Morgan (2008). *Capacity, Change and Performance*. Discussion Paper No 59B. Brussels, Belgium, European Centre for Development Policy Management.
29. Ibid.

CHAPTER 8

Learning from experience: Lessons for success

We've now had two decades of experience with GANs (Global Action Networks). Drawing from that experience, what lessons emerge for anyone thinking of undertaking a global, multi-stakeholder change strategy? Valuing parsimony, eight are described here.

Lesson 1. Change mindsets from organization to network

"Many in GPPAC (the Global Partnership for Prevention of Armed Conflict)," comments Executive Director Peter van Tuijl, "are at the very beginning of knowing what it is to be part of a network. It's something that needs to be learned. The fact that GPPAC is there and provides a school to learn, that is a great function of GPPAC in itself."

In fact, networking as an active verb for global change is something that we are still in early days of exploring. In a great little paper, a networked mindset for social change is described as "working wikily": "characterized by principles of openness, transparency, decentralized decision-making, and distributed action."[1]

Of course networks can come in many forms – some are purposely structured to facilitate control. However, here are six points I find arising from GANs' change strategy.

Share power

"A GAN sits in middle (of the network) to facilitate interactions – not on top of it," comments GRI Chief Executive Ernst Ligteringen. But in this position, GANs have very few carrots or sticks. They really require voluntary energy and enthusiasm. People and organizations have lots of ways they can spend their time and resources. They won't bring all of that to the table, if they don't feel like they have an appropriate amount of influence. Through a *leaderful* culture and liberating structure with an inspiring vision, people become engaged.

An exception to the lack of carrots is with the financing GANs (usually in health care). For them, the challenge to appropriately share power is even greater. Power is traditionally associated with controlling allocation of resources. To avoid this requires emphasizing peer-like relationships and decision-making. One rule the Global Fund has instituted is that both recipient country representatives and donor country ones on the Board must agree to the person hired as Executive Director.

Sharing power requires resisting many learned proclivities. For example, Ernst comments: "Standard-setters have centralizing tendencies." One role of GANs is to point out when participants bring anti-network assumptions and behaviors.

Sharing power means *empowering* stakeholders who have traditionally been marginalized. And for the powerful sharing power means changing behaviors to encourage participation. This often involves building the capacity of the traditionally marginalized and the powerful to interact productively.

And sharing power involves sharing information as well. I recall the huge impact legislation in the US had upon community development organizations aiming to influence banks. Until the banks were obliged to share information, the NGOs could not make the strategic and helpful arguments about how the banks could do better. Alexander Kashumov, with The Access Initiative (TAI) in Bulgaria, further points out that "Trust is dependent on how satisfied the participants are about sharing information. And that's what TAI is mostly about – lessons sharing, information sharing."

Sharing power does not mean denigrating leadership. Indeed, taking a lead is the very heart of GANs' change strategy.

Be accountable, maintain integrity

In a network, peer-like relationships dominate. No one is above questioning by other participants. But accountability must be facilitated through regular meaningful reference during decision-making to not just objectives, but also principles and values. In the hectic action of daily life, these are easy to sideline.

GANs' reputation is one of their critical assets. Often reputation is associated with "brand management," particularly when used in labels to help sell merchandise. When asked about the key qualities for success,

Ania Grobicki, Global Water Partnership (GWP) Executive Secretary, comments: "The first and most important quality is personal integrity. For people to be able to trust what you do and what you say. It's absolutely essential."

The topic of accountability is a great example of the distinction between the GANs as networks of participating organizations, and GANs as a Secretariat that functions much more like a traditional organization. In the latter, there are traditional reporting relationships.

Partner yourself

The networking drive for GANs comes from the scale of the issues they are tackling and the range of participants needed to address them. Paul Faeth, Global Water Challenge President, comments: "None of us in the network is going to have the resources to solve this issue, but we can identify the innovative approach and spread it beyond so lots of people can pick it up and contribute to it."

Particularly when a network realizes some success, it can become inward looking. It may increasingly feel it does not need others. However, we have seen how in Stage 4 growth, openness to partnering with others is critical. This requires listening and identifying opportunities, as well as responding to those proposed by others.

The partnering also means pushing the boundaries about how you work with participants. Cobus de Swardt gave a great example of this, of being leaderful, and of giving up power in preparation of Transparency's annual report. "Some years ago, our annual report had four pages on National Chapters and about 40 pages on the Secretariat. We changed that to reflect the work of our movement, yet it still followed the organizational structure of the Secretariat. This year the report was prepared with very clear involvement by the network and you can't even see that there's a Secretariat."

Acknowledge the roles of individuals and hierarchy

The *dominate* dynamic of GANs is networking, but that does not mean that individuals and hierarchy have no role. Let's remember the Chapter 2 description of networks as entities that integrate partnerships and, in their nodes, hierarchy. They also depend upon energetic individuals to challenge and try new things.

A nuanced balance is needed. In an article titled *The Ignorance of Crowds*, Nicholas Carr writes: " . . . peer production is a good way to mine the raw material for innovation, but it doesn't seem well suited to shaping that material into a final product. That's a task that is still best done in the closed quarters of a cathedral, where a relatively small and formally organized group of talented professionals can collaborate closely in perfecting the fit and finish of a product. Involving a crowd in this work won't speed it up; it will just bring delays and confusion."[2]

Create coherence

Remember that social change networks are about creating alignment in direction and collective energy of all the participants. Don't get lost in trying to coordinate the activities of the network, although you may do that for a subset of participants. In the midst of great complexity a network steward's role is to identify strategic projects that can cause shifts in speed and alignment amongst and beyond direct participants.

Be role-centric

If there is one thing that Verna Allee has taught me through her work with value-networks, it is that networks are not the sum of the organizations within them. Rather, they are the sum of the roles that participating organizations play. The focus is on defining the roles that are necessary for the network to be healthy, and stimulating participating organizations singly or collaboratively to play the needed roles. Understand the role that organizations play *vis-à-vis* the network's purpose, and encourage them to play the role really well collectively.

Lesson 2. Be clear about your theories of change

If you feel uncomfortable with "theory," simply replace the word with "strategy." A wonderful short report in the peace-building field called *Designing for Results* explains that "Theories of change help ... (people) stay aware of the assumptions behind their choices, verify that the activities and objectives are logically aligned, and identify opportunities for integrated programming to spark synergies and leverage greater results."[3] In short, articulating a theory of change is critical for developing effective strategies.

GANs have change theories embedded in their seven-point definition, as described in Chapter 5. Yet, few GANs articulate these or *really* integrate them into their actions. And even fewer recognize the lack of integration or articulate why they have not integrated it.

Some of the basic change theory questions involve *who* you aim to involve. GANs are multi-stakeholder with the change theory that must engage all the system stakeholders to implement their strategy. An articulated exception is with (usually certification/assessment) GANs who have decided not to include government as co-owners because some owners are afraid this will lead to either co-optation or mandatory standards rather than voluntary ones.

Other change theory questions involve *how* you aim to realize the change. GANs are also based upon the belief that a multi-stakeholder platform is needed to realize the change goals. An unarticulated exception to this is with those GANs that do nothing to nurture multi-stakeholder platforms beyond the global level. Their actions suggest that at the local level change is simply a technical matter of applying technical standards, rather than a social matter of changing relationships. Their actions also suggest that a single global platform is sufficient to realize their change goals, which seems highly dubious.

Other change theory questions involve the *what* – the definition of what you are aiming to change. For example, people addressing climate change focus upon carbon emissions and people addressing conflict prevention focus upon civil unrest.

The theories of change are dynamic and change with changing circumstances, with success and with deepening understanding about issues. For example, in the late 1980s in the climate change community there was a debate between wealthy-country NGOs who said the basic problem was over-population of the developing countries. Developing countries said the problem was the high consumption of the wealthy countries. Transcending these perspectives produced the concept of "ecological footprint."

Another example is with the GWP. It framed its original strategy around integrated water resource management. However, even as it realized success in developing application of and capacity for this approach, it realized it was insufficient to realize its vision of a *water secure world*.

Lesson 3. Take an entrepreneurial development and learning approach

Global change of the scale that GANs are addressing is not going to occur overnight or even within a few years. These are multi-decade processes. Moreover we do not really understand how to realize the change goals.

They are highly complex change processes. This emphasizes the importance of taking a development and learning approach. These points are reflected in the following comments.

Berangere Magarinos, former Partnership Manager for the Global Alliance for Improved Nutrition, comments: "You need entrepreneurial mind and to be willing to continual test new things. It's a very risky business, you don't work from manuals, you're writing protocols and frameworks while you're doing it. We learn by doing . . . don't come with just problems, let's talk solutions!"

Peter Eigen, reflecting on the development of Transparency International (TI) says: "TI was not 'designed' by me. We never set out to build a civil society organization. I just got people from everywhere to stick together. We developed guidelines for national chapters . . . right now it looks very logical and coherent, but it was a very organic process."

Marcos Espinal of the Executive Secretary Stop TB Partnership Secretariat explains: "In life if you want to be successful you have to take risk. Just do it and apologize later if necessary. You have to be smart, and not expose yourself. I work with the board . . . rather than fight on my own."

Andre de Freitas, Forest Stewardship Council (FSC) Executive Director, points out: "One of the key changes (since he became ED) is the conscious decision to shift from a hands-on to a more strategic board. It's a fairly natural process, and important to happen. In the past the Board approved national standards, now we have a technical committee to do these things."

Paul Faeth, Global Water Challenge President says: "We learn, connect, invest . . . 'learning' is the most important part. We talk a lot about 'good practices.' "

A development approach also means starting with people where they are – not where you wish they would be. When the UN-backed Principles for Responsible Investment (PRI) began, some suggested that it should set a social–economic–environmental impact and governance standard for the investment industry to commit itself to. Executive Director James Gifford comments: "When we launched, no one would sign a standard. So we have an aspirational framework with principles, not a standard. We wanted to push things along and capture big players. Today we have over $20 trillion in assets signed up to the Principles." Now James is in a new development phase, and focusing on how to raise signatories' commitment to giving life to the principles.

The GANs are very organic, moving organizations as they grow through the four stages identified in Chapter 3. They must have an entrepreneurial, pushy edge. The change they aspire for will never be realized without being pushy. Neither conflict avoidance nor unskillful change management are options.

This requires actions that often seem harsh. People who are good at one stage of development in leadership positions often need to step aside as the challenges and leadership skill needs change. Peter Eigen is already foreseeing his departure from the Extractive Industries Transparency Initiative (EITI): "When someone takes over from me, it will be a more normal manager. In the beginning having to dream up how to operate, you need a totally different personality."

Also as GANs develop, they must change their routines and structures. "You need extremely flexible people, people need to be willing to change the process every six months.... people with large bureaucracies won't survive," comments Berangere who thrives on the change. Many people find the constant change very difficult.

Lesson 4. Keep work focused

"The common ground has to be about members wanting and working to change the system for the better – not just a study group or a research group but a group working for change for the better," says Ritwick Dutta of TAI in India. "Research findings should be the basis of evidence-based advocacy. For the vast majority, research makes sense only if it leads to direct visible changes in their lives."

There are many distractions from this change focus. At one point in TAI, some became overly concerned about the "scientific quality" of the assessment tool and they focused upon its further refinement. However, any tool of a GAN is as good as the change it provokes. The crucial question was "would expending resources on further refinement be the best way we can realize our goal?"

Another great distraction is to focus upon structure. "Don't waste your time with endless discussions on structure such as should this country be in this region," says GPPAC Executive Director Peter van Tuijl. His further reflection that conflict crosses borders all the time points to the disconnect between the question and the issue they are dealing with.

Talking about how to do some specific project in the context of a change theory and specified values is worthwhile. Implementing the projects produces key lessons about how to organize the work. If a project requires engaging diverse local actors, then something is learned about how to do this and should be incorporated into future development. However, theoretical arguments about how a GAN should be organized without sufficient experience is another way people can lose the work focus. The formal structural questions, as emphasized earlier, should follow and draw from experience.

This further emphasizes the importance of *learning as a core part of GANs' work*. This is perhaps the hardest of all lessons, since by nature GAN people are action-oriented. This results in repetitive mistakes and actions that are significantly below strategic optimum – how do you know if what you are doing is the most strategic? That the tools you are using are the best available? That the way you are doing it is the best way of doing it? These questions cannot, of course, be asked for every action and you cannot let the perfect be the enemy of the very good. However, the "just do it" approach often ends up with very inefficient and ineffective results.

Lesson 5. Be comfortable with ambiguity and paradox

Working in global multi-stakeholder change processes means working with uncertainties, lack of clarity, diverse perspectives, and seemingly conflicting goals. I remember from my decade working for a labor union that this situation can actually be one for great creativity and innovation. Sometimes it is actually best not to try to hammer everything out to "be clear." Often as new activities take place and discussions continue, new options simply emerge that transcend original positions and imaginations of what is possible.

Ambiguity and paradox arise from the entrepreneurial quality of GANs. GANs are often trying to do something new, and they cannot reference a "how to" manual. These qualities also arise from the very nature of the "squishy" and "messy" issues that GANs deal with. As Marine Stewardship Council (MSC) Standards and Licensing Director Andrew Mallison comments: "Fisheries science is not exact...how can you measure fish that move? Many factors effect biomass so how do you measure that? And when you have experts not from industry experience, they have trouble envisioning what is 'perfect enough'. (But) our standard has to evolve and in five years the standard will be different and more complicated...how we manage that expectation is important."

But ambiguity and paradox arise simply as a quality of networking with such diversity and without control. Sam Daley-Harris, Director of the Microcredit Summit Campaign, succinctly comments: "When the cat's out of the bag, you don't control the directions." This emphasizes the importance of participants' trust in the GAN, and development of its processes to carry on difficult conversations.

Lesson 6. Keep the appropriate geographic center of gravity

GANs have a complex "glocal" (global-to-local) mission. Usually they begin with a global concern, a global strategy, and some type of global representation. Sometimes they remain there, and become more like global policy networks; the World Economic Forum has established a number of these. However, a GAN is about local impact and this means going beyond global.

Often the next development focus is national, sometimes because the issue and strategy require engaging national governments, and sometimes simply because people traditionally think in terms of national units. But also often the next stop is with organizations like corporations and NGOs that have local and regional activity. Projects are piloted with individual participants or collections of them, and the GAN shifts its focus to more local activity. In the final stage of development, the GAN aims to be pervasive, and this usually requires engaging very local organizations and even individual citizens as well, such as TI is doing with its Advocacy and Legal Advice Centers where ordinary citizen raise corruption complaints.

Georg Kell, Executive Head of the Global Compact, describes this process: "We started practically, leveraging large global corporations with the assumption that with their value chains we would have a big multiplier effect. That's still a good practical strategy. In the meantime engaging SMEs (small-medium enterprises) and building their capacity is key to transforming the economy and that's why our country networks are also focusing upon them. Each year they get a little bit more robust. We are giving even more priority to country networks and they are the main vehicle to engage the SMEs. Now with our current membership SMEs are accounting for roughly 50 percent of the total."

Thinking of this constellation as "global-to-local" will not work. It also has to be "local-to-global." One important quality in response to globalization is the need for putting the local back into a very influential position as explained in Chapter 7 with the policy competency.

Another important goal of GANs is to create a world where globalization works for all. Much GAN action is driven by Albert Einstein's insight that solutions to a problem cannot be resolved at the level that they have been created. Therefore, the GAN is created as a different level in response to a problem in order to influence other levels. This means ending the nation-state based decision-making processes where nations fight for their own interests rather than the global good – in many cases producing global commons disasters and decision-making paralysis. Engaging NGOs and corporations that have other geographic and non-geographic frames of reference is an important strategy.

GANs' usual development process means they shift their geographic center of gravity toward the local. This means that "the global" that started the GAN has to give up power, which is often difficult. But for success, the overriding guideline is "subsidiarity." Subsidiarity describes the principle that a bigger aggregation of participants should only intervene in the work of a smaller aggregation to the extent that it is necessary to achieve a specific purpose. The Council of Europe defined "subsidiarity" as " . . . endeavour(ing) as far as possible to manage affairs as closely to the citizen as possible and to depart from this principle only for reasons of absolute necessity."[4]

For GANs the concept of "citizen" should be thought of in the context of "participants" and the discussion about membership in Chapter 6 on formalizing relationships. Enabling the subsidiarity principle is a development goal of GANs. Sometimes the smaller aggregation (e.g.: national chapter) has demonstrated incapacity and therefore needs help; sometimes it is acting in a way that has negative impact upon others, so that a larger aggregation (e.g.: global board) must intervene.

Georg Kell describes the Global Compact strategy in terms that resonate with subsidiarity: "We focus upon empowering the networks in exchange for them proving that they have the functional capacity to deliver. So the burden of proof is with them. They have to show that they can meet the minimum criteria for what constitutes a network and in exchange for that they get the brand for one year but only for dedicated purposes."

The global–local balance will depend upon the GAN and its strategy. The Microcredit Summit Campaign's core strategy was to create alignment of organizations providing microcredit (practitioners) around specific goals. Sam Daley-Harris, Director of the Campaign, succinctly comments: "We want to know what BRAC (a Bangladesh practitioner) would do, not what the global Council of Practitioners would do. So there was recognition that the nexus of action was the institutions and the clients they'd reach out to, to use a poverty measurement tool . . . that was the smart part of the light touch putting the locus at the institution level."

Lesson 7. Create and maintain sufficient diversity

A key role of GANs is their ability to be boundary-spanner. GPPAC Executive Director Peter van Tuijl comments: "That is the thing in networking, the ability to move from local to global and create configurations of people and organizations that are of value." This takes real, solid work. The participants that a GAN needs to engage to be effective do not automatically come forward. And when they do, they do not naturally know how to interact with diverse partners productively. Ger Berkamp, World Water Council (WWC) Director General, says: "People have sometimes rather different views on how to manage and govern the organization."

Diversity is not just a nice thing to say a GAN possesses. It is an important source of its legitimacy with its issue's stakeholders. As well, it is the driver of innovation. The challenge of diverse views, articulated in a productive process, is the source of new approaches that integrate and transcend traditional approaches.[5] Creating a market for sustainable forest products and a label with credibility required a multi-stakeholder solution.

The diversity issue is a critical staffing one too. A global organization must have a global complexion. But this sets up its own challenges since really tapping the advantages that can provide is complicated work. Cobus de Swardt, Transparency Managing Director, explains: "We have as a Secretariat often failed to really make diversity a strength. We have people from 40 countries working here and we have all the negatives of living in a central European international city (Berlin) and few advantages of having such a diverse group together. This remains a challenge to us."

Cobus sees they need to improve on the personal level by encouraging inter-personal exchanges; on the organizational level by empowering people to do things in different ways; on the process level by tapping much more into "who people are" and what they bring. He believes that this will increase efficiency of processes. "There is no discrimination by design, but by default," says Cobus. "If you don't allow diversity to bloom you discriminate by default."

This value of diversity can again come up against the strategies of GANs. "The challenge of dealing with growth is one of providing consistency," comments MSC Standards and Licensing Director Andrew Mallison. "If you're a client in Gambia, how do you engage with standard? We need global coverage, and consistency anywhere." In fact, this gets back to local versus global standards, and identifying the level of specificity absolutely required for respecting the principle of subsidiarity. For example, MSC works to address small artisanal fishers as well as large corporate ones. How to accommodate artisanal diamond miners is a big concern for the Kimberley Process (KP). Similarly, to be successful the Global Compact and Global Reporting Initiative (GRI) must address the different needs of small and medium enterprise as well as global corporations.

One of the greatest challenges is with language. It produces its own dynamics, explains Tomas Severino, TAI Mexican Team Member: "The regional meetings are especially valuable because we can all speak Spanish, meet people and build relationships, and learn from each other. Global meetings are also important but regional ones have been primary in Latin America."

Lesson 8. Persevere

GANs are not an easy strategy to implement and the issues they address take many years to impact meaningfully. The incremental, small wins are key to recognize and celebrate to keep energy and enthusiasm for the longer haul.

Sam Daley-Harris recalls in late 2009 a series of these types of celebratory events: "We got a video 24 yrs ago about microcredit and the Grameen Bank, and by 1986 we had legislation introduced on micro-enterprise and had 100 editorials on the topic. Yunus (of Grameen, future Nobel Prize winner) joined our Board in '88. In 1994 I attended a breakfast briefing with Juan Samovia (then Chilean Ambassador to the UN) and during the Q&A, I said 'We'd like you to adopt the goal to reach 100 million of the world's poorest families with microcredit by 2005.' He said 'We're not taking any new goals to (1995) Copenhagen (Social Summit) . . . we're repackaging other goals from previous summits.' That was the moment we decided to do a civil society-organized summit. It happened in February '97 with 1400 practitioners. In 1998, a year after our original Summit, the UN passed a resolution declaring 2005 the year of microcredit . . . the year our goal was due. We got marginalized. We had little to do with the Year of Microcredit. Yunus wasn't even invited to be on the Board. It's all back to politics." But the Microcredit Summit Campaigns practitioners' reached their goals in 2007, and established new ones for 2015.

When Cobus de Swardt was asked about impediments to success, he responded with enthusiasm: "There are some challenges that we don't know how to address quite yet. Like all things, it's our own inabilities to push faster. To take political risks that are absolutely essential to accelerate social change. The ability to choose the political risks you are willing to take."

Notes

1. Scearce, D., et al. (2009). *Working Wikily2.0: Social Change with a Network Mindset.* Cambridge, MA, USA, Monitor Institute.
2. Carr, N. G. (2007). "The Ignorance of Crowds." *Strategy + business* (47, Summer).
3. Church, C. and M. M. Rogers (2006). *Designing for Results: Integrating Monitoring and Evaluation in Conflict Transformation Programs.* Washington, DC, USA, S. f. C. Ground.
4. Local and Regional Authorities in Europe (1994). *Definition and Limits of the Principle of Subsidiarity*, Council of Europe.
5. Waddell, S. (2005). *Societal Learning and Change: How Governments, Business and Civil Society are Creating Solutions to Complex Multi-Stakeholder Problems.* Sheffield, UK, Greenleaf Publishing.

CHAPTER 9

Foreseeing a future

Scenario for a plausible future

The year is 2022. The Council of Global Action Networks (GAN) has just completed its week-long Global Biennial. Juanita Tariq, Chair of the Network of Global Health GANs, is pleased. "The governments finally understand that they are only one of the stakeholder groups, and don't have the final say on everything. And we're finally addressing the good of the global commons, rather than dealing with nation-state blocs. They are finally organizing in response to the transnational perspectives of business and civil society."

The week-long event was not called a "meeting," but simply "The Global Biennial." It was not like meetings of United Nations representatives – there were no grand-standing speeches, no need to carefully mete out formal time by nation state and ego, and few back-room discussions of "the real decision-makers." Nor was it like the annual World Economic Forum, with its many panels of experts, keynotes, and the all important hallway discussions. Nor was it like the World Social Forum, with its focus upon defining what to tell others to do, and its chaotic scheduling.

This Biennial was part of a two-year cycle of processes, crafted to bring in diverse perspectives in a sophisticated rhythm of various face-to-face and virtual platforms. "There's still a lot to learn," Juanita reflected, "but this last couple of years was a big improvement over the previous cycle. We've now got a really great group of global facilitators . . . no, they're really process masters, the way they create impressively in-depth dialogue and action with such a variety of interests."

"I think for this next cycle, we've really got to improve the integration across issues. Getting the local, national, regional and global meetings is pretty easy . . . although we've really got to do better with the translation options. But the connections across issues are much more complicated."

In particular, Juanita reflected with disappointment on the connections between the Coalition of Finance GANs and her own Network of Global Health GANs. "Well, it's true that the health GANs had a lot more experience working across diseases and types of care. And we've done pretty well partnering with some other obviously pertinent groupings of GANs like the water ones. The connection between safe and secure drinking water and health *is* more obvious," she thought. "But I think the real problem is that there are so many prima donnas in the finance domain. Big egos and testosterone," she grimaced to herself. "But in health care the common good *is* much more obvious."

People arrived at the week-long discussions not so much in anticipation that this is where "decisions were going to be made," but rather that this is where they would clarify how what they were going to do to address the critical themes. It was framed as a global community planning event, and it was dominated by small group dialogues. Participants were already steeped in local, regional, and issue dialogues and joint Highly Strategic Projects. These were designed as learning projects that also created both social connections across divides and joint experiences to develop collective direction much more easily.

"Energy wasn't such an issue at this biennial," Juanita thought to herself. "It was overshadowed by all the climate change disasters that really pushed up the issue of disaster management and climate change adaptation.

"If only there had been real action on climate change before that final break-through in 2020. By then it was simply too late and now it's all costing us trillions of global credits. But at least it's invigorated the drive to take real action on carbon emissions. The health care GANs are leaving this meeting with real clarity about how to cut their own emissions a further 20% over the next five years. And support for the carbon tax is now strong."

"And the global taxation issue had made significant progress, despite the ongoing bickering between China and the United States. Most of the OECD countries have converted their development aid to global public goods production, and that's really helped. And now we have some decent revenue coming from the global tax on international finance flows. It's really such a tiny amount we're talking about, in comparison to what the financial crises of 2008–2009 and 2015–2016 cost us, but at least we have some real revenue. And the Global Finance GAN council finally has developed a real global strategy and power."

The 2015–2016 crisis was the last nail in the coffin of the financial insiders power elite – the government–finance industry alliance. Unlike 2008–2009 when there was neither a vision of an alternative option nor real political will for change, by 2015 the situation was different. Tax-payers, consumers, asset owners, non-finance industry business, critical academics, and other stakeholder groups were ready and created the political will for a different strategy. That led to a four-year multi-stakeholder Commission on Global Finance that organized stakeholder meetings around the world, did some useful traditional research, and undertook some meaningful action projects. The Global Finance GAN was a major product, and was implementing reforms globally.

"But," Juanita sighed, "we're still going to have lots of difficult dialogue and maneuvering around allocation of funds from the new taxes to the GANs. *That'll* give a lot of energy to our next cycle!"

The next Biennial was scheduled for Jakarta. Competing for hosting the Biennials was beginning to resemble competition for the Olympics. "This year's Santiago sponsors did a really great job. I think Samuel was probably right, that the atmosphere of the meeting is somewhat a cross between the Olympics and meetings of the G-20. I really look forward to coming to the next one," Juanita realized with a bit of surprise.

Challenges to the scenario

Of course this scenario is highly speculative. It's designed to stretch imaginations about how we *might* organize ourselves to make globalization work for all. For this future to become more likely, there are some significant challenges that need addressing.

Challenge 1. Increasing competence

Cobus de Swardt, Transparency Managing Director, provides a self-critical view: "We have not delivered on the pace of professionalization." He is similarly critical about the ability to create much more inclusive processes. "I saw a beautiful picture of a car of 2015 that was designed using open interface where everyone could log in and add their ideas. (By contrast) our interface, and this I believe is true for civil society at large, is a very old-fashioned one that is not truly an empowering one so people feel that they are really shaping the agenda."

Similarly, World Water Council (WWC) Director General Ger Berkamp, asked about on what they need to become really good at to realize their goals, responds: "How to become more effective with this wide range of stakeholders, and how to build with them an approach that leads to more action-oriented results from their work together."

What we have now, to use the vernacular, is GANs v1.3. We've got the outline of what GANs look like and significant experience with them, but to take us to 2.0 requires dramatically increasing the competencies as described in Chapter 7. The fact that we are at such an early stage of developing good methodologies for measuring impact, for example, is a great indicator of GANs' level of development. How do you make really good decisions and identify priorities, if you don't have good information about what works?

This requires a significant effort. In Chapter 1, I pointed to the history of development of schools of business, public administration, and for NGOs. Today for GANs, in terms of the competencies, the focus is still on "Network Development," a little bit of Leadership, and people with change expertise are pushing to be recognized. The others are remarkably underdeveloped.

This effort is about developing new knowledge, but the real focus must be on work-based development. This is much more speedy, it reinforces the badly needed learning culture, and ensures the knowledge is useful.

However, today many GANs are so dominated by such powerful "do is good" cultures that they cannot integrate learning and reflection to ensure that what they do is the smart thing to do. As only one illustration of this: I was introduced by the head of one GAN to a staff member in very laudatory terms, with the suggestion that the staff member talk with me about their network development strategy. When I got back to the staff member, he explained that he could not talk until an event he was helping to organize was over – in four months! I suggested that if we talked, it would probably cut down on his work because I could share some knowledge. He said "Yes. But I don't have time to talk".

Challenge 2. Realizing scale

Can GANs get large enough to realize the tipping point? And how large is that? Do we measure big by numbers of participants? Market share? Global reach? Is the "tipping point" theory a valid one, or will even a few global commons poachers be able to wreck havoc on the issue areas? Can GANs grow to realize the influence they aspire for? Can they do it fast enough?

Although leaders in the GANs are enthusiastic about their work and achievements, they also realize they are far from their objectives. Cobus de Swardt, Transparency Managing Director, says: "From where we are now at this level with TI to get our issue over the tipping point, we need to build our organizational capacities a lot and even if we were

10 or 100 times bigger we would still not get our issue over the tipping point."

Global Reporting Initiative (GRI) Chief Executive Ernst Ligteringen comments: "We need a sea change, quantum leaps. . . . this stuff is urgent. It's still too much about whether or not it should be voluntary. It should be about 'can we afford to have companies impose costs on the global commons?' And if the answer is no, how are you going to come to a good strategy to address that? If voluntary is sufficient, I'm in favor. And I think best practices and innovation, that is voluntary, you can't legislate that. But the floor, that I've never seen voluntary. Why the shyness to say this is serious?"

Julia Marton-Lefevre, Director-General of the conservationist GAN IUCN with 1,100 members comments: "Our membership can grow much larger, of course, but we will need to be careful not to threaten the cohesion of the Union." And yet, on a global scale, 1,100 NGO and government members seem very modest.

Most of the GANs are only now at an age where the scale question is really pressing. Are there assumptions and histories that inhibit our imaginations about how to reach the scale needed? Whether GANs can be sufficiently imaginative and aggressive with Stage 4 challenges remains to be seen.

Challenge 3. Avoiding bureaucratization

One big drive for the development of GANs is their promise for decentralized, network action that can be highly efficient and accountable. However, we do not have great models of doing this at the global level at scale. The default is to go back to what you are used to and that people understand, which is institutional bureaucracies.

Berangere Magarinos, former Partnership Manager for the Global Alliance for Improved Nutrition (GAIN), sees two options for its developments: "Compared to others in our field, GAIN has good financial capacity, but the smallest delivery capacity. Our model was to deliver programs through partners, but the problem is partners have other programs to deliver. We can either become the UN of nutrition with field offices, or you work through the network mentality. But right now the network is not very rooted where the issues are."

The GANs will often face this type of challenge. Even when they have rooted networks, there is a chance that with change of a few top leaders who feel more comfortable with hierarchy than network, things will tip to hierarchy. Concerns about standardization and control can become calls for centralization. Desire for growth in numbers can push out the innovative spirit.

The "inter-governmental organization" secretariat model has been very influential in GANs' development. Although elements of it are very useful at a certain stage of a GAN's development, it can inhibit development through Stage 4. The goal of being successful as an institution may dominate the original vision.

Georg Kell, working so intimately with the UN, has fully experienced these dangers. He says his biggest concern is "... to avoid being captured by individual governments and the UN bureaucracy. I spend much of my time making sure the special space we've developed over the years is maintained. We have to avoid being captured by individual governments, the bureaucracy and its inter-governmental machinery that would suffocate us."

Challenge 5 argues that governments must be more engaged in GANs, but one downside is that this could further support bureaucratization. Government members naturally feel more comfortable with that model. In their search for legitimacy and funding, the GANs face demands to be conventional and like other organizations. Their distinctiveness can be worn down by the pressures to be like others.

The bureaucratization is also expressed with the debate between being a movement and being a management system. Living and organizing the latter is much more comfortable for most people than the former. The chaotic craziness associated with movements can be chased out in favor of the safe predictability of bureaucracy and management. GANs combine both movement and management system, efficiency and effectiveness.

Challenge 4. Defining "successful business models"

Can GANs create income sources of sufficient scale and predictability? GANs should be lean because fat will further support a bureaucratization. However, most GANs are anorexic. They have incredibly ambitious global change goals, and budgets of a few million dollars. A big notion driving their business model is their ability to leverage, influence, and access the resources of others. They are doing this pretty well considering such things as voluntary time contributions of all the participants, but how does that fit with a business model and their actual needs?

The basic elements of the business model are voluntary and project-based financing. Applying the multi-stakeholder logic to funding suggests tax funding from governments, private sector donations and sale of some services, and civil society funding from foundations.

Current models are all over the map. The Global Water Partnership (GWP), founded and supported largely by Northern funders, raises money from wealthy-country national governments and channels most to Regional Water Partnerships. The country level participants then raise money from their national governments and ODA (overseas development assistance) with country-level focus.

Ernst of the GRI comments: "We jump through all kinds of hoops to get ODA money. But it's really a square peg in a round hole. And governments are not interested in new funding schemes (like global public goods)."

Another problem for GANs is to have balanced support from stakeholders, to maintain their independence. When governments see large corporations are members, they often justify their own lack of support by saying that the corporations should be funding the GAN.

Andre de Freitas of the Forest Stewardship Council (FSC) points to another option. "We had some hard choices . . . one was increasing our fees and we made an assessment and concluded that our system was undervalued and so we made a significant increase in fees, doubling the fees for most certified companies. But are we sustainable now? That depends on how able we will be to resource our network in the future."

The Marine Stewardship Council (MSC) model currently is to raise half its budget from certifiers and half from foundations. The Global Compact has created a trust fund to accept donations from corporations at arm's-length for projects, and funds the core operating expenses through grants from governments. "We follow the 'Obama model' with many small contributions," explains Georg.

But the products of GANs are global public goods. GANs have arisen as a new and better way to produce them. As GAIN's Berangere says: "You can use grant money to start processes, create awareness . . . . but as soon as that's done, you have to think of sustainability . . . " GANs have gone through their pilot start-up process demonstrating their capacity to produce global public goods. The current approach is no way to finance them long-term. Without a different approach, GANs will have a hard time realizing their potential.

Globalization has brought enormous economic benefits. But it heightens stress on many systems from environmental, social, and justice perspectives. These new demands must be addressed by funding strategies that are sustainable and predictable.

One action in this direction is the campaign for a Global Framework for Action on Water and Sanitation. The campaign basically is calling for something like the Global Fund to Fight AIDS with a common fund for the water and sanitation sector.

In the late 1970s one such scheme was proposed by Nobel Laureate James Tobin. He described a tax that would limit speculation and fluctuations on foreign currency markets. A 2010 review pointed out: "There is a total flow of USD777.5 trillion. With a minimal impact on transactions caused by the introduction of such a tax, a levy of 0.005% would guarantee approximately USD33 billion for solidarity programmes to combat hunger and extreme poverty."[1]

Another approach is already helping the comparatively well-funded health care GANs, including Stop TB and the Global Fund to Fight AIDS. In 2005, some countries participating in the Leading Group for Innovation in Development Financing began applying a small tax on international air travel, with the funds dedicated to "scaling up access to treatment for HIV/AIDS, malaria and tuberculosis primarily for people in low-income countries, by leveraging price reductions for quality diagnostics and medicines and accelerating the pace at which these are made available."[2] In its first 2 years it raised $730 million. In January 2010, voluntary contributions were promoted with most ticket purchases; McKinsey estimates the voluntary contributions could produce another $1 billion annually. The tax and voluntary contribution levied with support of private business is the type of multi-stakeholder model that could provide sustainable and predictable financing for GANs.

Challenge 5. Engaging government

The recipient of this new flow of funds from air travel – UNITAID – is a weak form of a multi-stakeholder partnership. It reflects the traditional problem that GANs have with engaging governments: government's assumption that they should control. The UNITAID Executive Board is composed of eight people from participating governments or their agencies, and only three from other organizations. Can GANs engage government as a peer amongst diverse stakeholders? Will governments be willing to be a peer?

When governments enter a GAN field, one GAN leader commented that sometimes they have the attitude that: "We're the big boys, we'll take over now. And later they discover that taking over is not so easy or effective, and their appreciation for the GAN's work increases."

Governments' argument is that they should control because citizens elect them and they are the only organization accountable to all. Moreover, in the case of the travel tax, they are accountable to the citizens who pay it. This is pre-globalization and pre-GAN thinking. Globalization has ushered in the need for global public goods, and there is no global government to vote for. For a national government to say that it individually, or any collection of them, is/are solely responsible for the production of global public goods is simply disingenuous. GANs have arisen because governments have not proven able to produce them.

Nevertheless, taking the position that governments should not be involved in GANs is equally nonsense. "We need government back at the table," comments Auret van Heerden of the Fair Labor Association (FLA), which does not have government formally as a participant. "There are systemic problems in many markets that government needs to address." As an example, he refers to FLA's attempts in Northern India to address corruption in social security and to include provisions so migrant workers can transfer benefits.

Some GANs specifically exclude government from membership, concerned about inappropriate influence or, in the case of standard-setting ones, that voluntary schemes will be seen by industry as mandatory ones. But this produces very odd "stakeholder" outcomes. For example, the FSC does not have government members. However, government not only has a critical policy-setting influence in forest issues, but it also literally owns most forests and is a major consumer of forest products. This means the FSC is considerably less than a "whole system" entity, and that it is deprived of some significant strategic options well short of mandatory standards.

The Compact's Georg Kell comments: "We had to prove at the country-level that a voluntary initiative is not a substitute for what governments do, nor does it compete with governments . . . it's a complement to good government efforts. Voluntary initiatives often fill governance voids . . . of what governments don't do." Indeed, that is what research suggests. After looking at some GANs, Pieter Glasbergen concludes that GANs help governments more effectively realize their goals. And for GANs: "There are two reasons why GANS perform better when they are able to involve governments and international organizations in their mission and activities. First, mainstreaming of concepts can only be realized by governments or by their recognition of the private governance mechanisms as an alternative tool to solve a collective action problem (such as production of global public goods). Second, governments are also important because most GANs operate in an issue field with many competing private and public initiatives ... and the competition poses a threat to their performance. It requires a form of meta-governance that only governmental organizations can deliver."[3]

On the other hand, Georg echoes the fears of some of the GANs like FSC when he says his biggest fear is "that governments embrace us too strongly. We have a principle-based versus legal compliance approach."

There are some innovative ways in which GANs are experimenting with engaging governments. Both Transparency International (TI) and the GRI gain global legitimacy with government through their formal relationship with the Global Compact. At the GRI, Ernst does not have government members, but is experimenting with a government advisory group. The MSC indirectly engages government, by using standards of the Food and Agriculture Organization (FAO). "FAO compliance isn't of direct value," says Andrew Mallison, Standards and Licensing Director, "But there's 'green insurance/cover' with the NGO community. And (for business) it provides evidence that our standards are recognized."

The Kimberley Process (KP) with conflict diamonds might provide an outline for the future. It obtained a UN resolution of support to give it global credibility with government. It then developed a structure with governments, business, and NGOs as members, including nations producing 99.8 percent of the world's diamonds.

The Principles for Responsible Investing (PRI) are similarly endorsed by the General Assembly of the UN. It also has a memorandum of understanding between the two UN partners and a UK-based charity (the PRI). The charity is tasked with fulfilling the objectives of the partnership including reporting to the Secretary General annually. Its Board is 11 representatives from asset owner signatory organizations and 2 representatives from the UN.

For the Compact, Georg sees two other particular potential issues with government. "If the world were to turn inward and protectionist, the Compact could not function. If we turn national or too regional, forget about it."

Challenge 6. Becoming glocal

What does a network that is truly global-to-local and vice versa look like? How does it function? Peter Van Tuijl at the Global Partnership for the Prevention for Armed Conflict (GPPAC) points to a relatively easy but important point: "At the very first GPPAC International Steering Group meeting I attended I said the network cannot be represented at the global level by two white Dutch males." As one measure to address this situation, the Chair, Emmanuel Bombande from West Africa, became much more active.

But there are systemic and cultural hindrances to GANs becoming global. One problem is the United States. Compared to most countries, it is much more inward-focused and its organizations are more difficult to entice into partnering. The Global Compact had to work for years to make inroads because of American companies' fears about litigation if they signed the Compact's principles. China and the Arab countries present real challenges when trying to organize a multi-stakeholder platform since the governments are so dominant. This is one reason that the Extractive Industries Transparency Initiative (EITI) put Tunisia on the back burner for membership. The global imbalance between wealthy and poor countries also creates problematic dynamics. The countries implementing EITI's standards are from the latter, and financial supporters are from the former. Norway is in both camps, but Australia and Canada, for example, are just supporters. This division is also an important dynamic in the health GANs and the GWP.

Peter at GPPAC further points out: "You cannot be global only. Then you are floating. We know enough people who are completely absorbed by global processes, but lack any form of national accountability. You must make the connections between local, national, regional, global. If you miss local you really miss something." GANs are now making progress in this direction. The Climate Group is much more active with state/provincial/city governments than with national; Transparency is now expanding to have local Advocacy and Legal Advice Centers; and the Global Compact's national networks are embracing small and medium enterprises. Stop TB Partnership's Marcos Espinal illustrates their own shift to local: "In Uganda . . . we knew there were three districts where it was not reaching people, and that there were three NGOs in those districts, so we brought them around the table and in the end the NGOs took responsibility to help and facilitate for the government TB treatment."

Challenge 7. Maintaining the cutting edge

Innovative people and organizations often get worn out. Can the GANs maintain a cutting edge? They need energy and drive. Ernst at the GRI, reflecting on the lack of action at Copenhagen's 2009 climate conference, comments: "This is the time to push on! People started visionary and now there's the demand. The business response to climate change is 'timid' and 'sleepy'." They also need productive conflict. The founding innovative drive for GANs comes from the conflict of perspectives and people's commitment to work together to transcend them. But as they get to know each other, the energy can deflate into politeness or become flat from familiarity. Constant renewal is important, which emphasizes the importance of vibrant Board election processes and processes to expand and bring in new perspectives.

Pushing for scale and quantity can also water down the cutting edge. GANs have to ensure that they compose organizations that are pushing for significant change. Georg Kell Executive Head of the Global Compact says being choosy is important: "It pays to focus upon quality, which ultimately drives quantity. Initially in the Compact we were just focused upon numbers – let's get from 300 to 500 (companies), but soon we discovered that stressing the quality notion makes the (Global Compact) brand that much more attractive and its value so much greater. The network managers can then leverage the brand that much better and are in a much better bargaining position when they discuss partnership. And globally it's much easier to recruit companies when their brand conveys quality. We made pretty tough decisions recently on delisting companies that failed to communicate their progress (on implementing the principles – a member requirement). In some countries like the Philippines and Mexico membership fell by up to 80%."

GANs must continually survey their issue arenas for emerging people and ideas and actively recruit them or they will be replaced. Can they resist the seductive siren calls to become "institutions" and to continue to be audacious with goals, break rules, and push boundaries?

Challenge 8. Managing competition

Competition comes in two forms. One is external, typically with unisectoral schemes such as the Sustainable Forestry Initiative (SFI) of the American forest industry. At times, these can gain a multi-stakeholder complexion, such as with the International Organization for Standardization (ISO) which is really a business services organization but does a reasonably good job of integrating stakeholder consultation into its standard-setting processes.

NGOs also compete with GANs. Will Martin, MSC Chair, comments: "Some NGO programs are trying to mimic MSC but they are not independent third-party assessment programs, and they often are more focused on penalty than reward. The NGO itself makes its subjective assessment of a fishery. Sometimes, this assessment is a continuation of their campaign against a particular fishery or fisheries . . . the focus is too negative, with too much emphasis on 'failing' a fishery. Some of these programs give a green listing to only a handful of fisheries, with the rest either yellow or red. The obvious message is negative, punitive. Ours is a totally positive program that is focused only on recognizing and rewarding sustainable fisheries. We don't attack bad fisheries, we promote the good ones. There are so few situations in life where a totally positive approach works, but I think the MSC program falls into that category."

Can GANs respond to this form of competition? The evidence suggests "yes," although they need to become more skillful with their response. Their core comparative advantage is their multi-stakeholder quality. This greatly broadens their legitimacy. As well, it provides them with unique marketing leverage as their members also represent consumers. For example, fair trade has been quite successful in a campaign for local government in the United Kingdom to integrate fair trade standards into their purchasing policies. This multi-stakeholder advantage is also proving potent in competition between SFI and the FSC labels.

Another form of this external competition is perhaps more worrisome. This can be referred to as the "Corporate Social Responsibility (CSR) challenge." Typically CSR is based upon the notion that a business or modest collection of them can take the high road and shift the standards within an industry. This is a version of the "tipping point" theory. However, this has proven extremely difficult.

Why this CSR challenge is worrisome is illustrated with the Chapter 1 story that I presented of the Fair Labor Organization (FLA) in Honduras. It appeared a resounding success. The company not only re-hired its 2,000 workers with compensation, it also agreed to phase out "collective pacts" covering 8,000 other Honduran workers. These were seen as anti-freedom of association, and their elimination allowed for unionization in all facilities. But FLA's Auret van Heerden says: "Right now we have a pretty gloomy picture where global supply and demand that undermines standards like wages. So while the company has been forced to open the factory, I'm not sure that factory is viable. The company may be forced to subsidize it for a while because politically they have no choice. But I don't know that it's a sustainable solution." Buyers need to agree that price is not the sole concern, governments need to ensure a living wage floor, and companies need adopt a CSR strategy. Can GANs meet these conditions?

This brings us to the second form of competition: between the GANs themselves. Both the Global Compact and GRI are promoting frameworks and strategies that include labor rights. In the labor rights arena specifically, there are:

- The International Labour Organization (ILO), distinguished by its formal government participation in addition to NGOs, labor, and business that make up the three other GANs;
- Social Accountability International (SAI), distinguished by a workplace/plant-level certification strategy;
- The FLA, distinguished by a buyer-driven strategy of American universities that want the goods they sell to meet certain standards;
- The Ethical Trading Initiative, distinguished by a strategy focusing upon supply chains of major corporations.

As the GANs push for membership expansion, the NGOs and corporations in them are going to increasingly raise the questions about why there are so many and why they would want to participate in several networks. That question was the original drive behind the founding of the GRI with respect to triple-bottom-line reporting.

In the water arena there also are many GANs and other global actors. Ania Grobicki, GWP Executive Secretary, comments: "In the water arena you've got a multiplicity of more actors emerging, so we have to find new ways of cooperating and creating coherence. Developing countries face a bewildering array of organizations operating at the global level."

Can the GANs working in the same issue arena collectively reassess their learnings and strategies, and to think how to really scale up for impact? That doesn't necessarily mean a merger, which in many ways is contrary to "network thinking." It might be best to have relatively distinct strategies and networks, but with a collective understanding of how they relate and their "piece" of the puzzle. This is already happening to some extent with the GRI-Compact relationship defined in a Memorandum of Understanding.

In a pre-network organization world, the *interests of organizations as institutions* are dominant. In a world of multi-stakeholder global networks, the *vision for an issue* like labor rights is dominant and that is the reason organizations become participants. The central question might be: "what is the role of each GAN in the issue arena?". What *roles* do we need filled for the labor rights-and-corporations domain to be healthy? Undoubtedly the lessons from networks to date would reveal these, and provide the basis for developing a more effective collective strategy. (One way to get at this role question is through Value Network Analysis described in Chapter 4.)

Challenge 9. Building accountability, reputation, and legitimacy

Can GANs develop their role of responding to people's and organizations' emerging global action needs? Can they respond to the diversity of perspectives and needs, in ways that build their reputation? Successfully dealing with these challenges requires GANs becoming much more sophisticated with communications and action development processes, and greatly increasing the numbers of participants.

We are still "stuck" in a relatively formal interpretation of "democracy" at the nation-state level that equates it with the dominant Western paradigm with multi-party systems and one-person-one-vote. There is a tendency to import this interpretation into the workings of GANs with the rationale of "accountability." But this mis-construes the role of GANs, and will condemn them to the same problems with bureaucratization and politicization that they were formed to address.

From the corporate side, there is a focus upon relatively short-term and linear outcomes. The concept of "brand" has gained significant traction with GANs. But simply imported from the corporate world this can, in fact, undermine the glocal and diversity strategies of GANs. Behind corporate branding is centralized standard-setting. GANs have to be particularly careful about the subsidiarity nature of decision-making, and distinguish between detailed corporate product-definition branding and branding around principles. They cannot allow efficiency concerns to become the major driver.

On the other hand, the civil society side promotes a focus upon processes of engaging the marginalized, giving them equal voice, and creating long processes of discussion to determine action. Particularly well-developed are consensual mass actions of coalitions to pressure others to change. This is indeed important, but simply importing those mechanisms to GANs will undermine their collaborative action logic.

Successfully addressing the accountability, reputation, and legitimacy challenge will integrate and transcend these valid distinctive traditions. This challenge is one that really requires successfully addressing all the other challenges.

Trends supporting the scenario

As well as challenges to the scenario opening this chapter, there are trends that support its development. These are pressures for change to the status quo and historic decision-making processes and institutions.

Trend 1. Continuing globalization

Globalization – the process of developing transnational inter-connectedness socially, politically, and economically – is increasing. Consider these ways of describing pressures and trends for creating global strategies.

- There are an estimated 214 million international migrants in the world today (2008) and migrants comprise 3.1 percent of the global population.[4]
- In 2008, transfers by foreign worker to their home country were estimated at USD 444 billion worldwide, USD 338 billion of which went to developing countries.[5]
- In 2009, an estimated 1.02 billion people were classified as undernourished, 12 percent more than in 2008. Almost half the world – over 3 billion people – live on less than $2.50 a day.[6]
- After years of stagnation, health assistance from industrial to developing countries has risen sharply over the past decade, setting a record in 2007 of nearly $10 billion. A major factor cited was health care GANs.[7]
- January 2000 to December 2009 was the warmest decade on record. Throughout the last three decades, the surface temperature record shows an upward trend of about 0.2°C (0.36°F) per decade.[8]
- Extinction rates (of plants and animals) are rising by a factor of up to 1,000 above natural rates. Every hour, three species disappear. Every day, up to 150 species are lost. Every year, between 18,000 and 55,000 species become extinct. The cause: human activities.[9]
- Annual total merchandise trade growth rate from 2000 to 2008 was between 12 and 16 percent.[10] In 2009 trade declined 12.2 percent, and was projected to increase by 9.5 percent in 2010.[11]
- Between 2000 and 2010, some 13 million hectares (the size of Costa Rica) of forests were converted annually to other uses, such as agriculture, or lost through natural causes.[12]

These are big changes and challenges that require global strategies. But let's not forget the other side of the equation: globalization also presents opportunities to create a much more equitable, healthy world of connections. History suggests that these opportunities have an irresistible allure.

Trend 2. Inability of traditional strategies to address globalization

Is it reasonable to expect international government organizations like the UN and the World Bank to be able to address them? History suggests no. Think of the difficulty of *arriving* at agreements – Copenhagen and failure to reach a climate accord, the financial crises and appropriate change, and the continuance of war. And also think of the difficulty of *giving inter-governmental agreements real life*, such as with the Kyoto Accord, the Convention on Biodiversity, and the 1992 Rio Declaration on Environment and Development.

It also seems unreasonable to expect business to be able to address these challenges. We tried that with the rise of the Washington Consensus[1] in 1989 that led to promotion of business as the lead agent in solving critical issues. That brought on rising inequality and increasing environmental problems.

In the language of international bureaucrats and academics, we are in the midst of a "global governance" crisis. What they mean in everyday language is that things are out of their control (probably a good thing), spinning in a direction that does not spell a pretty future for anyone (although some people think that they individually will do well), *and* that no one knows what to do about it (which is a really big problem).

Of course governments and business have important roles in developing the solutions, as do NGOs. But let's be reasonable about what we can expect of them working on their own. This situation can be compared to the period preceding the rise of today's nation state. John Ruggie, referring to work by Garrett Mattingly, says that "... he shows persuasively (that) the modern state did not *evolve* from earlier experiences; rather, it was *invented* by the early modern Europeans."[13] We need to invent new ways

---

[1] The term "Washington Consensus" was initially coined in 1989 by John Williamson to describe a set of ten specific economic policy prescriptions that he considered should constitute the "standard" reform package promoted for crisis-wracked developing countries by Washington, D.C.-based institutions such as the International Monetary Fund (IMF), World Bank, and the US Treasury Department. Subsequently, the term has come to be used in a different and broader sense, as a synonym for market fundamentalism.

to approach these challenges and opportunities, and GANs represent one of those inventions.

Trend 3. Disruptive impact of new technologies

Sometimes the impact of technology is overblown, but at times it has the power to fundamentally shift societies. Think of the impact of European ship and navigation technology on North American aboriginals; the role of the car on people's relationships and lifestyles; the role of the printing press on education and communications. All of these examples provoked fundamental changes in the way we relate to one another, opportunities, and the way we organize society.

By new technologies, I am referring to our transformed ability to gather, manage, produce, and exchange goods and information. In terms of societal impact, particularly important are information and communications technology revolutions that began with the personal computer. Access to information is power, and its increased availability is changing power structures. The role of mobile phones in displacing people who were intermediaries between agriculture producers and markets has had a profound impact. Being able to learn about market prices and directly connect with retailers and consumers has led to great shifts in power and wealth to the producers.

The impact of social media and the low-cost of communications facilitate more easily developing relationships across geography. The geographically bounded government organizations are going to be big losers in the power shifts this portends. We must find new ways of asserting the common good. We are already developing strategies with the help of communications technologies. GANs can be an important part of the solution, since the communications technologies so obviously support their network strategy.

Trend 4. Shifting assumptions about the way the world works

Perhaps the most important impact of these first three trends is that they are changing the way we see and think about the world. In the chapter on change, I referred to Thomas Kuhn who popularized the concept of "paradigm shift." These shifts occur when we change basic assumptions about the way the world works, and our theories that guide our action. As an illustration I described the impact for Europeans when they shifted from thinking of the world as flat to thinking of it as round. These sorts of shifts are critical to our future directions.

I see six important ways that people's thinking is changing. Collectively, these six changes suggest a paradigmatic shift.

Assumption 1. From addressing issues in parts to whole systems thinking

Responses to global challenge are dominated by a Western science tradition that divides up a problem into various slices, analyzes them, and then assumes that by ensuring the slices are addressed, the whole will also be successful. For example, the failure to address global challenges has political science, sociological, and economic slices.

From a political science viewpoint, the failures have to do with global public policy – we do not have a sufficiently effective way of making and implementing rules globally. This was the point of departure for the 2000 report to Kofi Annan, *Critical Choices,* which looked at the future of the UN and the emerging role of global public policy networks and stimulated my work with GANs.[14]

From a sociological viewpoint, in part the failures have to do with "norms" – we do not have sufficiently strong people and environmentally sensitive values integrated into the way people and organizations act. Failures also have to do with difficulties in crossing big differences such as social, cultural, professional, and geographic ones, as social capital theorists such as Robert Putnam point out.[15]

From an economic perspective the failures are associated with market rules, and getting them right on a global level so that business can play a more effective role. As the World Business Council on Sustainable Development (WBCSD) reminds us: "The market system did not come about by accident; it is very much a human construct."[16]

This cacophony of perspectives is like the blind man touching different parts of an elephant and concluding that he is touching different animals. The political science, sociological, and economic perspectives are all right, and the problem is that we do not approach global action from an integrated systems perspective. The key point is that the political, social, and economic systems are all *interdependent,* and focusing on just one part will not solve "societal" problems. But how to coordinate across all of them is a big challenge.

One historic example of trying to do this is with the big business – big government – big labor paradigm that dominated post World War II strategies to define the social contract. For example, in the United States the wage increases negotiated by the United Auto Workers and the auto makers was generally enjoyed the support of business and the government well into the 1960s. This "corporatist" nation-state approach is still influential in contemporary Germany and Sweden. It presumes that government is the final arbiter, but that big government and big labor should be able to work out differences about dividing benefits between investors and workers.

GANs are trying to create global social contracts with respect to some specific issues, by creating multi-stakeholder platforms for this to occur. The importance of thinking in terms of the "whole" as well as their specific issues (parts) stresses the importance of the Stage 4 development activity described in Chapter 3 when GANs connect to each other to integrate their issues.

Assumption 2. From inter-national structures for addressing global issues to multi-stakeholder ones

There is no global government structure for decision-making with respect to issues of public concern. Rather, there is an inter-*national* structure. To address a problem or matter of public concern that crosses national borders, nation-states are the only structure that we have to take collective action. Nation-states run the UN, the World Bank, the World Trade Organization, and the International Monetary Fund; they are the signatories to the regional and global agreements that define the rules for trade and other international relationships. The primary concern of a nation in these forums is its individual national interest. There are no organizational structures that focus on global interests and what will generate the best outcomes for the world as a whole.

This lack of strategy structure generates the negative dynamic of the tragedy of the commons. All of the nation-states focus upon what they can get out of the global whole, or how they can minimize the effort they put into maintaining it. This leads to predictable problems with respect to the more obvious commons such as air and the oceans; but the dynamic is the same with respect to other transnational interests, as well.

The solutions to these types of problems require thinking beyond them. Earlier I referred to Albert Einstein's comment that "Problems cannot be solved at the same level of awareness that created them." In this case, the government level is the nation-state. The solution will be found either at a level "below" nation-states, with the elements that make up a nation-state such as people and their organizations, provinces/states – or at a level beyond the nation-states, one that does not operate within the confines of national boundaries.

These other levels should not be thought of as simply "legal" entities such as "citizens" and legally constituted organizations, for those entities themselves owe their definition to the nation-state. This critique suggests that although those entities probably will be involved in defining the solution since they are required to operate within the current inter-national system, in fact what is needed is an *invention* that is not limited by or dependent upon the concept of the nation-state for its existence.

The motivations to persist with the inter-national rather than global approach are very strong. A sense of control (power) over the situation is one obvious incentive for nations to persist in their actions. The United States has made this particularly clear with its rejection of multi-lateral action and new transnational entities such as global courts. To create a global decision-making framework suggests that nations will give up some of their power.

Further, individuals involved in representing nations receive many personal benefits that make them want to support the inter-national system. These benefits include prestige, sense of self-importance/self-worth, good salaries, and lots of privileges. Rather than seeing places where something is to be done, many representatives appointed by nations to inter-national organizations see either rewards for something or ways to get rivals out of the way.

However, John Ruggie who is a Harvard professor, Assistant Secretary General for the UN and a chief architect of the Global Compact sees this state tradition changing " . . . (due) to the beginnings of a fundamental reconstitution of the global public domain: away from one that equated the public in international politics with states and the interstate realm, to one in which the very system of states is becoming embedded in a broader, albeit still thin and partial, institutionalized arena concerned with the production of global public goods."[17]

GANs are a strategy development structure that gets beyond this conundrum and yet recognizes the important role of the nation-state by creating global multi-stakeholder platforms. Civil society and business do not operate with a geographically defined limit like governments. Engaging them brings in transnational and global concerns.

Assumption 3. From assuming the natural environment to nurturing it

To say at the beginning of the twenty-first century that the natural environment is important seems obvious. The third world summit on environmental issues was held in Johannesburg in 2002. There followed nearly two decades of climate change negotiations. Numerous international treaties and conventions dealing with environmental issues have been negotiated. However, the fact that human society and activity is dependent on the natural environment is still far from being recognized as a core principle in global decision-making.

In some ways this problem is the reverse of the problem of not seeing the forest for the trees and the need to think about the interaction of the parts. The problem is that the framework for thinking about the interaction between the parts needs to have as its fundamental frame of reference the impact upon the natural environment. Although sustainability as a concept has been expanded appropriately to include the triple-bottom-line of social, economic, and environmental impacts, both the social and economic systems are dependent on the health of the natural environment – whereas the reverse is not true.

If this principle were reflected in inter-national decision-making and action, there would no longer be, for example, a fight to make trade policy within an environmental framework. As it is, those fighting on the trade and sustainable development front know that economic decision-making frameworks are the ones that still dominate the World Trade Organization, the International Monetary Fund, and the World Bank. Asserting the environmental imperative is the core work of the International Centre for Trade and Sustainable Development.

Many GANs have arisen specifically in response to the environmental crisis. All of them integrate sustainability into their work as a principle of fundamental importance. Figure 9.1 aims to describe this and the first two shifts in assumptions. We can see that this draws a very different picture about how to create the social contract, in comparison to the post-World War II paradigm as is presented in Figure 9.1.

Assumption 4. From change that can be addressed by linear approaches to complex systems strategies

Western approaches to solving problems are also dominated by linear strategies based on the ideas of task division and "expert" knowledge that

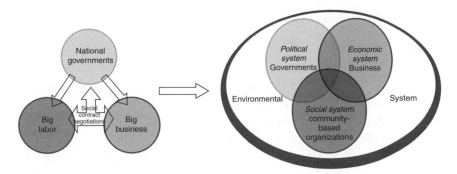

Figure 9.1 From a "Government" world of parts to a governance world of the whole

cannot be easily shared. The task of describing an issue falls to researchers. They write up a report and pass it on to a second group, consultants (sometimes with senior managers as internal consultants), who take the data and match it up with how they think things can work differently. The consultants design a solution that they then pass along to a third group. This third group – practitioners – then takes the design and tries to implement it. The researcher–consultant–practitioner linear production model shown in Figure 9.2 is the basis of business consulting, public policy development, and product innovation processes.[18]

As anyone who has tried to implement a consultant's report knows, there are a couple of problems with this approach – problems that are magnified when the issue involves complex global problems. One problem is that the issues are so complex, even defining what you need to know is difficult, let alone gathering the appropriate data. What are the causes of poverty? Of environmental degradation? There are such complex webs of causality behind these mega-problems that understanding them is ongoing work.

Another problem is that this model takes a long time to complete, particularly when dealing with complex problems where data gathering can

Figure 9.2 Linear development process

go on forever. President George W. Bush still insisted that more data gathering is needed to prove global warming is a problem. In the traditional public issue model, the solution designers are government public policy makers who are not known for speed themselves, and the implementers are everyone else in society. When dealing with production of a new car, the time implications of this linear model are problematic. When dealing with complex issues like climate change where shifting directions can take years, the repercussions can be disastrous.

An associated problem with the linear model is that the underlying conditions that produce the data collected have often changed by the time implementation occurs. This means that implementation may actually be harmful in the new context, rather than helpful. This is a common problem in strategies to address poverty, for example, which have been dominated by mega-schemes – whether government- or business-led. Nobel Laureate economist Joseph Stiglitz points to the use of old data as a reason that solutions of the International Monetary Fund lead to disaster.[19]

But perhaps the greatest problem with this model applied to global problems is that the implementation very often never gets done. Those who are supposed to do the implementing do not have faith in the data, they question the design, and they have problems adapting it to their situation. The data and design often do not go beyond the reports that summarize them.

Perhaps the most incredible example of this implementation problem is with the UN's attempt to breathe life into the commitments that governments made at the 1992 global environmental meeting in Rio de Janeiro. These were summarized as Agenda 21, which is described as " . . . a comprehensive plan of action to be taken globally, nationally and locally by organizations of the United Nations System, Governments, and Major Groups in every area in which human impacts on the environment."[20]

Implementation progress reports of this plan were due a decade later, at the World Summit on Sustainable Development in 2002 in Johannesburg. As that date neared, it became obvious that very little of substance had been done. When the UN's Commission on Sustainable Development (CSD) finally turned attention to implementation, a solution was identified in the form of "Type 2" partnerships. Type 1 partnerships were those between national governments – the big, important idea people who made the plans and commitments in the first place. Type 2 partnerships were to be with business and civil society organizations that were going to implement the governments' commitments. Naturally enough, the CSD had few takers to form Type 2 partnerships – the potential "partners" saw it as doing governments' work and many disagreed with the plans to start

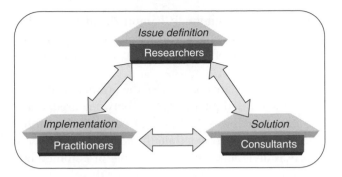

Figure 9.3   Problem-solving as a cycle

with. (Also the CSD only gave 6 months for partnerships to form, and made promises of funding a major driver. These are both conditions for multi-stakeholder partnership formation that are highly likely to produce failure.)

In the world of global problem solving, Figure 9.3 is the one that GANs are developing. Each of the three key steps is linked to the others. This model emphasizes the importance of integration of new data, the experiences of practitioners, and the solution designs. It reflects the well-known learning model discussed in Chapter 5 as experiential learning. It emphasizes that learning and change must be closely connected. Defining people as experts solely with respect to one part of the process means that their work will be poorly informed by the other critical parts. Production must be a collaborative process. Scientists, researchers, and politicians as designers – and those from business and civil society as implementers – must all be engaged as teams throughout the whole process for the change cycle to occur. Although the tasks require distinct activities, they must be occurring concurrently.

Assumption 5. From negotiating our way to solutions to envisioning futures

Historically, inter-national exchanges have been dominated by issues of trade and land. Agreements between nation-states focused on either regulating commerce or settling territorial disputes. Only with the founding of the UN and Bretton Woods institutions after World War II did human rights and international development start to become important. And only in the 1960s did the environment begin making its way onto the inter-national stage. This admittedly simplistic historical description is useful for two reasons. It explains *who* was historically involved and *how* they work together – and another source of difficulties in addressing global issues.

Issues of land and trade are concerns of the political and economic elite. Medieval Europe witnessed pitched battles between aristocracies fighting for control of land, which was the basis for power and wealth. Merchants and bankers of the time were continually negotiating access to jurisdictions of sovereigns and their subjects. The role of commercial exchanges increased, and that of the landed aristocracy declined, with industrialization in the late eighteenth century and the substantial rise in global trade in the nineteenth century. Inter-national boundaries became less fluid as borders between nations became more stable.

These changes were reflected in the emergence of the modern nation-state where the workings of foreign ministries and those of trade and commerce are closely entwined. Ministries dealing with military affairs became supportive appendages of industrial rather than land interests.

This history of inter-national affairs explains in part why pursuing concerns about poverty and the environment through traditional nation-state bureaucracies is so difficult: nations' bureaucracies responsible for inter-national action – their tools, processes, and mental models – were shaped in response to economic interests. The global networks built between governments were largely built to reflect industrial and trading concerns. Representatives of those interests have the personal networks of influence and information that have long dominated inter-national affairs. When short-term economic interests are pitted against long-term concerns about the environment and poverty, the non-economic interests are at a structural, procedural, and network disadvantage.

The historic economic-based inter-national mindset is one cause of economic globalization. Transnational actions by economic interests are much more powerful than globalization of other concerns. The key tool of economic globalization is negotiation, very much in the commercial trading tradition. This means that relationships are framed in terms of give and take, personal benefits, and utilitarian objectives.

This commerce mindset is not appropriate to address the complex, long-term issues of globalization. These types of issues require a set of *transformational* strategies as described in the change chapter. In this strategy parties actually get together to share their different perspectives and build common understanding with respect to an issue of public concern. This attitude requires building mutual commitment to work together in the context of hard-to-define goals, and producing outcomes that are often of unequal benefit to parties. The benefit to developed nations for their work to alleviate global poverty is rather hard to define or ratio-nalize in traditional economic terms. Environmentally, developed nations can actually benefit by dumping their pollutants and their contaminating industries on developing countries – which is exactly what happens when an economic globalization mindset dominates.

Only in the 1950s with concerns about development and human rights, and from the 1960s onward with concerns about the environment, did non-business people begin to be significantly involved in international affairs. Naturally, to break into the close business–government club is not easy. International negotiations are shrouded with traditions of secrecy. They are expensive, since they require travel. They often require knowledge of other languages. They require specialized expertise about not just the issue of concern, but about the other countries involved. And perhaps most impor-tantly, they require access to people who are the decision-makers and who historically come from the social and business elites. After all, foreign ser-vice in government, as witnessed by patronage appointments, continues to have a glamorous and attractive aura.

The social and environmental issues at the forefront of the economic globalization backlash today are ones that require commitment to a higher vision rather than narrow self-interest. Unlike trade traditions of secret negotiations based on competitive interests, current global issues require openness and sharing of information so people can coordinate, create syn-ergies, and co-operatively work together in the public interest. This, too, is the challenge for effective global action networks.

This explains why change strategies that go beyond negotiations and arise from the transformational change processes of visioning described in Chapter 5 are such a critical part of GANs' work. It also explains the importance of their communications work and the technological revolution that facilitates connections and sharing of information.

Assumption 6. From an enforcement focus to a collective values focus

Conversation about global problems usually quickly turns to conversations about how to enforce agreements that nations have signed. There is an underlying assumption that the major difference in global public policy making in comparison to national public policy making is that there is no final authority to enforce the agreements. However, to propose that the major gap is simply enforcement suggests that the only reason anyone obeys national laws is because of the threat of being fined or thrown into jail. The national public policy development process is a sophisticated procedure involving several steps and many organizations to bring about alignment between the aspirations of citizens and the way a country works. In fact, there is a whole range of weaknesses in global public policy making in comparison to national, that needs to be addressed.

In the policy section of the Competencies Chapter 7, I described the global public policy-making process. As pointed out, there are actually four major gaps that need strengthening:

The Participation Gap: Strengthening the ability of citizens to influence global policy.

The Ethical Gap: Ensuring that responses to citizens are legitimate and just.

The Operations Gap: Developing mechanisms to give life to global policy.

The Communications Gap: Effective nation-states do not depend upon enforcement as the major means for ensuring that citizens abide by laws and regulations. Rather, they depend upon a process to first of all ensure the laws and regulations reflect what makes sense to citizens through the first three steps of the public policy process. The next step focuses upon moral suasion and education.

This is not to suggest that enforcement mechanisms are not needed in international decision-making. Clearly they are important as a final option. However, they need to be placed in the context of a range of weaknesses in global public policy development, rather than as the only element, or even the dominant one.

GANs aim to address these gaps by substantially increasing participation in global public good debates and responses. Agreement on principles and values is one of the common basic conditions for participation. These are integrated into their core work to take action to address their issues. And through their participatory processes, they educate and apply moral suasion as well as economic and other arguments to fill the communications gap. They remain voluntary, and do not have enforcement mechanisms.

Summary

The scenario at the beginning of this chapter is only one plausible future. Other commentators have identified other possibilities. For example, one describes six possible dominant scenarios for the future global architecture:

(1) multilateralism: intergovernmental organizations like the UN assert themselves;
(2) grassroots globalism: radical decentralization of authority with self-governing local communities become the norm;
(3) multiple regionalisms: regional units, such as the European Union and the Association of Southeast Asian Nations, become the major global players;
(4) world statism: world government with some form of global elections and military is established;
(5) networked governance with two versions:

   a. networks of politicians and officials of governments connecting across national boundaries, such as those from cities and ones with judges, become much more dominant.
   b. the GAN future.

(6) institutional heterarchy: organizations of various interest groups (e.g. religious, corporate, government) develop a democratic global complexion, individuals could associate with more than one, and the institutions would interact to create rules and norms.[21]

In a very impressive book, Saskia Sassen looks at the evolution of the nation-state and beyond. She starts in Europe in the twelfth and thirteenth centuries and points to the multiplicity of governance forms: kingdoms, "democratic" city states, the Catholic Church, feudal land arrangements, merchant cities, and more. Looking at this period, she asks: "Who would have guessed that the democratic populist nation state grounded largely in ethnic alliances would become dominant?"[22] In fact, there is reason to believe that we are truly at the tail end of this period.

We could, of course, simply collapse in the face of the challenges. Jared Diamond describes how that happened with the Mayans as they stressed their Central American ecology beyond its capacity.[23] That's a real possibility. To avoid such a possibility, we need to change the way we are, and imagine new possibilities that take us to a flourishing future.

Harvard's John Ruggie sees a major trend today is "... the emergence of a global public domain beyond the sphere of states".[24] I believe that the future of GANs is reasonably bright, given the trends and shifting assumptions. However, I have aimed to create here a framework for readers to do their own assessment. You might feel differently about some of the challenges, trends, and assumptions. And you might disagree with my view that GANs' values are attractive and their strategies offer a world where globalization works for all. I encourage you to become active in a GAN and with the challenge of global decision-making. Greater participation in both surely is critical for bending the curve into the future in the direction of a flourishing world for all.

Notes

1. Pochmann, M. and G. R. Schutte. (2010). "A Tax for Globalisation Based on Solidarity." Retrieved April 28, 2010, from http://www.leadinggroup.org/article540.html.
2. Douste-Blazy, P. and D. Altman (2010). "A Few Dollars at Time: How to Tap Consumers for Development." *Foreign Affairs* 89(1): 2–14; Diamond, J. (1997). *Guns, Germs, and Steel: The Fates of Human Societies*. New York, USA, W. W. Norton & Company; UnitAid. (2010). "UNITAID: Mission." Retrieved April 28, 2010, from http://www.unitaid.eu/en/UNITAID-Mission.html.
3. Glasbergen, P. (2010). "Global Action Networks: Agents for Collective Action." *Global Environmental Change* 20(1): 130–141.
4. United Nations. (2009). "United Nations' Trends in Total Migrant Stock: The 2008 Revision." Retrieved April 28, 2010.
5. World Bank (2009). *World Bank's Migration and Development Brief*. Washington, DC, USA, World Bank 11.
6. FAO (2009). *State of Food Insecurity*. Rome, Italy, Food and Agriculture Organisation.
7. Marszalek, E. and S. London (2009). *Health Assistance to Developing Countries Soars*. Washington, DC, USA, Worldwatch Institute.
8. NASA (2010). "2009: Second Warmest Year on Record; End of Warmest Decade." Retrieved April 29, 2010, from http://www.nasa.gov/topics/earth/features/temp-analysis-2009.html.
9. Djoghlaf, A. (2007). *Press Release*. Montreal, Quebec, Canada, Convention on Biodiversity.
10. WTO (2010a). *International Trade Statistics 2009*. Geneva, Switzerland, World Trade Organization.
11. WTO (2010b). "Trade to Expand by 9.5% in 2010 after a Dismal 2009, WTO Reports". *2010 Press Releases*. Geneva, Switzerland, World Trade Organization 598.
12. FAO (2010). *Global Forest Assessment 2010*. Rome, Italy, Food and Agriculture Organization.
13. Ruggie, J. G. (1993). "Territoriality and Beyond: Problematizing Modernity in International Relations." *International Organization* 47(1): 139–174.
14. Reinicke, W. H. and F. M. Deng (2000). *Critical Choices: The United Nations, Networks, and the Future of Global Governance*. Toronto, Canada, International Development Research Council.

15. Putnam, R. D. (1993). *Making Democracy Work: Civic Traditions in Modern Italy*. Princeton, NJ, Princeton University Press.
16. WBCSD (2001). *Sustainability through the Market: Seven Keys to Success*. Geneva, Switzerland, World Business Council for Sustainable Development.
17. Ruggie, J. G. (2004). "Reconstituting the Global Domain: Issues, Actors and Practices." *European Journal of International Relations* 10(4): 499–531.
18. Jasanoff, S. and B. Wynne (1998). "Science and Decisionmaking". *Human Choice and Climate Change*. S. Rayner and E. L. Malone (eds). Washington, DC USA, Battelle Press: 1–87.
19. Stiglitz, J. E. (2002). *Globalization and its Discontents*. New York, NY, USA, W.W. Norton & Co.
20. United Nations. (December 23, 2002). "United Nations Sustainable Development Agenda 21." Retrieved December 31, 2002, from http://www.un.org/esa/sustdev/agenda21.htm.
21. Khagram, S. (2006). "Possible Future Architectures of Global Governance: A Transnational Perspective/Prospective." *Global Governance* 12: 97–117.
22. Sassen, S. (2006). *Territory, Authority, Rights: From Medieval to Global Assemblages*. Princeton, NJ, USA, Princeton University Press.
23. Diamond, J. (1997). *Guns, Germs, and Steel: The Fates of Human Societies*. New York, USA, W. W. Norton & Company.
24. Ruggie, J. G. (2004). Op.cit.

INDEX